Rabbit Tales

Rabbit Tales
Poetry and Politics in John Updike's Rabbit Novels

Edited by
Lawrence R. Broer

The University of Alabama Press
Tuscaloosa and London

∞

The paper on which this book is printed meets the minimum
requirements of American National Standard for Information
Science–Permanence of Paper for Printed Library Materials, ANSI
Z39.48-1984.

Library of Congress Cataloging-in-Publication Data

Rabbit tales : poetry and politics in John Updike's Rabbit novels /
    edited by Lawrence R. Broer.
        p.   cm.
    Includes bibliographical references and index.
    ISBN 0-8173-0899-7
    1. Updike, John—Characters—Harry Angstrom.   2. Politics and
literature—United States—History—20th century.   3. Political
fiction, American—History and criticism.   4. Updike, John—
Political and social views.   5. Angstrom, Harry (Fictitious
character)   6. Middle class men in literature.   7. Updike, John.
Rabbit at rest.   8. Updike, John. Rabbit is rich.   9. Updike, John.
Rabbit redux.   10. Updike, John. Rabbit, run.   I. Broer, Lawrence
R.
    PS3571.P4Z85   1998
    813'.54—dc21   97-40344

British Library Cataloguing-in-Publication Data available

Updike is both poet and historian, so various in observation and so truthful, so inventive and adept, that he leaves one brooding on his scene and remembering his epithets.

V. S. Pritchett

For my basketball pals
Deke, Herb, and Jack

Contents

Acknowledgments

It is my hope that the good of these essays conveys my infinite regard both for John Updike and for Harry Angstrom, who surely takes his place alongside those other American icons, Ishmael and Huck, Babbitt and Loman, Gatsby and Caulfield. There are many people to thank for helping prepare this book. Nicole Mitchell's enthusiasm was inspirational from start to finish. The meticulous editorial advice of Linda Miller and Jackson Bryer was invaluable. For their devoted critical efforts, I am of course deeply grateful to the twelve scholars whose work appears here. I am grateful to the English Department and the Division of Sponsored Research of the University of South Florida for providing the research time to prepare this book. I wish also to thank the office staff of the English Department—Diane Meyer, Chris Eberhard, Yenira Tossas, and Aileen Jorge—for their assistance throughout this project. My sincere gratitude, finally, goes to my intrepid research assistant, Gloria Holland, to my friend and adviser, Gail Sinclair, and to Michael Kilgore for suggesting the title.

Rabbit Tales

Lawrence R. Broer

Introduction

As early as 1974, V. S. Pritchett lauded the "monumental" achievement of John Updike's "Rabbit" tetralogy, a body of work "which in substantial intelligent creation will eventually be seen as second to none in our time" (206). Capped by winning the National Book Critics Circle Award for *Rabbit Is Rich* and the Pulitzer Prize for both *Rabbit Is Rich* and *Rabbit at Rest*, the tetralogy—*Rabbit, Run* (1960), *Rabbit Redux* (1971), *Rabbit Is Rich* (1981), and *Rabbit at Rest* (1990)—represents not just the best of Updike's fiction, but a work of imagination rivaling Balzac's *Comédie Humaine*, Dos Passos's *USA Trilogy*, and Faulkner's Yoknapatawpha series. According to Donald Greiner, the Rabbit novels are John Updike's *Barchester Chronicles*, for like Trollope, "Updike uses his fiction to choreograph the social dance of our age" (*Updike's Novels* 84).

While the literary production of this "Mozart of our technological culture"[1] is prodigious—poetry, criticism, short stories, even artwork, and fourteen novels since 1959—it is Updike's creation of the former high school basketball star Harry Angstrom and the latter's evolution over four decades of volatile change in American life, from the time of Ike through the rule of Reagan, that stands as Updike's magnum opus. Echoing the sentiments of numerous fellow writers, Thomas Disch asserts that with Harry "Rabbit" Angstrom someone has finally, albeit inadvertently, written the great American novel ("Rabbit's Run" 690). Jonathan Raban concludes that Americans finally have a modern American work of fiction they can set beside the work of Dickens, Thackeray, George Eliot, and Joyce and not feel the draft (15).

The essays by prominent Updike scholars that make up this volume illuminate the unique achievement of these novels in numerous ways, demonstrating that a character and a world so ambiguous and diverse can be understood only through multiple perspectives and interpretations. The perceptions here are theoretical, textual, and cultural—multilayered interpretations that explore Harry Angstrom's ever-shifting attitudes toward sex and women, war and peace, politics and religion. Becoming more specialized as they go, the essays yield an increasingly larger yet more focused understanding of Harry's predicament. They show him in all his dimensions—emotional, social, historic, psychological, religious, philosophic, and artistic.

While these essays often focus upon one work in the tetralogy, each essay examines the relationship of that novel to the series and to the literary traditions that shape all of Updike's work. Opinions vary as to the individual merit of the four novels, but *Rabbit at Rest* receives special attention because it is generally considered the most artistically successful, because it brings to fruition the essential themes of the series, and because it provides a paradigm of the methods used to create all four novels.[2] In assessing the scope and nature of Updike's achievement, commentators address Updike's detractors, considering those issues that typically give offense to Rabbit/Updike critics— what is generally seen as Rabbit's progressive disillusionment in the course of the tetralogy, and his careless amorality, his rabbity philandering.[3] But all agree that in the Rabbit novels, Updike discovers a character and a dramatic situation that produce one of the most compelling and complex literary tapestries of our time. They agree that in the character of Harry Angstrom, Updike has created an archetypal American hero, one strikingly real and individual, yet emblematic of his class, his country, and his era. This echoes Updike's own affirmation, in his introduction to the Everyman Library edition of the novels, that Harry was "a way in—a ticket to the America all around me" (ix).

The subtitle of this book refers to Updike's remarkable dual achievement in these novels as both poet and historian—his ingenious weaving of art and politics, lyric and epic—that causes these books to be read on a variety of levels and to lend themselves to diverse critical approaches. Ralph Wood thus sees Updike examining the spiritual state of the entire nation, erecting in Harry Angstrom a figure no less culturally definitive than Twain's Huckleberry Finn, Hemingway's Nick Adams, or Faulkner's Ike McCaslin. Calling Harry a "historical artifact," Donald Greiner views him as inseparable from the political and socioeconomic circumstances that shape him. The country's social history and Harry Angstrom's personal history are "coterminal," Edward Vargo explains. Angstrom's personal loss of vitality and moral direction reflects the larger picture of national decline.

Charles Berryman and Jeff Campbell show how the social and economic forces that shape this prototypical American are deeply rooted in our national heritage. With ties to Natty Bumppo, Hester Prynne, Ishmael, Jay Gatsby, and Tom Joad, Harry Angstrom is perhaps more representative than any of them. Yet the anxiety and lostness that give Angstrom his name are shown as the product of an age whose materialism and spiritual emptiness stifle Harry's questing spirit. Unlike Huck Finn, Harry, as Matthew Wilson contends, has no new territory to which to flee the constraints of a society that offers him no place for his abundant energies. According to Greiner and Jack Moore, what the river is to Huck, the forest to Leatherstocking, or the sea to Ishmael, the basketball court and golf course are to Harry—an arena where the individual's skill and courage combat the tyranny of circumstance, but also a world where the opportunities for freedom have become increasingly less hopeful. In Wilson's view, only death—and four novels of preparation for it—will free Harry from the American "cul-de-sac" that traps him.

Ralph Wood and Judie Newman similarly attribute the dilution of Harry's heroism to the fact that as a citizen dwelling in the age of anxiety, the dominating presence of technological wonders provides no real substance for the spirit. Greiner explains that each Rabbit novel records the tone of a decade: *Rabbit Is Rich* is about the late 1970s, but the rainbow Harry chases in the 1950s and 1960s has "shrunk" as the American dream goes sour with the bad taste of advancing age and aimless youth.

While these essays establish the Rabbit novels as pertinent social history in the tradition of Edith Wharton and F. Scott Fitzgerald, the novels also demonstrate their "cunningness" of technique. As ingeniously crafted as any novels in our time, Updike's tetralogy weaves a fabric of changing hues and textures, of social realism and something of grandeur. As these essayists provide insight into Updike's use of irony, complex characterizations, multilayered image patterns, competing tonalities and juxtapositions, and subtle shifts of point of view and authorial distance, they demonstrate how his technique changes appropriate to the respective phases of Harry Angstrom's life. Most importantly, they reveal the metaphoric and symbolic dimensions of Updike's art that move it beyond social realism to poetry. As Edward Vargo explains, the novels stitch together statement and interpretation, both of which incorporate the literal, the synecdochic, and the metaphoric.

Donald Greiner echoes the general view that it is Updike's particular combination of realism and metaphor—what Edward Vargo calls the "art of the usual" and what Thomas Mallon has dubbed a "marriage of dailiness and poetry" (17)—that most distinguishes the style of these novels. Appropriate to Updike's personal brand of realism, the author's gift for projecting felt life allows him to produce what Henry James called "the illusion of real life" in vivid, authentic terms. Updike refrains, as George Hunt says, from distorting the world and our commonsense perception of it. Several of these essayists see Harry Angstrom defined by relived historical moments, everyday situations in suburban America where conflicts are enclosed in trivial and apparently insignificant daily routines. As Charles Berryman says, Updike not only incorporates the mood of the times, but he also dramatizes events that dominate the headlines. The cold war, the Korean War, the Vietnam War, the civil rights movement, the moon landing, the Ted Kennedy accident, the oil crisis, the hostage crisis, the Toyota invasion, and the explosion of Pan Am flight 103 over Lockerbie all enter into the characters' conversations such that, as Ralph Wood suggests, historians will consult these books as barometers of post–World War II American life.

Dilvo Ristoff and Edward Vargo look closely at the artistic implications of Updike's use of the artifacts of popular culture—newspaper clippings, highway numbers, real estate flyers, medical pamphlets, sports highlights, car ads, brand names, and popular songs. This "meticulous taxonomy" of the material world contributes to Updike's brand of verisimilitude—concreteness and visual precision that combine fictional narrative with historical lecture. These dubious icons of chaotic and discontinuous culture—what Joseph Waldmeir calls "the slick, the superficial, the artificial"—provide a double-edged mirror that both defines and limits Harry, and which reflects as well his country's declining attitudes and values. Harry turns neither to scripture nor to the church for wisdom, but to the triviality of television commercials and advertisement jingles. As Wood suggests, Harry's popular religious culture offers little solace for the aching absence of God.

Although these essayists admire these novels for their referentiality and topicality—their "dazzling thingness"—they are more concerned with Updike's self-acknowledged role as a poet who valorizes and redeems the commonplace. Referring to a sensibility that makes an "epiphany of each suburban minute and twinge" (Eder 3), V. S. Pritchett remarks that "Updike has the extraordinary gift of making the paraphernalia of, say, the Sears and Roebuck catalogue sound like a chant from the Book of Psalms" (202). Far from mere "documentary" creativity, these novels are not just about history but a historical process, a unique kind of personal/historical record that shimmers and changes, a "magical evocation" in which common objects and characters are imbued with value and importance that, as James Plath says, transcend their "ordinariness in our ordinary world." For many of these essayists, what triumphs most in these novels is the exhilaration of Updike's poetic style, the exuberance that continues to take the world, despite all doubt and gloominess, as an object worthy of praise. Campbell speaks of the "regenerative images" that carry Harry's redemptive possibilities at the end of the series. Wood describes Updike as a "rapt witness" to the world that surrounds and transcends. In his essay on Proust, Updike describes his own affirmation of style, viewing the French writer as "one of those rare men . . . who lost the consolations of belief but retained the attitudes and ambitions of a wor-shiper" (qtd. in Cooper 321). So, too, Updike himself "substitutes for tran-scendental reassurances the small answers of texture, mastering the artistic paradox by which even deathly realities are redeemed in the vivid life of prose" (Cooper 321).

While Updike's art is the art of the commonplace, it is also the art of "the inconclusive," the vision and method of a historicist consciousness that points always toward the multiple. Greiner expresses the prevailing view in these essays that the very core of Updike's art is a refusal to absolutize the world. Thus we have a richly contradictory character and multiple histories being developed to such a degree that an actual "subversion" of truth, a sort of "Bakhtinian carnivalization" (Wood xvii), takes place, which Updike calls the "yes, but" quality of his fiction, a subversiveness that resists closure—re-fusing to place the truth in the hands of a Rabbit, an Eccles, a Skeeter, a Jill, a Stavros, or a Mr. Springer. The truth has no fixed place and no permanent owner; it can be found in the text's capacity to decentralize authority and in its contribution to an understanding of Harry and the problematic Amer-ica he signifies. Thus the Rabbit novels reveal "worlds within worlds," what Vargo calls the "broad discontinuities" of the American scene, and in Harry a plurality of selves that makes him more dynamic and complex than can be suggested with any single label. Harry becomes exceptional yet unexcep-tional, spiritual yet nonspiritual, individual yet social—a dialectic of oppo-sites that reveal him as one of the most troubling heroes in twentieth-century literature. Such oppositions, Wood concludes, make Harry a protagonist who poses a problem rather than a solution, who queries his readers more than he teaches them a lesson. Underscoring the view that it is the author's purpose to urge acknowledgment of the complexity of Harry's dilemma, Greiner quotes Updike's declaration that "I don't wish my fiction to be any clearer than life."[4] Greiner explains that Updike's critics want him to take a stand, to blame either social pressure or individual whim, but to do so is to ignore the ambiguity of Updike's sense of culture and, in a larger sense, what Wood calls the "irreducible ambiguity" of the human condition.

Charles Berryman cautions at the onset of his essay against a too simple acceptance of the series as a continuous story.[5] However, most agree to a theme that unifies all four novels: how to reconcile the individual's need for freedom with the demands of society. The question is more specific: "How best does an American translate freedom into fulfillment? Through commit-ment to others or by going it alone?" (Farney A10). Most interpret the epi-graph to Rabbit, Run as Updike's personal expression of the moral dilemma that confronts Harry in all four of his incarnations: "The motions of Grace, the hardness of the heart; external circumstances" (Pascal, *Pensées* 507). Suggesting that it is this clash of dialectical opposites that gives the series its mythic dimensions—bestial and angelic, material and spiritual, mortal and immortal—Campbell views Harry's heart as a "battlefield of good and evil," and Wood sees Harry's moral adventure as "a pilgrimage through anguish." As Harry quests for the mysterious "it" that beckons him from novel to novel, struggling with what he calls in *Rabbit, Run* the "right way and the good way"—the life of instinctual gratification versus that of self-denying responsibility—readers watch to see whether it is Harry's frequent flintiness of heart that will ultimately define him, or instead his movements of grace—a willingness, as Wood says, to accept responsibility for one's own life and for those other lives one has been entrusted with. Whether Harry Angstrom grows or declines over the course of the series defines the "moral debate" of these critical essays. What does he learn or not learn along the way, and where does he finally "rest"? Some argue that Harry overcomes his early self-centeredness to grow in moral discernment and sympathy, while others stress Harry's "inner dwindling," seeing him as increasingly selfish and diminishing toward death. Others view him in terms of unresolvable paradox—simultaneously fertile and fearful, harmful and loving, vital and dreadful, a deeply religious soul who leaves death and grief in his wake.

It is not the purpose of this book to favor one view of Harry Angstrom over another, but to demonstrate the richly multidimensional nature of Updike's subject, a mixture of the epic and the lyrical, the traditional and the postmodern. Updike writes with the common reader in mind, but also offers ample rewards to those who probe deeply into subtle implications, what Roland Barthes calls "enigmatic disposition of text." What becomes clear from these diverse interpretations is that each individual creates his or her own version of Updike's elusive hero, that it is less Updike than the reader who mediates between the text of reality and the text on the page. What matters most is not that readers see Harry as noble or ignoble, progressing or regressing, but that, as Campbell says, they accept Updike's challenge to enter the debate, weighing "alternatives of heart" that tell them who they are and where they are going.

Notes

1. Alfred Kazin qtd. in Kilgore (20).
2. Updike acknowledges that it is in *Rabbit at Rest* that "so many themes convene" (introduction to *Rabbit Angstrom*, xxii).

3. Bernard Schopen aptly describes the uneven, if not perverse, nature of Updike criticism: "The novels of John Updike have spawned a criticism rather remarkable in its contentiousness. His books have evoked critical outrage, bewilderment, condescension, commendation, and an enthusiasm approaching the fulsome. The same novel might be hailed as a major fictional achievement and dismissed as self-indulgence or as a failure" (523).

4. Updike describes his artistic mission as presenting "sides of an unresolved tension intrinsic to being human." Rather than a straightforward portrait of Harry, Updike strives for "the imprint of a beautiful and useful truth" (introduction to *Rabbit Angstrom*, xiii).

5. Updike provides his own account of the complex evolution of Harry's character from novel to novel, explaining how the shifting terrain of the author's personal life shapes and reshapes his artistic vision (introduction to *Rabbit Angstrom*).

1

Donald J. Greiner
No Place to Run
Rabbit Angstrom as Adamic Hero

When, at the end of *Rabbit at Rest* (1990), an apparently dying Harry Angstrom thinks the word "enough,"[1] John Updike not only concludes one of the most remarkable achievements in contemporary American literature but also terminates one of the most troubling literary heroes in traditional American culture. To assign heroic stature to Rabbit is to invite controversy, for Harry is often careless with his health, reckless with his family, and heedless of his friends. Yet the extent of his heroism is not to be measured by classical paradigms. Rabbit does not, after all, perform astounding feats of strength and skill. But he does "believe," and he does seek grace in all the connotations of these ambiguous words; and thus in the course of his thirty years of literary life Harry Angstrom personifies Updike's understanding of how, in America, personal aspiration is always compromised by cultural decline. I want to suggest two primary points in the following pages: first, that Rabbit is Updike's variation on the canonical American literary hero, and second, that Updike foresaw Rabbit's defeat even before the publication of *Rabbit, Run* in 1960.

I

Late in *Rabbit at Rest*, Harry looks at his overweight, middle-aged body and sees "an innocuous passive spirit that doesn't want to do any harm, get trapped anywhere, or ever die" (381). Rabbit shares these desires—and their frustrations—with Cooper's Leatherstocking, Hawthorne's Hester, Melville's Billy Budd, Twain's Huck, Fitzgerald's Gatsby, and Salinger's Holden. With Rabbit Angstrom, Updike adds his name to the short list of American authors capable of successfully creating immortal characters who first absorb and then define the national culture.

The list is distinguished, and the novelists on it feature the peculiar brand of American literary heroism defined years ago by R. W. B. Lewis: "Tragedy, in American literature, was generated by the impact of hostile forces upon the innocent solitary, who had sprung from nowhere, and his impact upon them" (92). Naming this kind of character an American Adam, Lewis observes that the hero usually takes "his start outside society; the action to be imitated may just as well be his strenuous efforts to *stay* outside as his tactics for getting inside; and if he does get inside, it makes a difference whether he is walking into a trap or discovering a setting in which to realize his own freedom" (101). Although Harry Angstrom cannot think in Lewis's sophisticated terms, he nevertheless intuits Lewis's point: that he is a relative innocent trapped in the American culture of 1950–1990; that he seems to have sprung from nowhere and thus stands outside the accepted norms of the culture; and that his goal—especially in *Rabbit, Run*—is to maintain his freedom by *remaining* outside despite the costs, which are always great. Updike's essential paradox in the Rabbit tetralogy is that Harry is distanced from yet wholly exemplifies his culture. Lewis summarizes what he calls "the matter of Adam" as "the ritualistic trials of the young innocent, liberated from family and social history or bereft of them; radically affecting that world and radically affected by it; defeated, perhaps even destroyed, but leaving his mark upon the world" (127–28).

By the end of *Rabbit at Rest,* in sharp contradistinction to Hemingway's Santiago, who is an earlier version of "American" heroism, Harry is first defeated and then destroyed. Although surely responsible for his own predicament, he is nevertheless at odds with the American cultural malaise that he defines as "Reagan's reign." In *Rabbit at Rest,* as in the other novels of the tetralogy, Updike describes the hairstyles, the inane pop songs, the dismal television programs like *Roseanne,* the physical fitness nuts, and the racial prejudices both to illustrate the uneasiness of the culture that Rabbit would like to flee and to generate sympathy for a character who reflects many of the people who will read the novel but whom those readers will not much like. At age fifty-six, Harry still worries about sex and death, religion and grace, but he is not as certain as he used to be, not as confident. His personal limitation mirrors the national decline as Updike suggests that America is depleted and that dreams are deferred. Looking at the imported Toyotas that have brought him the "easy" life (surely Updike's deliberate contrast with Jay Gatsby's magnificent, pretentious car), Rabbit thinks not of success but of the eerie presence of lurking death.

No longer the hopeful Rabbit of his basketball-playing youth in the Eisenhower 1950s, the Harry Angstrom of *Rabbit at Rest* is similarly distanced from the grace he once pursued with inarticulate fear. Like many Americans of his indulgent generation, he suffers from heart trouble, Updike's physical sign of Harry's spiritual dread. Never well spoken, he continues to define abstractions with the metaphors of sports in an effort to maintain separation from—to stay "outside"—the culture. Golf, he reasons, now has a greater relevance to his life than basketball: starting wide before falling into a small hole in the ground. For all his fear, Angstrom continues his quest to run free of society's limitations. He is Updike's American dreamer, a mundane Natty Bumppo or Jay Gatsby, whose persistent dissatisfaction cloaks a lifelong spiritual yearning.

Despite Harry's transgression of adultery with his daughter-in-law, then, the reader cheers when, in the last movement of *Rabbit at Rest,* he runs one final time—away from complications, away from culture, away from a catastrophe that he himself has helped cause. He no longer runs toward the ill-defined goal of "it" as he does in *Rabbit, Run,* but at least he is on the move, as are Leatherstocking and Huck, "jostling for his space in the world as if he still deserves it" (*Rest* 442). He even returns to the basketball court despite his weight, his age, his heart. In short, he tries, as the solitary American hero always does. But his fear presages the final stillness, and the last word of the tetralogy is "Enough."

II

Updike foresaw Rabbit's defeat. Indeed, he prefigured it in a short story and a poem that antedate the publication of both *Rabbit, Run* (1960) and his first novel, *The Poorhouse Fair* (1959). Quite early in his career, in other words, Updike had Rabbit Angstrom in mind—or, at least, an Ur-Rabbit. Initially published in the *New Yorker* for April 9, 1955, before being collected in *The Same Door* (1959), the tale "Ace in the Hole" appeared within six months of Updike's first professional short story ("Friends from Philadelphia," *New Yorker,* 30 Oct. 1954). The poem "Ex-Basketball Player" appeared two years after "Ace in the Hole" in the *New Yorker* for July 6, 1957, before Updike collected it in *The Carpentered Hen* in 1958.

Both an impressive story in its own right and an early version of *Rabbit, Run,* "Ace in the Hole" touches on the details of popular culture in the 1950s that Updike later stresses in the first Rabbit novel. Fats Domino's "Blueberry Hill" is a hit tune, the jitterbug is the dance of choice, and "ducktails" are the male hairstyle of the day. Fred "Ace" Anderson prefigures Harry "Rabbit" Angstrom as the small-town basketball hero who finds himself on the sidelines after graduating from high school. With the future nowhere in sight, Ace survives on a combination of past memories and present motion. Like Huck floating down the river, Leatherstocking walking west, or Billy Budd sailing the ocean, Ace seeks motion to sustain life. But Updike's irony is apparent: the American 1950s feature diminished heroes and restricted move-ment. Indeed, throughout his canon Updike suggests a relationship between the loss of space in the United States and the dilution of heroism. The sound of the axes that Natty Bumppo deplores is a staple in Ace's culture. Clearly worried but unable to define his problem, Ace pulls a cigarette from his pack, moves it to his mouth, strikes a match, lights up, inhales, and blows out the flame, all in time to "Blueberry Hill." Yet the motion is deceiving, for like Harry in *Rabbit at Rest*, Ace Anderson is as out of shape as his culture: one half-block sprint and two flights of stairs make him pant.

Unlike *Rabbit, Run*, "Ace in the Hole" does not permit Updike the room to fully develop the complex reader response that he nurtures in the novel, a response predicated on the reader's disapproval of the hero's longing to be a basketball star again and the reader's sympathy with the hero's instinct to en-joy life, to lash out at the predictable cultural routine that cramps his easy motion and natural grace. Ace is in danger of becoming what Huck Finn calls "sivilized," and Updike fears the change. What arouses readers' sympa-thy for Ace is his refusal to give up, the very trait that Ruth attributes to Harry Angstrom in *Rabbit, Run*. Ace is one of the earliest characters in Up-dike's fiction to experience what will become a general dilemma: how to rec-oncile the need for freedom with the demands of culture. Like Rabbit, Ace is married, but domestic compromise seems impossible because it suggests a fa-tal loss of momentum.

So Ace does what American literary heroes have done for two centuries and what Rabbit does throughout four novels: he seeks freedom in motion. Grabbing his wife for a dance, Ace does not so much jitterbug away his prob-lems as keep himself on the move. The crisis will remain after the record stops, but for the moment he can dance within the freedom of the impro-vised pattern, marking time with the only rhythm he is willing to acknowl-edge: "He spun her out carefully, keeping the beat with his shoulders. . . . [H]e could feel her toes dig into the carpet. He flipped his own hair back from his eyes. The music ate through his skin and mixed with the nerves and small veins; he seemed to be great again, and all the other kids were around them, in a ring, clapping time" (*Same Door* 26).

"Ace in the Hole" is not a typical initiation story like *Adventures of Huckleberry Finn* and *Billy Budd*, because the hero neither learns nor be-comes disillusioned. Despair may set in later, as it surely does for Rabbit, the result of early fame too easily won, but for the time being momentum is all. Perhaps Ace's mother is too indulgent and his wife too plain. Perhaps his ca-pabilities are limited and his job dull. But none of this is to the point in Up-dike's first manifestation of the American Adamic hero. Convincing the reader to sympathize with Ace, Updike also persuades the reader to regret the already stalled life of a young man whose joy at graceful movement will join his inability to cope and lead him presently, the reader senses, into the same American cul-de-sac that traps Rabbit, the cul-de-sac from which only death—and four novels of preparation for it—will free him.

Two years after "Ace in the Hole," Updike published the second trial run of the Rabbit tetralogy. The poem "Ex-Basketball Player" is a somber piece of social observation, a quiet commentary on an American culture that cannot sustain its heroes, no matter how mundane they are. Part of the long tradition of poems about the loss of youthful prowess couched in the metaphor of past athletic glory, "Ex-Basketball Player" is a deliberately prosaic rereading of A. E. Housman's "To an Athlete Dying Young." Housman's unnamed hero and Updike's Flick Webb are "runners whom renown outran," but unlike Housman's youthful performer, Flick is not yet forgotten. Still, the memory of Flick's triumphs is Updike's irony: Webb occasionally dribbles an inner tube for laughs, but "most of us remember anyway." He is Updike's solitary, a man outside the society that once idolized him, a hero of motion without space in which to move.

Housman, Cooper, Melville, and Twain may write about depleted heroism, but at least they concede the possibility of heroic action on a grand scale. In Updike's post–World War II America, however, heroic deeds are nearly always local and usually diminished. A few years ago Flick Webb was good, but like the avenue that runs past his high school, he is "cut off." His name foretells the paradox of his fate: natural movement inextricably entangled. Now alone, as American literary heroes usually are, and unassimilated by his culture, Flick sits in a netherworld between the cigars of adulthood and the syrupy drinks of adolescence. Note the pun on "tiers" in the final stanza:

Off work, he hangs around Mae's luncheonette.
Grease-gray and kind of coiled, he plays pinball,
Smokes those thin cigars, nurses lemon phosphates.
Flick seldom says a word to Mae, just nods
Beyond her face toward bright applauding tiers
Of Necco wafers, Nibs, and Juju beads. (*Carpentered Hen* 3)

III

Ace's "hole" and Flick's "web" become Rabbit's net. "Ace in the Hole" and "Ex-Basketball Player" set the stage for *Rabbit, Run,* one of the great novels in American literature and Updike's first full-length consideration of the way sexual dissatisfaction and marital tension mask spiritual questing in a society that claims to be religious. The imperative voice of the title suggests Updike's sympathetic advice to his hero to break free from confining apartments and mediocre lives, but by the end of the novel, and eventually of the tetralogy, both author and reader know that Rabbit's momentum, his motion, is as stale as the convention he has fled. His defeat already augured in the earlier poem and story, Harry Angstrom has no borders to cross, even though he keeps on running.

Always moving uphill as if questing toward the unseen and thus the unknown, Rabbit has what Updike calls "the beauty of belief" (*Run* 366). A solitary in the midst of Middle America, Harry would not use such terms as "beauty" and "belief," but he knows that something, what he calls "it," is up there. Rabbit's intimations of religion and his pursuit of grace separate him from Ace and Flick and shift him closer to Lewis's definition of the American Adam. Yet a first reaction to Angstrom's haphazard quest is likely to be not admiration but disapproval bordering on disgust. It is not, a reader might argue, that Rabbit intends to cause pain, but that he wrecks the lives of others in a single-minded break for freedom. Updike hopes to convey both the shock and the necessity of Harry's running, for this is a novel of paradoxes. As Updike remarks, "There is a certain necessary ambiguity. I don't wish my fiction to be any clearer than life" ("Desperate Weakling" 108).

In no way can Rabbit call his own predicament clear. Willing to lose his life in the social sense in order to find his individuality, he does not know how to search. Leatherstocking can keep walking west, and Huck can take off down the river, but the highways of Harry's American culture trap him. When he denies his guilt in the burial scene, the reader's dismay at his apparent insensitivity is magnified, but Rabbit senses that the true believer in God need feel no guilt. The faithful need only "cast every care on Thee," which is exactly what Harry does. A believer who cannot define belief, Rabbit feels threatened when family and friends urge him to join their shared expression of guilt for the baby's death, their humanistic ideal that people survive by relying on each other. But Rabbit rejects their appeal to what a theologically astute character in *The Poorhouse Fair* calls "busy-ness," goodness without belief.

Updike's lost America is a nation of lost faith. Updike himself asks the key question about Rabbit in a preface to the 1977 Franklin Mint edition of *Rabbit, Run:* "Rabbit is the hero of the novel, but is he a good man? The question is meant to lead to another—What is goodness? . . . In the end, the act of running, of gathering a blank momentum 'out of a kind of sweet panic,' offers itself as containing a kernel of goodness; but perhaps a stone or a flower at rest holds the same kernel." Updike refuses to answer his question directly, but he implies that goodness is a large part of Rabbit's makeup when he calls him "fertile and fearful and not easy to catch . . . wild and timid, harmful and loving, hardhearted and open to the motions of grace" (n.p.).

Harmful and loving, Updike's hero personifies D. H. Lawrence's famous definition of "the essential American soul," the American Adam, as "hard, isolate, stoic, and a killer" (73). Rabbit's harmful, loving pursuit of grace is especially unsettling because it is a product not of the 1960s, the drop-out decade, but of the 1950s, the so-called tranquil Eisenhower years. As Updike explains in the foreword to the Modern Library edition, "*Rabbit, Run* was written in 1959, in the present tense. The time of its writing contained the time of its action" (n.p.). That is, the songs and news and styles that Harry hears and sees are those that Ace Anderson, Flick Webb, and Updike hear and see in the 1950s. The present tense also allows Updike to stress the immediacy of Rabbit's sensations, which in turn calls attention to the primary trait of his character: Harry feels but he does not think. Rabbit reacts to every stimulus as if it exists only in the present, without development from the past or reverberation toward the future. He is Lewis's literary hero, springing from nowhere into the present, affecting the culture before being defeated or destroyed by it. In this sense he is also an extreme product of the hermetic Eisenhower years. Updike comments: "My fiction about the daily doings of ordinary people has more history in it than history books" (qtd. in Samuels 106).

The broader historical context of the Rabbit tetralogy frames the traditional American conflict between the rights of the individual and the demands of society. Probing the complexity of the American experiment, Updike asks the same question that intrigued Cooper, Melville, Hawthorne, and Twain. Should the hero define himself by social convention, or should he indulge his yearning toward individual belief? Harry sees the conflict as either a nine-to-five job and dinner in the kitchen or the freedom to run but with no place to go. Updike calls this clash of values the "yes, but" quality of his fiction: "Yes, in *Rabbit, Run,* to our inner urgent whispers, but—the social fabric collapses murderously" (qtd. in Samuels 100). Although Rabbit is not intelligent enough to realize it, the unsolvable problem that Updike sets him is cultural. The reader may applaud Harry's reluctance to give in, but the reader also shrinks from the pain that his running causes. As Updike explains, "There is no reconciliation between the inner, intimate appetites and the external consolations of life. . . . [T]here is no way to reconcile these individual wants to the very real need of any society to set strict limits and to confine its members" (qtd. in Gado 92).

Rabbit's refusal to allow culture to absorb self may be either the courage not to relent to "sivilization"—an intuitive realization that what is right socially may be wrong personally—or it may be individualism bordering on selfishness. But the rightness or wrongness of Rabbit's run is not the issue; rather, the tetralogy urges acknowledging the complexity of the dilemma. The Rabbit novels do not offer answers, but they do pose problems; and one problem, as illustrated by the epigraph to *Rabbit, Run*, is how do people find grace when the little demands of living crowd their lives? Ace, Flick, Harry—and Updike—do not know. The epigraph—a quotation from Pascal—reads, "The motions of Grace, the hardness of the heart; external circumstances." Rabbit may be many things, but his heart is not always hard. What he does have are the culturally sanctioned forms of school, family, work, and church, all of which fail him. The epigraph suggests that grace and hardness are in tension and that the relation between social obligation and internal need is determined by the external circumstances of one's life. Culture shapes personality. Social forces clash with the promise of possibilities. The demands of others deny the motions of grace. It is not that culture is malignant or that Harry is a saint, but that neither can prevent the slow disintegration of the other. Updike's negative critics want him to take a stand, to blame either social pressure or individual whim, but to do so is to ignore the ambiguity of Updike's sense of culture. If Rabbit could understand the harmony of Pascal's thought, he would stop running. Rather than wait for the grace that would reconcile both external circumstances and nonspiritual internal needs, he runs. Yet even though he runs, he is the only character to intuit the motions of grace. He cannot translate his intuition into words, but his inarticulate yearning is more valuable than the Reverend Eccles's insistence on demythologizing belief to the level of humanistic cooperation and, finally, compromise.

All Updike's Adamic hero can do is transfer his pursuit of grace to the realm of athletics, where he was once a star with motion and glide. Rabbit's forcing himself into the sandlot basketball game at the beginning of *Rabbit, Run* is Ace's dancing the jitterbug and Flick's dribbling the inner tube writ large. If, in the later volumes of the tetralogy, Rabbit plays less basketball and more golf, he still pursues "it" in the guise of a perfect tee shot. At various times he feels "pinned," trapped by a "shark," "glued-in," "manipulated," and "threatened." In each case the sensation of being crowded challenges the desire for fluid rhythm, graceful action. Significantly, when he tries to renew his stalled momentum at the end of the tetralogy, he does so on a basketball court. To return home to a family in chaos would be to embrace the external circumstances of culture. Like Huck, Harry can't stand it—he's "been there before."

Late in *Rabbit, Run*, Angstrom has what I consider the key insight into both the social dynamic of the entire tetralogy and Updike's sense of American culture as a whole. Deserting the mourners at the grave, Harry sets out on his last but undetermined run, and as he does so he glimpses the conflict between the right way of cultural expectation and the good way of individual need: "On this small fulcrum he tries to balance the rest, weighing opposites against each other: Janice and Ruth, Eccles and his mother, the right way and the good way, the way to the delicatessen—gaudy with stacked fruit lit by a naked bulb—and the other way, down Summer Street to where the city ends" (433–34). Beyond the city lies, to Updike's lament, not Leatherstocking's forest or Huck's river but concrete highways going nowhere. Yet even Leatherstocking and Huck cannot resolve the conflict between the right way and the good way in American culture. They just have more room to run.

The "yes, but" quality that Updike brings to his fiction determines the tone of the Rabbit tetralogy. One feels the urge to say "yes" to the lure of graceful motion, but to do so one must say "no" to the demands of the social contract—often at catastrophic cost. The clash between internal yearning and external circumstances could paralyze a thinking person into stasis, but Rabbit rarely thinks. Relying on feeling and an instinct for life, he tries to maintain his momentum through the net. Updike's sympathy—but not his unqualified approval—goes with him.

The irony is that Rabbit is defeated even before he lights out for the territory, as "Ace in the Hole," "Ex-Basketball Player," and the high points of American fiction show. Saying good-bye to Harry Angstrom at the conclusion of *Rabbit at Rest* is like saying good-bye to Leatherstocking and Hester and Huck and Holden and Augie March. It's like saying good-bye to ourselves.

Note

1. I use the following editions: *Rabbit, Run* (New York: Modern Library, 1965); *Rabbit at Rest* (New York: Knopf, 1990).

2
Charles Berryman
Updike Redux
A Series Retrospective

There are several challenges inherent in a retrospective of the Rabbit novels. Is the series coherent despite its interrupted creation over three decades? Does the main character reflect important changes in the culture of America? Do the repeated scenes of adultery give a basic design to the series? What terms are suggested by Updike for an evaluation of the protagonist? The four novels together have been described in the 1991 award from the National Book Critics Circle as "a work which will stand as one of the major achievements of American fiction in the 20th century." If the series is now complete, as Updike has promised (assuming he will resist the urge to add "Rabbit Resurrected" as a fifth title), it is time for a retrospective.

Each volume in the series was received with a mixture of praise and criticism, but the growing reputation of the author follows an ironic pattern. The most daring novel, *Rabbit Redux* (1971),[1] with its interracial cast and scenes of apocalyptic violence, was dismissed by one critic as "jarring and offensive to both mind and taste" (Lyons 44), while the third novel, *Rabbit Is Rich* (1981), which tends to probe deeply into the surface of things, won the triple crown of book awards and the most public acclaim.

Updike was close to the beginning of his career when he introduced the character Harry Angstrom in *Rabbit, Run* (1960). Both author and character were still in their twenties, and the novel was well received as a portrait of a young man who follows his instinct to run away from the confines of marriage and responsibility. This early novel, the second in Updike's career, thus helped to establish his reputation for the dramatic study of adultery in terms of psychological realism. Not much critical attention, however, was paid to how the protagonist may be a representative American figure. Updike includes a very detailed and realistic description of the sights and sounds of a small American city during the late 1950s, but the conduct of Harry Angstrom appears to be driven more by his personal history than by any larger political sense of American destiny.

Updike published three further novels before he returned to Harry

Angstrom a decade later in *Rabbit Redux*. The success of the early novel had become a particular challenge for the author. "I got sick of people talking about Rabbit, sick of them asking me what happened to him. So I decided to revisit my old friend" (*Picked-Up Pieces* 510). Updike wrote the sequel, he tells us, when "the Sixties pressed heavily upon me," and the social turmoil so obvious at the end of the decade speaks from every page of *Rabbit Redux*. Author and character, both a decade older, feel invaded by the chaos of the time. By having Skeeter and Jill come into the life of Harry Angstrom, Updike expands his fiction to include the social problems America is experiencing in the late 1960s. By narrating the novel again in the present tense, Updike continues to offer a form of consciousness that hovers between author and character. The action of the novel unfolds against the television news of Apollo 11 and the war in Vietnam.

Rabbit Redux was received as "a paradigm of contemporary American history" (Uphaus 80), but a number of the critics were not pleased. No doubt the second book in a series is a natural target for criticism, and the growing career of an author tends to invite a closer scrutiny. In any event, the novel was described as "a guided tour of virtually every negative cliché that can be applied to America today" and was dismissed for its "breathtaking ineptitude" (Lyons 49). Perhaps the audience was not ready for Harry Angstrom to be talking politics with Jill and Skeeter, who represent class and racial concerns not imagined in the earlier novel. Nor ready for the familiar subject of adultery to be presented in metaphors of space exploration and the rape of Vietnam. Thus a bold picture of what Updike has called "the most dissentious American decade since the Civil War" (*Hugging the Shore* 858) remains the least appreciated novel in the tetralogy.

Updike again published three more novels before returning after yet another decade to a more comic version of his familiar character in *Rabbit Is Rich*. The education of Harry Angstrom continues as he makes love on a bed full of gold coins and discovers the unexpected dividends of wife-swapping, but at forty-six he enjoys more sex and money than he deserves, and the events of the novel are less violent and tragic. No child drowns or burns to death. Only the gas pumps have shrouds to mark the energy crisis of 1979. This time around, however, the critics were ready to cheer and celebrate a "brilliant performance" (Kazin 3). Updike was treated to a second appearance on the cover of *Time* to mark his success at fifty, and the magazine reported the good news that "Rabbit has evolved into a quintessentially American character" (Gray 81).

Looking back on the success of *Rabbit Is Rich,* the author makes a self-mocking apology for winning so many prizes. "Why some books win prizes and others don't is a mystery. In part it was that by this time, I'd been around so long, and was obviously working so hard, that people felt sorry for me and furthermore hoped that if Rabbit and I received a prize we would go away and put an end to this particular episode in American letters." Updike knows, of course, the advantage of talking about his own work with modest good humor. When he describes *Rabbit Is Rich* as "an upbeat book in spite of itself" or cheerfully admits that "it's a big, basically bouncy book that won prizes," the tone of self-mockery is meant to disarm the potential critics ("Why Rabbit" 24).

The same pattern continues with the next decade of Updike's career: three more novels and then a return, in 1990, to the fate of Harry Angstrom. This time, however, the author insists that "*Rabbit at Rest* will be the fourth and last of my so-called Rabbit books" ("Why Rabbit" 1). Updike also admits that "it's a depressed book about a depressed man, written by a depressed man" (24). While that hardly sounds like much of an advertisement for a new novel, the tone does reveal the level of personal involvement the author feels with his creation. Indeed, Updike confesses that "deciding to wind up the series was a kind of death for me" (24). The writing of the novel, in fact, was interrupted by several visits Updike made in 1989 to be with his dying mother in Pennsylvania. Her death occurred shortly after the first draft of the novel was finished, and by the time of its publication the next year Updike felt ready to acknowledge that "her dying became interwoven with my own sense of aging and my hero's even more severe sense of aging" (24).

This final novel about the author's fictional self from a suburb of a small city in Pennsylvania thus reads like an extended meditation on the shadows of mortality. After Angstrom's initial heart attack, thoughts of dying are seldom absent from his mind. The news on television is full of disasters, including a major plane crash and reports of a coming hurricane. The novel has more than its share of worried doctors, intensive care units, and technical descriptions of how the heart does or does not work. The same realistic detail that Updike used to represent the passion of a young athlete in *Rabbit, Run* is now lavished upon the physical decay of Angstrom, who thinks of himself as "fifty-five and fading." The reader may weary of hearing about every medical symptom that concerns Rabbit during the more than five hundred pages in this final novel, but it is all an occasion for Updike to represent the complex layers of memory. Author and character are recalling decades of experience in the anxious form of present-tense shared consciousness. Neither is quite ready to face the end of daydreaming or the paradox of consciousness being at rest.

Rabbit at Rest was received with the respect that might be appropriate at the funeral of an old friend. The novel did win a National Book Critics Circle Award and the Pulitzer Prize, but the celebration of Updike's achievement was less enthusiastic than had been the case a decade earlier. There was no reappearance on the cover of *Time*. Perhaps the fate of Harry Angstrom had come to seem rather provincial when compared with major changes in the world. The novel ends just before the collapse of communism in Eastern Europe, but Angstrom is more concerned with his boring retirement in Florida. Updike and his main character have lived their adult lives in the context of the cold war, but the news of its passing is minimal in *Rabbit at Rest*. Angstrom does feel rather uncertain of himself when he parades on the Fourth of July in an Uncle Sam costume, but his anxiety is typically directed more at the palpitations of his own heart than any larger political meaning. Gone are the days of *Rabbit Redux* when Angstrom would debate with Jill and Skeeter about racial issues and international politics.

The most daring scene in *Rabbit at Rest* is no doubt the sexual encounter of Angstrom and his daughter-in-law. Adultery is a major theme in all the Rabbit novels, but the progression of Ruth, Jill, Thelma, and now even his son's wife, Pru, follows a rather mindless path. When Harry left his wife in *Rabbit, Run* and started living with a part-time prostitute, the move may have been impulsive and selfish, but at least the moral implications were explored in a complex dialogue of conscience. When he casually sleeps with his daughter-in-law, however, there appears to be no more presence of mind than when he eats birdseed from a dispenser at the zoo. Perhaps it is true that Angstrom has never been very clear about his motives or conduct, and his misadventures throughout the series have been depicted with more than a little dark satire of modern America adrift without a moral compass, but his conduct in the final volume tends to match the nihilism of his thought that "nothing matters very much," together with its equal, "we'll all soon be dead." After such knowledge, what forgiveness? Any reader who has followed the adventures of Rabbit for more than fifteen hundred pages is apt to feel at least a bit disappointed by the banality of his end.

A major problem inherent in the critical task of measuring the achievement of a finished series is the changing perspective that comes from a second reading of the novels in sequence. The opening basketball scene in *Rabbit, Run*, for example, appears to have a deeper sense of fate when the reader happens to know where Rabbit will fall victim to his final heart attack. Any second reading of a novel, of course, is apt to upset the timing of expectation and surprise that may have informed the initial response. Perhaps no later encounter with Rabbit's sudden flight from his daughter's funeral will recapture the shock and excitement of the initial reading. The repeated scrutiny of a series, however, is apt to complicate the problem that comes with hindsight. If the pleasure of reading Updike's work depends in part upon the fresh encounter of a narrative in the present tense, any retrospective study should at least acknowledge its difference from the experience of following the adventures of Harry Angstrom for the first time.

The problem of altered response is compounded with a series that extends to four volumes and moves ahead in decade-long leaps. How consistent are the different incarnations of Harry Angstrom? Indeed, were all four novels written by the same author? Updike is mindful of such questions when he compares the writing of *Rabbit Is Rich* with that of its predecessor: "I was in a different town, I had a different wife, a different sense of myself . . . I was at home in America, all right" ("Why Rabbit" 24). If the consciousness of each novel does hover between author and character in the unusual style of present-tense narration, then Updike's progressive sense of himself is important to our understanding of the sequence. If the final volume was "written by a depressed man," as Updike admits, how does it alter our response to the earlier book that was created when the author "was feeling pretty good . . . at home in America"?

If character and author are apt to change from novel to novel, the same is true of America itself, and that further complicates the task of reconsidering the series. Nothing has been more common in the critical study of the Rabbit novels than to view their protagonist as a representative American. Perhaps the most extensive view of this sort is Dilvo Ristoff's *Updike's America: The Presence of Contemporary American History in John Updike's Rabbit Trilogy*. The apparent realism of Updike's style, of course, encourages the reader to believe that the author is holding a mirror up to contemporary America, but the images of history are not stable, nor is Updike's style a mere reflection of the American scene. Indeed, the essays in this collection, from Donald Greiner's view of Rabbit as an American Adam to James Plath's analysis of form and content in terms of a Vermeer painting, suggest the wide range of critical approaches for Updike's creation of history.

"Although the first novel had a few overheard news items in it," Updike explains, "it wasn't really in a conscious way about the 50's. It just was a product of the 50's . . . written by a sort of helplessly 50's guy" ("Why Rabbit" 24).

A decade later, however, *Rabbit Redux* was written as a "vehicle in which to package some of the American unease that was raging all around us." Updike was then ready to identify the political dimensions of the novel: the "echoes and ramifications of the national and international disturbances that were so preoccupying in the late 60's" (24). If the angst of Harry Angstrom in *Rabbit, Run* is seen initially as more personal than political, a reading informed by the later novels is apt to reinforce our sense of the character as a political symbol. When he plays golf, for example, is it merely an innocent expression of his role as Adam in the Garden, or should he remind us of Eisenhower in the 1950s gazing down the green fairways of indifference? Such questions are inherent in any reconsideration, but with a series in which the political and social perspectives unfold over a span of three decades, the reader with perfect hindsight is left with multiple choices for the image of America.

The opening scene of *Rabbit Is Rich* introduces an America running out of gas in the late 1970s, but the narrative unfolds with enough irony and optimism to guarantee its popularity. Although Updike describes the third novel in the series as "a national picture" of a decade with America feeling a "general sense of exhaustion," he admits that his own good mood produced a "cheerful" and "upbeat book" ("Why Rabbit" 24). If the fortunes of the main character are more closely tied to the well-being of the author, what happens to our view of the character at a time when the author is doing well but America may be in decline? "That the America of the Rabbit novels has seen steady decline," claims Stacey Olster, "is no secret to any reader of Updike's works" ("Rabbit Rerun" 47). Perhaps, but the comic success of Angstrom making love on a bed full of gold coins may remind us that whatever views of self, character, and country are blended together for the perspective of *Rabbit Is Rich,* their coherence is informed by a pervading irony.

Coming to understand the ironic distance between a cheerful author and a depressed America in the late 1970s may help us to read either forward or backward in the series. The next book—"about a depressed man"—takes place a decade later, when a new American president is talking about a new world order. There is no comfort, however, for Harry Angstrom in the possible end of the cold war. His version of Uncle Sam in *Rabbit at Rest* is too aware of his own failing health. Angstrom may somehow represent the United States, but Updike wants us to enjoy the irony of Harry marching out of step in the Fourth of July parade. Nor was he in step with American history back in the late 1960s. In the very decade that Norman Mailer was arrested during the protest march on the Pentagon, Angstrom was supporting the Vietnam War in several conversations with an angry veteran. And how did Rabbit respond to the most prominent American success in 1969? The news of Americans walking on the moon only made Angstrom feel more lonely and deserted. The report on television is "all about space, all about emptiness" (*Redux* 22).

Thus it could be argued that Updike creates a protagonist for each decade who runs contrary to the prevailing mood of the country. Angstrom feels trapped by the conformist 1950s and repeatedly tries to run away, but a decade later, when the rebellion of the next generation tends to dominate the news, he feels led back home to stand for order and responsibility. Angstrom is rather optimistic and rich in 1979 despite announcements from Washington about American malaise, and a decade later he is depressed and dying just when his fellow Americans are told to welcome a new world order.

The critical practice of interpreting the character of Harry Angstrom, either in harmony or discord with some prevailing American mood, is an invitation, of course, to traffic in vague estimates of national attitudes and character. Even if there is a degree of sense in describing Angstrom from time to time as irresponsible, reactionary, self-satisfied, and depressed, the images of American culture that form the background of each novel are more detailed and complex than what can be suggested with any simple label of a decade. No doubt the fresh reading of a novel as close as possible to its present-tense setting is more likely to be faithful to its complex life than any later critical attempt to measure a pattern of changing attitudes or ironic displacement. Nevertheless, the public record does include remarks Updike has made at award ceremonies when he not only reviews the different incarnations of Harry Angstrom in terms of American history, but also identifies himself with the life stages of his fictional character. "His sense of being useless," Updike says of Angstrom, "has this political dimension, then. Like me, he has lived his adult life in the context of the Cold War. He was in the Army, ready to go to Korea, hawkish on Vietnam, proud of the moon shot" ("Why Rabbit" 25). The last phrase suggests that Updike may no longer remember the emptiness Rabbit felt in response to the moon shot back in 1969. Any critical effort to reconsider the Rabbit series is therefore subject to the possible confusion of author and critic alike, especially when both are reviewing the progress of a character who may or may not represent Updike's ambivalent self-projection across forty years of American history.

The differences between author and character are more apparent than the underlying similarities. Whether he is a Linotype operator for a local paper in *Rabbit Redux* or the manager of a Toyota dealership in *Rabbit Is Rich*, Angstrom does not appear on the surface to have much in common with the professional author who left Pennsylvania for Harvard, Europe, an early job with the *New Yorker,* and more than one appearance on the cover of *Time.* The fact, however, that Updike uses the local setting of his own childhood for Angstrom's home territory suggests that the fictional character is deeply rooted in the author's vision of himself. Perhaps the character should be interpreted as an alter ego who represents that part of Updike doomed to be at odds with the world, the part that could neither escape the stubborn ties of his childhood setting nor be content with their limited rewards. Just as Angstrom runs away in the first novel, only to travel in a circle back to his point of origin, Updike also returns again and again to the pain and hopes of his alter ego in Pennsylvania.

Rabbit's goals are not very clear when he first attempts to escape from his hometown. He would like to drive south until coming to a beach on the Gulf of Mexico, but even with the help of a new map he cannot follow a route in that direction. "The only way to get somewhere," a local farmer tells him, "is to figure out where you're going before you go there" (*Run* 28). This is the first advice offered to Rabbit in the novel, and he replies, "I don't think so." Nor did Updike have a map that he could follow to create the series of Rabbit novels. Indeed, during the writing of the first volume there was no thought at all of a sequel. Updike admits instead: "The way the novel expanded under my hands forced me to abandon a certain determined modesty in my literary ambitions. *Rabbit, Run* was originally to be one of two novellas bound into a single volume; with its companion, *The Centaur,* it would illustrate the polarity between running and plodding, between the rabbit and the horse" (*Hugging the Shore* 849). So much for road maps! Not only does Updike circle back three times to re-create the area of his childhood for the further adventures of Harry Angstrom, in the final novel he ironically gives him a retirement in Florida almost within sight of the Gulf of Mexico.

The changing intentions of the author make it difficult to chart a coherent route through the Rabbit novels, and the "way the novel expanded under my hands" into different books may serve to remind us that any reconsideration of an Updike work should take into account a possible relationship with "companion" volumes apart from the series in question. Given the appearance of three other novels during each interval in the Angstrom series, it is hardly possible here to explore the many promising connections. Nor is it feasible to survey the large number of poems and stories created by Updike over three decades that may have influenced in progress the changing incarnations of Harry Angstrom. However, two prototypes for the character of Rabbit are discussed by Donald Greiner in this volume, and a few links to other works should be mentioned.

Given the importance of adultery in each of the Rabbit novels, it is more than likely that Updike's view of the subject was influenced by his concurrent treatment of it in a trilogy based on the *Scarlet Letter*. In this series he retells a modern version of the Hawthorne story from the point of view of each main character. The minister's account comes in *A Month of Sundays* (1975), which is the novel that follows *Rabbit Redux*. There is also a minister, however, in *Rabbit, Run* whose lustful wife is ready to tempt the young and unfaithful Angstrom. The story of the betrayed husband in the tradition of Hawthorne is told in *Roger's Version* (1986), and the modern rendering of Hester Prynne's account is given in *S.* (1988). These volumes appear during the final interval in the Angstrom series and may challenge Updike to present the most extreme act of adultery in *Rabbit at Rest*. The heroine of *S.* leaves her husband to join a fake religious master at a commune in Arizona, but adultery with a pious hypocrite, as Hester Prynne discovered, only leaves her "in the dark labyrinth of mind with a home and comfort nowhere." The road to nirvana for Updike's heroine in *S.* is both a sad and comic journey into a contemporary maze of self-deception and betrayal. The road of adultery for Harry Angstrom leads him into a very similar mental landscape.

Updike has talked and written about Hawthorne a number of times, but his address to the American Academy of Arts and Letters in 1979 makes clear that his interest is in the contest of spirit and flesh in Hawthorne's fiction. Updike begins his address with the question, "What did Hawthorne believe?" and then goes on to explore how the Puritan ideas in Hawthorne's imagination are challenged by the material world (*Hugging the Shore* 73–80). The solution for Hawthorne was to bring together the real and imaginary in the basic design of a romance. Updike would soon attempt such a design in *The Witches of Eastwick* (1984), where adultery with the devil is the aim of three different women. This novel clearly owes as much to Hawthorne as the trilogy based on *The Scarlet Letter*, and it shows again how the subjects of adultery and faith, which were combined in the first Rabbit novel, have developed in Updike's imagination during the intervals of the Rabbit series.

The contest between spirit and flesh is most apparent in the first novel as Angstrom moves back and forth between marriage and infidelity. While the minister and the prostitute vie for the soul and body of our hero, he is further tempted by the minister's wife, and his refusal of this second chance for adultery sets off the chain of events that leads to the tragic drowning of his infant daughter. Adultery is a matter of concern in each Rabbit novel to follow, but never again does it have the force of a moral dilemma worthy of Hawthorne. Neither the minister nor his wife appears in the later Rabbit novels. Updike continues instead to explore such types in the concurrent series based on *The Scarlet Letter,* and that leaves Angstrom more or less stranded in a secular world. As a result, his adultery in *Rabbit Is Rich* is merely a comic scene of wife-swapping on a Caribbean vacation, and sleeping with his daughter-in-law in the final volume only happens when Rabbit is preoccupied with the shadows of his own mortality. By then Angstrom no longer has any will to resist adultery, and hardly any moral sense to comprehend why his wife and son are shocked by his conduct.

In *Rabbit Redux,* when Harry's wife has an affair with a salesman at the Toyota dealership, the shock and betrayal Angstrom feels are shown by Updike in full sympathetic detail. On the same day that Apollo 11 lifts off for the moon, Harry comes home to find his wife absent and his teenage son talking about the rocket launch. The news on television about space travel matches the journey that Angstrom must suffer into the new loneliness of his heart. He must cope with jealousy, fear, lust, and defeat just as the television screen shows the first Americans walking on the moon. If the moon is traditionally associated in literature with love and madness, it may be that Angstrom learns more about both of these subjects than the two astronauts with their footprints in the moondust. Rabbit and his wife, however, are ready to come back together again at the end of the novel, and the consequences of adultery are treated with less sympathy in the rest of the series. Updike in the meantime explores what happens to the descendants of Hester Prynne in novels like *S.* and *The Witches of Eastwick.*

Another interest that Updike explores between Rabbit novels also takes him back to the time of Hawthorne's success before the Civil War. If the 1850s begin with the bringing together of the real and imaginary in Hawthorne's definition of romance, the decade ends in politics with the failed compromise of James Buchanan to hold together the United States of America. After completing the first Rabbit book, Updike admits, "I wanted to write a historical novel about James Buchanan . . . a fascinating man, at least to me. I did so much research I began to dream about him" ("Why Rabbit" 24). The research, however, would not lend itself easily to fiction, and Updike returns instead to follow the adventures of Angstrom in "the most dissentious American decade since the Civil War." Nevertheless, the fate of the mid-nineteenth-century president is still so much on Updike's mind during the writing of *Rabbit Redux* that a minor character in the new book is given the same name. The last president to compromise the issue of slavery is thus ironically transformed into a black co-worker for Angstrom at Verity Press. The presence of Buchanan in the novel then allows Updike to introduce the black Vietnam veteran, Skeeter, who returns from the war and moves in with Rabbit. Their conversation often resembles a debate on the radical politics of war and race relations, subjects that bewilder and frighten Rabbit as much as they did the American president a century earlier.

Updike is amused by his own compromise with the research on Buchanan. "Having told a number of reviewers I was writing a book about Buchanan, I painted him black and put him in [*Rabbit Redux*], too" (*Hugging the Shore* 858). The separation of the Angstroms during a "most dissentious" decade thus has a distant parallel in the fate of America's only bachelor president on the eve of the Civil War. Rabbit feels more than loneliness and frustration—life as he knows it is falling apart: "He put his life into rules he feels melting away now" (*Redux* 53). The fire that destroys his house when Jill and Skeeter are living with him is no surprise and no accident. The violent death of Jill in the burning house is another tragic loss of American youth and idealism, no matter how foolish and pathetic, at a time when the rules of society are indeed melting away. Near the end of the novel Angstrom loses his job at Verity Press, but the management is afraid to fire Buchanan.

During the next interval in the Rabbit series, Updike found a different way to express his interest in Buchanan. The only play in Updike's career, *Buchanan Dying*, comes in 1974. Although it is also rooted in Pennsylvania, this play may have served to disentangle the historical figure in Updike's imagination from the fiction of the Rabbit series. At least no black or white character named Buchanan appears again in the Rabbit novels.

The research on Buchanan, nevertheless, is used again in *Memories of the Ford Administration* (1992), the first novel to appear after Angstrom was left close to death in *Rabbit at Rest*. If a retrospective of the Rabbit series is now informed by a reading of Updike's more recent work, it needs to be acknowledged that *Memories of the Ford Administration* is a comic parody of such an academic project. The narrator of this novel is a professor at Wayward College who is stranded midway between a broken marriage and his research on the life of Buchanan. *Memories of the Ford Administration* is supposed to be a report on its title subject to an association of historians, but instead the professor/narrator tells the story of his own confused life against flashbacks of the unhappy career of Buchanan, and as far as the Ford presidency is concerned, the narrator confesses, "I remember nothing" (369). The joke, of course, is not merely on the easy-to-forget Ford administration, but on the confusion of history and fiction at the heart of the Rabbit series, and finally on the presumption of reducing either to some academic discourse.

Updike has not served time as a professor of literature or creative writing. He prefers, for better or worse, the solitary confinement of authorship. His satire of academic life in *Memories of the Ford Administration*, however, does indicate some dialogue between his fiction and its critics. Thus it may be the case that some of the hostile criticism of *Rabbit Redux* is finally answered by Updike in his novel *Brazil* (1994). The major complaints about *Rabbit Redux* include charges of misrepresenting America in the 1960s— "image follows predictable image of ugliness, sterility, decay, hostility, and betrayal" (Lyons 50)—and failing to satisfy the critics with a main character who is "the quintessence of the non hero" (Detweiler, *John Updike* 50). The most negative criticism, however, has to do with the black veteran who announces himself as the Christ of the new Dark Age. "Seldom, if ever," says Eugene Lyons, "has any white writer been paralyzed into sentimental and self-contradictory blather quite so foolish in attempting to deal with a black character" (57–58). The self-proclaimed religious prophet in *Rabbit Redux* is last seen trying to escape from the police by running in the direction of Galilee. Updike merely reports the character's death in the next Rabbit novel, thus escaping further criticism on this score for the rest of the series, but in *Brazil* the main character is a black man who continues to run with the burdens of violence and alienation that exposed Updike to such earlier criticism.

Updike's return in *Brazil* to the image of a man on the run from his fate may take us back to the initial conception of Harry Angstrom in *Rabbit, Run*, but the racial identity of the hero in *Brazil* also reminds us that the angst of a man trying to escape his fate is transferred from Angstrom to a black character as early as *Rabbit Redux*. Indeed, it is the reported death of this figure in the next Rabbit book that leaves the rest of the series with a more stationary and less interesting protagonist. Updike's return to a black hero in *Brazil* is a rather bold move for a white author in the 1990s because it comes at a time when the critics are even more concerned about multicultural and racial issues. Although the social construction of racial identity is a current topic of literary criticism, Updike settles an old score by presenting a black hero who becomes a white man and then is murdered by the very image of his previous self.

Nothing is more common in Updike's fiction than the return of a previous self. Indeed, the very principle of return, whether in single titles such as *Rabbit Redux* and *Beck Is Back* (1982) or in multiple volumes about

Angstrom, Buchanan, and the characters of *The Scarlet Letter,* may suggest a design of repetition at the heart of Updike's work. The pattern of return, no doubt, shows how the demands of realism are supported by the power of memory. The need to remember is most apparent when Updike returns to former selves in his autobiography, *Self-Consciousness* (1989), or when the narrator in *Memories of the Ford Administration* is unable to resist the story of his own past, but it also drives the author and main character of the Rabbit novels. Updike returns to the scene of his childhood in Pennsylvania for the setting of the novels, and even in the first volume a young Angstrom is already characterized by the memory of his recent triumph as an athlete. Despite the present-tense narration used for the series, nostalgia remains a key to the mind of Angstrom, and each new decade merely adds another layer to his memory. Updike's last return to the aging Rabbit reveals a character who now reads history and carelessly ruins his heart with a vain revisit to the sport of his youth. The only closure for this cycle of repetition in the Rabbit novels comes when the resources of the heart are exhausted.

The pattern of return may also reflect the natural rhythm of sexual energy. Consider the dynamic movement in *Rabbit, Run,* for example, and how it follows the desire, frustration, escape, and return of the protagonist. The first novel in the Rabbit series, indeed, may be seen as a paradigm of Updike's creative work. It is therefore no surprise that a variation of the same pattern is used for the attraction, separation, flight, and return of the tragic lovers in *Brazil.* Is there another contemporary writer who has done more to explore the contours of the imagination in terms of human desire? "What the New World was to Renaissance cartographers," writes Alfred Kazin, "sex is to Updike. No one has put so many coasts, bays, and rivers where once there was only silence" (3). Kazin's topographical metaphor, no doubt, has some charm and truth on its side—Rabbit even tries to follow a map in *Rabbit, Run*—but it is the temporal nature of desire that has more to do with the rhythm of Rabbit's adventures.

If the tempo for the Rabbit novels is set by the pattern of desire in the first volume, Updike then plays a variation of the same dynamic for *Rabbit Redux.* This time Angstrom is separated from his wife during most of the novel, and his frustration builds to the climax of group sex with Jill and Skeeter—"Strip and get into it, she's full of holes" (298)—followed by the violent scene of fire and death. The return of Rabbit's wife near the end of the book allows a new start for their marriage, but even the closing scene of their reunion takes place in a roadside motel. Rabbit may not literally be on the run again at the end of *Rabbit Redux,* but the visit to a motel suggests once more how the pattern of desire is shaped by the temporary quality of the experience.

America is described as running out of energy at the beginning of *Rabbit Is Rich* a decade later. Perhaps the shrouds on the gas pumps are an indication that Rabbit's sexual energy is also wrapped up in the daydreams of middle age. He doesn't feel much desire for his wife; their son has a more active sex life; and Rabbit imagines sleeping with the young wife of a friend. Even his dreams are comically betrayed, however, when the fantasy goal of wife-swapping on a Caribbean vacation fails to pair him with the desired prize. The dream of a temporary escape from marriage instead brings Rabbit together with the wife of another friend. The game of musical beds anticipates the comic line in *The Witches of Eastwick* about the fate of a divorcée in a small town: it is "a little like playing Monopoly; eventually you land on all the properties" (25), but this game unexpectedly lands Rabbit with a new mistress who dies in the next and final novel of the series.

The relationship of sex and death, of course, underlies the rhythm of tragic events throughout the Rabbit novels, from the loss of the infant daughter in *Rabbit, Run* to the final exhaustion of Angstrom's heart in *Rabbit at Rest.* The last two books, however, chart the loss of desire in a more predictable and tiresome manner. When the young hero runs from his wife in the first novel of the series, his pattern of flight and return is rich with existential and even spiritual possibility, but his later acts of adultery with a friend's wife and then with his own daughter-in-law are evidence, at best, that Rabbit is running in ever smaller circles. At the funeral of his mistress in *Rabbit at Rest,* he meets the other woman from his dreams of a decade earlier, but now he feels beyond any desire, and the pattern of escape and return is focused instead upon his own death.

As the shadows of mortality darken Angstrom's life in the final volume, he may still have some moments of courage and grace. When the first heart attack comes, for example, while he and his granddaughter are off the coast of Florida in a small boat, Rabbit does show enough willpower and presence of mind to return safely to shore. Given the number of deaths caused in part by Rabbit's careless running through life, the safe return of his granddaughter in *Rabbit at Rest* might be interpreted as a gesture of redemption. The return to shore, however, only brings Rabbit back to more heart trouble, and the brush with death leaves him with more fear than enlightenment. His turn to the reading of history at this point might also be seen as a brave attempt to come to terms with the questions of his own mortality, much as his creator had done the year before with the writing of his memoir, *Self-Consciousness,* but for Rabbit neither history nor his own incessant nostalgia brings him any real peace of mind. He once again follows his basic instinct to run away when his wife blames him for the adultery with their daughter-in-law. Only this time his flight takes him to the final heart attack in Florida. Updike thus ends the series, as he should, with the question of redemption quite unresolved.

At the end of the Rabbit tetralogy, Updike is particularly mindful of the beginning. Thus any final judgment of the main character should take us back to the quote from Pascal used as the epigraph for *Rabbit, Run:* "The motions of Grace, the hardness of the heart; external circumstances." This epigraph proves to be a reliable indication of the double conflict that will define the character of Rabbit in all four of his incarnations. While a contest remains between Angstrom's better instincts and the hardness of his heart, there is also an ongoing debate between Rabbit and the changing circumstances of America. Despite all reconsiderations inherent in a second or third reading of a series published over three decades, the abiding concern is still with the character and fate of the protagonist. The power of Updike's tetralogy ultimately depends upon our continued identification with the adventures of Harry Angstrom. Will the motions of grace prevail despite the growing hardness of Rabbit's heart? Will any element of character withstand the nay-saying force of external circumstances? Both questions by design are kept open from beginning to end.

Updike's strategy to withhold any resolution of the double conflict may keep us reading to the last page of *Rabbit at Rest,* but our sympathy for the character and fate of Rabbit is still likely to decline in the process. How many times can we observe Rabbit run away after hurting someone and not conclude that his heart is selfish and hard beyond redemption? Are not we likely to have more sympathy for his youthful adventures, which are often marked by a quest for some elevation of spirit, and find less to celebrate when he turns to wife-swapping on a Caribbean vacation or sleeping with his daughter-in-law? Perhaps the need to re-create a more extreme version of the conflict in each novel eventually undermines its credibility. The problem is made worse by the failure of the word "grace" to grow in meaning as Rabbit moves through the latter stages of his life. His spirit only soars with the memory of athletic achievement, and his faith in human passion to recover the lost triumph of his youth naturally proves to be vain and disappointing. Therefore no deepening sense of grace is available to balance what appears to be a gradual hardening of the heart. While there is much talk about religion with the local minister in the first novel, there are only doctors in the last book to diagnose the failing body. Our continued sympathy for the dying character must depend almost entirely upon the pathos of his return to the sport of his youth because the diminished heart at the end has more to do with veins and blood than love or redemption.

The balance of concern also shifts in the conflict between Rabbit and his external circumstances. As long as he is running from the conformity of the 1950s or the radical politics of the 1960s, there is a real contest between individual desire and American destiny, but as soon as he becomes rich in the third novel, the tension between self and world is diminished. After we laugh at Angstrom when he makes love on a bed filled with gold coins, or respond with some amusement when he parades down Main Street in the costume of Uncle Sam, there is less incentive to find the hints of grace in his accommodation to the world. Perhaps we retain enough faith in the independent Rabbit of the first two novels to sense that his new wealth and respectability do not quite fit the underlying character, and thus our amusement is still mixed with sympathy. Nevertheless, as his waist expands with his bank account, it becomes more and more difficult to remember the young athlete and his dreams of glory. The world is too much with the older Rabbit. The golf games, for example, in the last two novels have become rituals of success and retirement. They no longer come even close to the motions of grace adumbrated in *Rabbit, Run.*

Not only is the main character of the series weighed down by his material success and the growing knowledge of his own mortality, but this inevitable compromise with the world is even represented by the growing mass of realistic detail in the final two volumes. From the beginning, of course, Updike has placed the character of Rabbit against a background described in images of popular culture, but as the series progresses, the novels grow in size, the mundane references multiply, and the individual character by the end is almost lost beneath the weight of the realistic detail. What happens, for example, to the spirit of Rabbit in the final volume when his fate is represented by the charts and predictions of the medical world? At the beginning of the series Rabbit is full of desire but cannot even follow a road map. At the end every beat of his failing heart makes a line on a medical chart. The individual is close to becoming a mere statistic of mortality.

What keeps our interest to the end, and what redeems the series if not the character, is the stubborn loyalty Angstrom shows to his old dreams and rebellious self. Despite the banality of success and the emptiness of retirement, Rabbit continues in his own way to yearn for the motions of grace. Another outrageous act of adultery, another pathetic return to the basketball court—these may seem like poor examples of a dream sustained, but they show us the core self that Rabbit holds onto in the face of all worldly disappointments. Updike does not give heroic stature to his main character, nor a very complex or perceptive mind, but he does endow Rabbit with a stubborn heart and a strong desire for life. These resources of character are then matched by the challenges of four decades. Nothing can be resolved short of death, because the terms of the contest are universal. The narrative continues to the end in the present tense because it is designed to represent a shared consciousness of author, character, and audience. Or as Updike says, "the Rabbit in us all remains both wild and timid, harmful and loving, hard-hearted and open to the motions of Grace" (*Hugging the Shore* 851).

Notes

1. All references to the Rabbit novels are to the Knopf editions.

3 Jeff H. Campbell
"Middling, Hidden, Troubled America"
John Updike's Rabbit Tetralogy

Commenting on the 1969 moon landing, Harry "Rabbit" Angstrom notes that "Columbus flew blind and hit something, these guys see exactly where they're aiming and it's a big round nothing" (*Rabbit Redux* 22).[1] Angstrom, hero of Updike's four Rabbit books, explores the America of the 1950s, 1960s, 1970s, and 1980s, believing that "there is something out there that wants me to find it" (*Rabbit, Run* 127), but in many ways he, too, is "flying blind," just as Columbus did. In his four-decade-long quest, Harry does indeed "hit something," but the contrast between the all-too-pervasive nothingness discovered by the man Updike has called his "angst-ridden Everyman" (*Hugging the Shore* 850) and the wonder and promise felt by the Admiral of the Ocean Sea provides ironic commentary on the five hundred years of so-called progress that have followed Columbus's first voyage.

When he published *Rabbit, Run* in 1960, Updike did not plan to continue Harry's story. But people kept asking him what happened next, and "a little over ten years later, as the interminable sixties were drawing to their end, the idea that Harry . . . was still out there and running suddenly excited me." So he returned to Rabbit, now a "paunchy middle American" whose "reluctant education" offered "the parable that nobody else, in those shrill years, was offering" (*Hugging the Shore* 858). After finishing the second book, Updike publicly committed himself to two more Rabbit books, and decade by decade he has produced the volumes that not only, as he has said, "plausibly portray . . . a specimen American male's evolution into grandpaternity" (*Odd Jobs* 872), but also explore what Alexis de Tocqueville in 1835 called "habits of the heart," that is, mores that "shape mental habits" and are "the sum of moral and intellectual dispositions of men in society" (287). For as Updike has pointed out, Rabbit's story is not just about a "specimen male": "America—its news items, its popular entertainment, its economic emanations—is always a character in the Angstrom tetralogy as well" (*Odd Jobs*

870–71). The Rabbit books, then, elicit not only a picture of a contemporary Everyman but also portray major characteristics of four decades of American culture.

Rabbit, Run, Updike's second novel, published when he was just twenty-eight years old, brought him immediate acclaim as one of America's most promising young authors. In it he invented and introduced Harry Angstrom, nicknamed "Rabbit" as a boy for his pale eyes and "a nervous flutter under his brief nose" (3). An angstrom is actually a unit of length equal to one hundred millionth of a centimeter, used primarily to specify radiation wavelengths, but in the 1950s angst was the existentialist catchword for the anxiety and despair many intellectuals felt as they considered the absurd nature of individual human existence. Rabbit becomes, then, Updike's angst-ridden American Everyman, an individual infinitesimally small in the cosmic scheme of things, but one who views himself as the center of his universe.

Updike has said that all his books are meant to be moral debates with the reader (*Picked-Up Pieces* 502). *Rabbit, Run* asks the reader to consider whether or not Rabbit is a good man, and suggests a further question, "What is goodness?" (*Hugging the Shore* 850). Updike explains: "There is a case to be made for running away from your wife. In the late Fifties beatniks were preaching transcontinental travelling as the answer to man's disquiet. And I was just trying to say: 'Yes, there is certainly that, but then there are all these other people who seem to get hurt' " (*Picked-Up Pieces* 502).

"Kerouac's *On the Road* was in the air," Updike has said, "and a decade of dropping-out about to arrive, and the price society pays for unrestrained motion was on my mind" (*Hugging the Shore* 850). In a more recent interview, Updike adds that the "threatening" success of *On the Road* and its preaching of the frenetic search for sensation was an impetus to his writing *Rabbit, Run,* which he admits was an "anti–*On the Road.* It tried to say, yeah, it's nice to get out on the road, but you tend to make a mess of the people you leave behind. That freedom carries its own cost" (qtd. in Farney A10).

The moral debate aroused by Rabbit's self-centered running is rooted in what de Tocqueville saw as the most distinctive of the "habits of the heart" of the citizens of the then-young nation. Chief among these "habits of the heart" (today we would use the term *mores*) de Tocqueville noted individualism, then a new word: " 'Individualism' is a word recently coined to express a new idea, . . . a calm and considered feeling which disposes each citizen to isolate himself from the mass of his fellows" (506). Such citizens, Tocqueville added, "form the habit of thinking of themselves in isolation and imagine that their whole destiny is in their [own] hands" (508).

In 1970, Philip Slater published *The Pursuit of Loneliness*, a landmark sociological study of the state of de Tocqueville's individualism in modern American culture. Although *Rabbit, Run* precedes Slater's book by a decade, it illustrates Slater's thesis that American society's emphasis on untrammeled individualism "increasingly frustrates and aggravates" three basic human desires:

> 1. The desire for *community*—the wish to live in trust, cooperation, and friendship with those around one.
> 2. The desire for *engagement*—the wish to come directly to grips with one's social and physical environment.
> 3. The desire for *dependence*—the wish to share responsibility for the control of one's impulses and the direction of one's life. (8)

Slater avers that when a society systematically frustrates these basic desires, the society's underlying fabric is threatened. Or, as Updike says, "freedom carries its own cost."

Robert Bellah, Richard Madsen, William M. Sullivan, Ann Swidler, and Steven M. Tipton banded together to produce in 1985 another sociological analysis of American culture that has taken its place alongside Slater's *Pursuit of Loneliness* as a key evaluation of American individualism. Basing their study on careful joint research and numerous interviews with Americans from coast to coast, Bellah and his associates turned to de Tocqueville for the phrase that became their title: *Habits of the Heart*. These writers agree with Slater that the individualism first clearly defined by de Tocqueville 160 years ago may threaten the fabric of our culture. In fact, they speculate that this individualism "may have grown cancerous" (vii).

Certainly Rabbit is to be admired for believing that there is meaning beyond Mickey Mouse and MagiPeelers. As Updike has said, he intended in the book to say "yes . . . to our urgent inner whispers"—to the positive side of the American habit of trusting the desires of one's heart. But at the same time, he was saying "but—the social fabric collapses disastrously" (*Picked-up Pieces* 503). So the reader is brought into the debate.

Updike used an epigraph from number 507 of Pascal's *Pensées* to set the tone for the book: "The motions of grace, the hardness of the heart: external circumstances." The motions of grace suggest the sense of something transcendental that Rabbit seeks and which lifts him in some ways above the others in the book. But the external circumstances must be addressed, and it is with a hard heart that Rabbit responds to those around him. An experience that Rabbit has on his initial flight gives us a helpful guideline with which to pass judgment on his actions—which grow primarily out of the habits of a hardened heart.

Rabbit stops at a filling station and asks for a map. The farmer-attendant asks, "Son, where do you want to go?" (26). Rabbit confesses that he doesn't exactly know. The man tells him, "The only way to get somewhere, you know, is to figure out where you're going before you go there." Rabbit, however, responds, "I don't think so" (28). Later he does pick up a map, but he sees it as a "net, all those red lines and blue lines and stars, a net he is somewhere caught in." He feels that the filling station attendant, with his reference to maps and plans, has been mocking him, deriding "the furtive wordless hopes that at moments made the ground firm" for him. He thinks: *Figure out where you're going before you go there:* it misses the whole point and yet there is always the chance that, little as it is, it says it" (37; Updike's emphasis). Harry is not ready to accept that little as everything, however, nor is he willing to accept the "going through" quality of Christianity as he hears it preached in the Episcopalian minister's sermon (237). He refuses to chart a course, to carry through on a commitment to others, and at the end of the book he is still running. He is searching for a new world of meaning beyond the old mediocrity of Ozzie and Harriet in Eisenhower America. Harry has found nothing, but Updike intended Rabbit's zigzagging odyssey to challenge readers to weigh alternative habits of the heart. Neither Rabbit nor his creator stopped searching, and ten years later Updike moved his American Everyman—and his readers—into the decade of the sixties to illuminate some very different American habits of the heart

Updike has claimed that his "fiction about the daily doings of ordinary people has more history in it than history books, just as there is more breathing history in archeology than in a list of wars and changes of government" (*Picked-up Pieces* 501). *Rabbit, Run* is an Eisenhower-era book, its society characterized by political and philosophical apathy and conformity. But *Rabbit Redux* is set in 1969, the first of the Nixon years and the close of a tumultuous decade. Harry (almost nobody calls him Rabbit anymore), the searching, exploring individual, now finds himself forced to confront his existence as part of a wider community characterized by the Vietnam conflict and its critics, black militants and race riots, the counterculture and drugs, women's liberation, technological changes in the job market, and the exploration of outer space. As Harry compares the astronauts' carefully planned and mapped discovery of the barren nothingness of the moon to Columbus's surprising find of a rich new world he died without ever really comprehending, the reader recognizes that Harry himself in this book is thrust into worlds he never dreamed existed.

The story opens on the very day of the moon launch, and the first chapter closes with the televised report of man's first steps on lunar soil. The Vietnam War and race riots in the cities are subjects for heated debates among the characters. And when Janice leaves to live with her lover Charlie Stavros and the runaway hippie Jill and fugitive black militant Skeeter move in with Rabbit, it is as if, as Updike has pointed out, "the television set invades the guy's life. That is, these are sort of headline figures who come upon him, and I think it was true of a lot of us in the late sixties that all the things we preferred not to think about became unavoidable." In this novel, then, Rabbit becomes "the middle class man whose living room becomes the scene of atrocities and teach-ins and all those things" (qtd. in Campbell, *Updike's Novels* 286).

So we have not only history but also sociology. Slater's *Pursuit of Loneliness* presented the 1960s as a struggle between two cultures, the old and the new. According to Slater, "the basic assumption of the old culture is that human gratification is in short supply; the new culture assumes that it is plentiful." Furthermore, he adds, "the old culture tends to choose property rights over human needs, competition over cooperation, violence over sexuality, concentration over distribution, producers over consumers, means over ends, secrecy over openness, social forms over personal expression, Oedipal love over communal love," while "the new culture tends to reverse all these priorities" (94–95). Jill, Skeeter, Janice, and Charlie all present and represent that new culture, while Rabbit represents the old-culture, Middle American competitive individualism confronted with these new challenges.

Part of Janice's newly-found sense of self (no longer just an extension of her husband), for instance, is her acceptance of the new-culture idea that pleasure is plentiful rather than scarce or rationed. She has come to accept her body as "her toy, how strange to have to learn to play, they used to tell her, everybody, the gym teacher, the Episcopal minister, Mother even . . . not to make your body a plaything when that's just what it was" (*Redux* 54–55).

Charlie Stavros represents the new culture in its challenging of American imperialism. Rabbit insists on displaying an American flag decal on the window of his Falcon, but Charlie challenges him: "I just can't get too turned-on about cops bopping hippies on the head and the Pentagon playing cowboys and Indians all over the globe. That's what your little sticker means to me. It means screw the blacks and send the CIA into Greece" (44).

Skeeter's somewhat biased view of black history stresses the old culture's disastrous emphasis on competition instead of cooperation, producers over consumers:

> You really had it here, you had it all, and you took that greedy mucky road, man, you made yourself the asshole of the planet. Right? To keep that capitalist thing rolling you let all those asshole crackers have their way and now you's all asshole crackers, North and South however you look there's assholes, you lapped up the poison and now it shows, Chuck, you say America to you and you still get bugles and stars but say it to any black or yellow man and you get hate, right? Man the world does hate you, you're the big pig keeping it all down. (234)

But it is Jill who gives the most articulate and most poignant voice to the new-culture concerns. Jill introduces Rabbit to a type of thinking totally foreign to his previous experience. With her he begins to venture out on a side of life suggested by the epigraph Updike has used for Chapter 2: "It's different but it's very pretty out here." The words are Neil Armstrong's as he orbited around the familiar but limited earth, but they reflect Harry's own reaction to Jill, a new entity brought into his orbit. He is fascinated by her description of matter as "the mirror of spirit. . . . [I]nside it are these tiny *other* mirrors tilted this way and that and throwing the light back the wrong way. Because to the big face looking in, these little mirrors are just dark spots, where He can't see Himself" (159). Even so, Harry has difficulty accepting all that Jill and the other new-culture voices say. He tells Jill that she's always had it too cozy, has had things handed to her, doesn't know about fear. "Fear," he says. "That's what makes us poor bastards run. You don't know what fear is, do you, poor baby? That's why you're so dead." Jill responds as true spokesman for the new culture: "People've run on fear long enough. Let's try love for a change." Harry is not ready to accept all that Jill and the others represent. He responds: "Then you'd better find yourself another universe" (170).

The contrasts between the two cultures, between competitiveness and cooperation, fear and love, are made very clear. Although Harry is not converted to the new habits of the heart represented by the new culture (and neither was his creator, who during the decade steadfastly and in rather lonely fashion supported such old-culture causes as the Vietnam War), he is now a more mature American Everyman whom Updike presents as tolerantly curious, open to education. Updike has commented that "America and Harry suffered, marvelled, listened, and endured. Not without cost, of course. The cost of the disruption of the social fabric was paid, as in the earlier novel, by a girl. Iphigenia is sacrificed and the fleet sails on, with its quarreling crew" (*Hugging the Shore* 858–59).

Rabbit genuinely responds to Skeeter's lectures on black history, is impressed by the new ideas he finds in Jill's books, and grieves deeply over Jill's death. The fleet and its quarreling crew may sail on, but at least this one member of the crew has been challenged to move beyond the self-satisfied solipsism that ten years earlier found no outlet but running. The final word of the novel—the question "O.K.?"—recalls the words of astronaut Neil Armstrong used as epigraph for the final chapter of the book. After following Buzz Aldrin's instructions for leaving the spacecraft to step onto the lunar surface, Armstrong said, "O.K., Houston, I'm on the porch." Everything about the moon shot was perfect. Outer space—empty as it may be—has been successfully conquered by man and his machines. Can inner space, the habits of the individual heart, be similarly conquered and successfully related to that outer world? Updike offers no clear answer, and has insisted that "the question that ends the book is not meant to have an easy answer" (*Hugging the Shore* 859). But Rabbit and Janice, in their small personal world, do seem to be, like Neil Armstrong, "O.K." and "on the porch." Since one of the meanings of *redux* is "cured," Updike seems at least to suggest that the steps Rabbit takes off that porch will be in the right direction. Harry has explored new worlds and has opened the way for further discoveries.

Rabbit Is Rich finds Harry the manager of the Toyota agency inherited from his father-in-law. He and Janice have lived with Ma Springer since their own house burned a decade ago. It is now 1979, almost the end of the Carter era, a time of runaway inflation, energy crisis, and long lines at gas pumps. Both America and Harry seem to be running out of gas. Harry is not worried, however, because his Toyotas get great gas mileage and bring in good money that allows him and Janice to be an active part of the country club set.

At forty-six, Harry is well satisfied with himself. He still pursues his habit of individualism, but now he is not so concerned with his inner longings or the challenges of a counterculture. He is, rather, a type of individualist that Bellah and his associates find uniquely typical of modern America: the manager. "With the coming of the managerial society," they write, "the organization of work, place of residence, and social status came to be decided by criteria of economic effectiveness" (46).

With a comfortable income, Harry feels himself rich and, like many Americans, measures happiness in economic terms. Harry's managerial, economically based lifestyle is clouded, however, by the pervading sense that all economic satisfactions are doomed by the force of entropy, sometimes called the Second Law of Thermodynamics, which hypothesizes that the basic tendency is for all matter in the universe to subside into a uniform temperature, effectively bringing about the heat-death of the universe. In social terms, entropy is the doctrine of inevitable social decline and degeneration.

Rabbit Is Rich opens on this entropic note: "Running out of gas," Rabbit thinks as he stands in the showroom of Springer Motors in the book's first line. Rabbit also notes that producing gas pump shrouds has become a new industry (20), and everywhere he looks in Brewer, "once the fourth largest city in Pennsylvania but now slipped to seventh, structures seem to speak of expended energy." There are "great shapely stacks that have not issued smoke for half a century" and "scrolling cast-iron light stanchions not lit since World War II" (32). On a personal level, Rabbit finds that his desires and wants have shriveled. "Freedom, that he always thought was outward motion, turns out to be this inward dwindling" (97). When discussing the decline of American industry with his son, Harry insists that "We used to be the best," but Nelson only responds, "So I'm told" (120). Thinking of his father, Nelson observes that Rabbit once "had this crazy dim faith about himself left over from basketball or growing up as everybody's pet or whatever," but now "that spark is gone, leaving a big dead man on Nelson's chest" (314). When a friend asks Harry if he's seen *Jaws II*, he responds in a way that allows Updike to turn the entropy imagery into a clever barb aimed at himself: "D'you ever get the feeling that everything these days is sequels? . . . Like people are running out of ideas" (403).

These images, only a sampling of many that could be cited, indicate that the "running out of gas" metaphor does have an important place in the book, especially in its first three sections. But, as always with Updike, there is another side. As Updike told me in our 1976 interview, *Rabbit, Run* was "a deliberate attempt to present both the escapist, have-it-my-way will to live versus the social restraints" (qtd. in Campbell, *Updike's Novels* 295). And we have seen that *Rabbit Redux* showed Harry venturing out into new worlds yet still inextricably rooted in the same self, and the book ended with a question rather than an answer. So *Rabbit Is Rich* presents a sociological analysis of the pervading presence of entropy in Rabbit's personal life and that of American culture in such loving and intimate detail that a shock of recognition forces us to say, "Yes, he's right; things are running down; time is running out." But there is another side to be examined. In an interview shortly after the book was published, Updike commented that the aim of his fiction was "bringing the corners forward, or throwing light into them." "I distrust books involving spectacular people, or spectacular events," he continued. "Let *People* and *The*

National Enquirer pander to our taste for the extraordinary; let literature concern itself, as the Gospels do, with the inner lives of hidden men." Echoing Arthur Miller's belief that modern literature must accept the common man as tragic hero, Updike asserted that "the collective consciousness that once found itself in the noble must now rest content with the typical." His goal, he said, was not "to write gushers," but "to write books that are hard and curvy like keys, and that unlock the traffic jam in everybody's head. Something like $E = mc^2$, only in words one after the other" (*Hugging the Shore* 873–74).

Clearly, Updike intended this novel not as a dirge but as an attempt to find an equation to unlock the unquestioning acceptance of degeneration and decay that entropy seems to predict. In 1968, Updike produced the long autobiographical poem "Midpoint," Part III of which, titled "The Dance of the Solids," brilliantly analyzed some of the insights into reality offered by modern physics. These Spenserian stanzas were so scientifically sound that they were also printed separately in *Scientific American.* One of those insights that fascinated Updike was Max Planck's $E = hv$ equation, a formulation that defines the relationship of energy and frequency. The equation does not deny that light is made up of particles, as Newton's experiments indicated, but asserts that light also must be understood as waves. I cannot claim to understand the many implications of wave theory and wave mechanics, but I do understand the assertion of physicists Ernest C. Pollard and Douglas C. Huston that the "sensational" successes of the applications of wave theory are "almost mystical" (313). And it is these "almost mystical" successes that offer Updike a way of saying "yes" to entropy while adding his customary "but," examining another side of the puzzle. Physics says, "Yes, light is made up of particles," and then adds, "but it also consists of waves." Quantum theory affirms that absorption of energy is continuous (suggesting entropy), but counters that emission proceeds discontinuously in quanta of energy that depend on the frequency of the oscillation of electrons. Just so, Updike sees a regenerative force that contradicts and counteracts entropy.

One of the epigraphs Updike uses for *Rabbit Is Rich* is from a poem by Wallace Stevens entitled "A Rabbit as King of the Ghosts": "The difficulty to think at the end of the day, / When the shapeless shadow covers the sun / And nothing is left except light on your fur . . . " In this poem, the light of the sun, representing objective perception, is gone, covered by a shapeless, entropic shadow. But there is still the "light on your fur," what Stevens elsewhere in the poem calls "a rabbit-light" (150), the power of the imagination. Through a quantum jump, the imagination emits new energy on a different frequency that transforms an insignificant rabbit to a self that, Stevens says, "touches all edges" (151).

So despite the darkness and emptiness promised by the continuing expending of energy, there is a counterforce represented by the "light on your fur," an interrelationship of the poles of individualism's self-concern and the world of social responsibility. Counterpointing the novel's rational and sociologically precise entropy imagery of growing darkness, there is contrasting imagery that suggests an individualism of a different kind that must be seen by a different light—the light of mystery and faith, the light of the "something that wants me to find it" (*Run* 127). Bellah characterizes this more promising type of individualism as one rooted firmly in our American origins, tracing back far earlier than the managerial, economically measured individualism that Harry and his country club friends superficially represent. Bellah calls this individualism biblical and finds its roots in John Winthrop and his fellow Puritans. For them individualism was taken for granted, but the individual was seen first of all as a member of God's covenant community, not as a mere economic functionary or as a solipsistic self-server. For this type of individualism, "the fundamental criterion of success was not material wealth but the creation of a community in which a genuinely ethical and spiritual life could be lived." According to Bellah, this type of individualism has given "the American experiment as a whole a utopian touch that it has never lost, in spite of all our failings" (28–29).

There are several scattered images in *Rabbit Is Rich* that suggest this more idealistic and biblical view of the individual. As Rabbit looks at the young woman who he thinks may be his daughter by Ruth, his mistress from *Rabbit, Run* days, he finds it "wonderful to think" of "a secret message carried by genes all that way through all these comings and goings all these years, the bloody tunnel of growing and living, of staying alive" (34). The world may be running out of gas, but the secret messages of the genes will continue the life process.

On another occasion, Rabbit reflects that "although the world keeps ending . . . new people too dumb to know it keep showing up as if the fun's just started" (*Rich* 88). He may echo fashionable ideas of decay and loss of energy, but fundamentally Harry affirms the continuation of human vitality. As he looks down the hill at the house in Galilee where Ruth now lives, for example, he cannot get the courage to confront her, but he crowds against a tree, struck with "the miracle of it: how things grow, always remembering to be themselves" (113). Later he comments, "What a threadbare thing we make of life! Yet what a marvellous thing the mind is, they can't make a machine like it, . . . and the body can do a thousand things there isn't a factory in the world can duplicate the motion" (139). And he thinks, "Funny about feelings, they seem to come and go in a flash yet outlast metal" (163).

It is in the fifth, concluding section of the novel, however, that the regenerative images are dominant. His granddaughter has been born, and Rabbit and Janice have just moved into a house of their own after having lived with Janice's mother for twelve years. It is January, the beginning of a new year and the new decade of the 1980s. Furthermore, it is Super Sunday, the day of the Super Bowl. Rabbit feels that the emptiness of his furniture-less new house is "a species of . . . new possibility" (431) that excites and pleases him. In this new house one has to step down into the den. Harry thinks that in this room he "might begin to read books, instead of just magazines and newspapers, begin to learn about history, say." The "small difference in plane hints to him of many reforms and consolidations now possible in his life, like new shoots on a tree cropped back" (453). Although he is aware that he has no habits (of the heart or otherwise) to cushion him in this new house, that his life seems to stretch emptily on all sides, and that "moving in any direction he's bound to take a fall," he nevertheless feels that on this Super Sunday he is "king of the castle" (456). He feels that "maybe God is in the universe the way salt is in the ocean, giving it a taste" (462–63). He also notes that even at this dead point of winter the days have begun "lengthening against the grain" and that "the planets keep their courses no matter what we do" (463).

But it is his new granddaughter, just born to Nelson and his wife, Pru, whose presence in the last paragraph of the book provides a final moment that manages to include the inescapable truth of the Second Law of Thermodynamics while challenging it with a quantum jump of new energy:

> [Pru] comes softly down the one step into his den and deposits into his lap what he has been waiting for. Oblong cocooned little visitor, the baby shows her profile blindly in the shuddering flashes of color jerking from the Sony, the tiny stitchless seam of the closed eyelid aslant, lips bubbled forward beneath the whorled nose as if in delicate disdain, she knows she's good. . . . Through all this she has pushed to be here, in his lap, his hands, a real presence hardly weighing anything but alive. Fortune's hostage, heart's desire, a granddaughter. His. Another nail in his coffin. His. (467)

Rabbit's daughter-in-law steps down into the new plane, which suggests reform, consolidations, and new shoots, and gives him what he has been waiting for—a sign that as the days lengthen against the grain, so does life; human individuality, uniqueness, keeps coming. A visitor, not unlike

Wordsworth's child trailing clouds of glory, the baby brings a new individual spirit into a world using up its energy prodigally, a world illuminated by shuddering flashes from Japanese rather than American technology. The stitchless seam of her eyelids, the bubbling of her lips, and her whorled nose defy and transcend all technologies, whether American or Japanese. Although she weighs little and has no force or energy to be measured in material terms, she knows she's good, has somehow pushed to be here—a real *presence.*

This new baby is what Rabbit has been waiting for. Updike has said that "ever since his baby girl drowned in *Rabbit, Run,* Harry has been looking for a daughter. It's the theme that has been pressing forward, without my willing it or understanding it exactly, through these novels" (*Hugging the Shore* 871). So this new baby is the daughter he has wanted, his heart's desire, a hostage to fortune—she is his; she can belong to no one else in quite the same way. Her presence does not change the outward reality of the empty house where he is bound to take a fall, nor does she reverse the aging process—she is another nail in his coffin, another sign of his moving closer to his own eventual death. Rabbit is running down. All things run down. But there is still the rabbit-light on one's fur that affirms the real presence of an audacious, unique, human, God-given personality looking out from the midpoint of its own universe. Or as Updike told me more succinctly, "Entropy may triumph in the eventual heat-death of the universe, but not in human lives" (qtd. in Campbell, *Updike's Novels* 146).

As it turns out, neither America nor Rabbit was even close to running out of gas in 1980. *Rabbit at Rest* opens just after Christmas 1988, "the last year of Reagan's reign" (6). Rabbit and Janice are spending their fifth winter in their Florida condominium since Nelson has taken over the Toyota agency in Pennsylvania. Nelson, Pru, and their two children arrive for a visit. Nelson explains the new philosophy of the 1980s to his father: "People don't make money an hour at a time any more; you just get yourself in the right position and it *comes*" (39). Although Nelson's as yet unrevealed cocaine addiction makes the younger man unusually jumpy, the visit goes well enough until Rabbit takes his granddaughter sailing and the boat capsizes. The exertion of righting it and getting them safely to shore precipitates a heart attack, and Rabbit is in the hospital when Nelson and family head back north.

Nelson's comment about getting oneself in the right position so that the money just comes is perhaps the ultimate expression of the managerial/economic individualism of the 1980s. Nelson's cocaine addiction, which leads him to sacrifice the family business for his personal indulgence, is also a telling example of the final results of a shallow individualism practiced not only by Nelson's father when he was seeking to avoid the mediocrity of Mickey Mouse and MagiPeelers, but by many Americans from the Eisenhower years on through the Bush era.

Nelson does, however, seem to learn something from his drug treatment program. He talks of becoming a social worker, thus devoting himself to helping others. Such a goal is certainly a real improvement in Nelson's habits of the heart, but the change may not be so positive as it might first appear. The role that Nelson seems to have adopted is what Bellah et al. label "the therapist" (47). The therapist is really not too different from the manager or economically determined individual, they insist. Both are "specialists in mobilizing resources for effective action," the difference being that the therapist uses internal resources and measures his effectiveness by "the elusive criterion of personal satisfaction." Like the manager, the therapist "takes the ends" of society "as they are given; the focus is upon the effectiveness of the means," not on any ultimate or absolute standards of value (47). For the therapist, according to Bellah et al., "the center is the autonomous individual, presumed able to choose the roles he will play and the commitments he will make, not on the basis of higher truths but according to the criterion of life-effectiveness as the individual judges it." By choosing the term *therapeutic,* the authors intend to suggest that the desire for cure is paramount in this paradigm; but they question exactly what is to be cured. "In the final analysis," they assert, "it is cure of the lack of fit between the present organization of the self and the available organization of work, intimacy, and meaning." The dubious value of such an approach to life "is that it enables the individual to think of commitments . . . as enhancements of the sense of individual well-being rather than as moral imperatives" (47).

Nelson does not follow through on his plans to become a therapist, but Rabbit does seem to achieve a significant revival of some of the earlier, more positive individualism he clumsily voiced in *Rabbit, Run*—one that recognizes a transcendent imperative. In saving his granddaughter's life, Rabbit overcomes some of his earlier self-centered hardness of heart. He selflessly pushes himself to the limit to be sure that at least this little girl is not drowned. In the midst of the struggle he remembers once telling "a prying clergyman, *somewhere behind all this there's something that wants me to find it.*" Now, he realizes, "Whatever it is, *it* has found *him,* and is working him over" (136). When Janice asks exactly what is wrong with Rabbit's heart, the doctor replies: "It's tired and stiff and full of crud. It's a typical American heart, for his age and economic status et cetera" (166).

But this American heart has habits other than bad dietary practices. When a friend urges Rabbit to consider bypass surgery because "You're just a soft machine," Rabbit thinks differently. He sees himself as a "God-made one-of-a-kind with an immortal soul breathed in. A vehicle of grace. A battlefield of good and evil. An apprentice angel" (237). Some of the biblical-type individualism is left.

This type of individualism does not dominate the modern American psyche, though, as Updike points out. He seems to agree with Bellah that there is much that is cancerous in contemporary American practices. The Japanese representative who withdraws the Toyota franchise offers some insightful comment on what has happened to American individualism since the days of John Winthrop and Thomas Jefferson. He discusses the struggle he sees between order and freedom. Everybody in America talks about freedom, he says. He mentions skateboarders who seem to want freedom to terrify elderly citizens on seaside walkways, youths with boom boxes who want freedom to surround themselves with "super-jumbo noise," and men who claim freedom to "shoot others on freeways in random sport." But his final example graphically illustrates the problem of rampant self-centered individualism. In California, he says, "everywhere, dog shit, dogs must have important freedom to shit everywhere. Dog freedom more important than crean grass and cement pavement." The Toyota company, in contrast, seeks to balance the "needs of outer world and needs of inner being, between what in Japan we call *qiri* and *ninjō*." In America, he says, there is "too much dog shit" (392).

The point of this little moral lecture is to inform Harry that in order to avoid criminal prosecution he must pay by the end of the month all debts accrued by Nelson's mismanagement of funds to support his cocaine habit. In any event, however, the Toyota franchise for Springer Motors will be canceled. Harry tries to gain some favor by pleading, "No one feels worse about my son's falling apart than I do," but the Japanese businessman/moralist interrupts to say, "Not just son. . . . Who is father and mother of such son? Where are they? In Frorida, enjoying sunshine and tennis, while young boy prays games with autos" (392–93). Again we have a conflict of values; again as readers we are drawn into the moral debate.

When Rabbit runs from family responsibility for the final time, heading for Florida alone, he tries to see again the station where the old man told him he should know where he was going before he went there, but the station is now a real estate office. Rabbit is not bothered because he thinks that now he knows the road and this time has figured out his destination. But his last words to Nelson indicate that he, like Columbus, dies without ever fully comprehending the meaning of his odyssey. Each book in his saga has an open ending. In the first he is running with no fixed destination. In the second we are left with a serious question about whether our American Everyman is really O.K. In the third we see a new life but one that heralds the passing of the older generation. In this final book all Rabbit knows is that "it isn't so bad" (512). And he believes that that is enough—maybe.

Updike senses a spiritual emptiness at the core of American life. "Our condition is basically one of anxiety, of lostness," he says. Life is a search for "a sense of having found home," yet the very dynamic that drives Americans to dream and to seek—the sense of "wanting"—"tilts against resignation and happiness" (qtd. in Farney A10). Robert Farney points out that "through Rabbit Mr. Updike poses the classic American choice. How best does an American translate freedom into fulfillment? Through commitment to others or by going it alone? By rooting down or by running away?" (A10).

As we have seen, Rabbit begins by running, and although he learns some valuable lessons, he never seems to *arrive.* Updike has commented, however, that he intended *Rabbit at Rest* "to show a happy death, at least a man content in some ways to die. . . . An arrival has been achieved" (qtd. in Farney A10). Achieving that sense of arrival is difficult for Americans always on the move, but the concluding scene of Rabbit's saga makes one final comment on America's habits of the heart. As Rabbit drifts in and out of consciousness, he marvels "that in its gaps the world is being tended just as it was in the centuries before he was born." When Nelson shouts at him, "Don't *die,* Dad, *don't!,*" Harry responds, "Well, Nelson, . . . all I can tell you is, it isn't so bad. [He] thinks he should maybe say more, the kid looks wildly expectant, but enough. Maybe. Enough" (512). Updike has pointed out that "the number of already rich men who were willing to commit crimes during the 1980s to get even richer proved there was no enough. Maybe that's one of the words Americans have a very hard time learning: The word enough" (qtd. in Farney A10). But his American Everyman *has* achieved an arrival of sorts, *has* learned that there is such a thing as enough; nevertheless, with his characteristic "yes, but," Updike adds, "Maybe."

Thus without ever leaving familiar American ground, John Updike's Rabbit Angstrom has explored and uncovered new meanings for readers willing to enter into the moral debate. Rabbit may lack the heroism and purity of Natty Bumppo, the moral depth of Hester Prynne, the breadth and tragedy of Ishmael, the naive but stubborn idealism of Jay Gatsby, and the communal commitment of Tom Joad, but he is perhaps more representative of

American society than any of them. For Updike has deliberately not sought the heroic, but has chosen to present the ordinary, or as he himself has put it, "the whole mass of middling, hidden, troubled America" (qtd. in Farney A1). In creating Rabbit Angstrom, Updike has challenged us to examine American habits of the last forty years. From the metaphorical hardness of the heart in *Rabbit, Run* through the literal hardened arteries of Rabbit's "typical American heart" in the final book, Updike calls us to explore with him the questions of what goodness is and how to balance the claims of the individual with the claims of community and order.

Notes

This essay first appeared in the *Journal of the American Studies Association of Texas* 24 (1993): 26–45, copyright 1993 by Baylor University. Reprinted by permission.

1. All references to the Rabbit novels and to *Hugging the Shore* are to the Knopf editions.

4

Dilvo I. Ristoff
Appropriating the Scene
The World of *Rabbit at Rest*

As with the first three novels of the Rabbit tetralogy, *Rabbit at Rest* starts on a very precise date. Ten years after Rabbit had been declared a hostage of fortune, we find him at the airport in Miami with his wife, Janice. They are on their way to meet their son, Nelson, their daughter-in-law, Pru, and their two grandchildren, Roy (four years old) and Judy (almost nine), who are flying in for a five-day visit. The year, we easily infer, is 1988, the month is December, the week is the last of the month, and it is a Tuesday, "the last year of Reagan's reign" (6).[1] To be more precise, it is December 27, 1988.

Virtually every incident of the story may be set precisely in time and space, so that not only may we say with certainty, for instance, that the first chapter starts on December 27 and ends on December 31, 1988, but we may also say, for sure, that (1) on December 28 Rabbit plays golf with his Jewish friends; (2) on December 29 he and Janice take their grandchildren on a tour of Thomas Alva Edison's winter home and the Sarasota Jungle Gardens, after which they watch the movie *Working Girl;* (3) on December 30, Rabbit, his daughter-in-law, and his grandchildren spend the morning at Omni Bayview, where and when Rabbit suffers a heart attack (we also know that the telephone rang in their condo at precisely 12:25 P.M. to inform his wife that he has been taken to the hospital); and (4) on December 31, Nelson, Pru, and the grandchildren fly back to Pennsylvania.

We find the same obsessive precision in every one of the thirty-five subchapters of the novel, so that, step by step, the reader is invited to read history into story and story into history, perceiving with little effort that one cannot exist without the other and that the characters are not only in history but are also as much its interpreters and proprietors as they are interpreted and owned.

Not all of the historical names, events, and circumstances in the novel have the same generative power in the story. Rabbit's life is especially influenced by those events, persons, and incidents that enhance the negative ideological frame within which he exists, namely, nationalism, racism, sexism, anticommunism, individualism, and religiosity. The forces that support this ideological frame have greater power and are, thus, of greater importance to the story.

Underlying this understanding is a conception of history as something more than a *locus* for action. It is, above all, a *motive* for action. It is such an integral part of the story that it would be no exaggeration to say that without history there is no story. It is not as if when one takes away the frame there is still the picture to be looked at; the fact is that without history there is no picture, for the historical scene has been melded into every moment of Rabbit's trajectory.

What are, then, some of these generative historical events or circumstances that populate Rabbit's world in *Rabbit at Rest* during the last year of Reagan's presidency and the first year of Bush's? Although there may be and, perhaps, should be disagreement on this, given the possible imprints produced by reader participation, it is safe to suggest the following as some of the major historical scenic components generating action in the story: (1) the various airplane accidents: (a) the midair explosion of a Pan American Boeing 747 on December 21, 1988; (b) the explosion on a jet flying from Atlanta to Rochester on December 27, 1988; (c) the DC-10 jet crash at Sioux City, Iowa, on July 19, 1989; (d) the USAir plane crash in New York River on September 21, 1989; (e) the crash of a French DC-10 on September 19, 1989; (2) the end of the cold war and the Japanese economic invasion; (3) feminism; and (4) AIDS and drugs.

The Plane of Death

The numerous airplane disasters are spread throughout the novel's more than five hundred pages, so that Rabbit is not sporadically but constantly reminded of the terror and death that accompany these catastrophes. It is easy, therefore, to perceive that the number of accidents acquires a qualitative significance, for it is the terror and death related to these accidents that Rabbit appropriates and makes his own.

Early in the novel, Rabbit recalls the deaths of television reporter Max Robinson and singer Roy Orbison and "then before Christmas that Pan Am Flight 103 ripping open like a rotten melon five miles above Scotland and dropping all these bodies and flaming wreckage all over the golf course and the streets of this little town like Glockamorra, what was its real name, Lockerbie" (8). The accident occurred on December 21, 1988, and was in all the papers the next day. Rabbit, like most Americans, carries with him, therefore, six days of bombardment by frequent news on the accident, knowing by now all the details—flight number, kind of airplane, height the airplane was flying, the name of the town where it fell, the probable causes of the accident, the reports of eyewitnesses, and so on.

As it must have happened with all those readers who, historically placed, read, watched, and heard the news, Rabbit uses the details as the basis for images or fictions of his own: the plane bursts open "like a rotten melon," the bodies dropping over Scotland "like wet melon seeds" (10). He imagines the terror of it all. He imagines what it must have been like, "sitting there in your seat being lulled by the hum of the big Rolls-Royce engines and the stewardesses bringing the clinking drinks caddy and the feeling of having caught the plane and nothing to do now but relax and then with a roar and giant ripping noise and scattered screams this whole cozy world dropping away and nothing under you but black space and your chest squeezed by the terrible unbreathable cold" (8).

Harry wonders how much the passengers and crew knew about what was happening as they fell through the dark and cold, their "hearts pumping," still alive. To the airline, as Rabbit sees it, people were nothing but "numbers on the computer, one more or less, who cares? A blip on the screen, then no blip on the screen" (10).

Rabbit also reacts to his own tendency to fictionalize the accident. He knows that for his granddaughter, Judy, it is indeed just another movie. For children these things only happen to other people, he thinks, but he is old enough by now to realize it may happen to everybody, himself included.

While playing golf with his Jewish friends on December 28, Rabbit cannot avoid mentioning the accident. To his surprise and disappointment, for them the event is merely a technical and political matter. Technically it is, as for Judy, a bomb; politically, they see it as a part of a larger issue—the Arab-Israeli conflict—a conflict that they now perceive to be affecting their lives more directly. But they miss his meaning:

> "I mean," [Harry] says, "how the hell do you think it feels? Sitting there and having the plane explode?"
> "Well, I bet it wakes you up," Ed says.
> "They didn't feel a thing," Bernie says, considerately, sensing Harry's personal worry. "Zero. It was over that quick." (69)[2]

And the discussion falls back to politics and then fades again into golf. Quite obviously, for Rabbit the meaning of the event is not merely technical or political. It has superseded these realms. He has appropriated an emotional, spiritual, personal religious dimension that he identified in the event. He can hardly read about it in the papers any longer. He cannot overcome the horror of "everything upside-down and void of mercy and meaning" (91). The terror of the passengers is his own. In his empathy, he metaphorically boards their plane, and their suffering and fate become his own:

> Up, up; the air thins, the barometer registers, the *timer begins to tick* as the plane snugly bores through darkness. . . . The image, like a seed at last breaking its shell in moist soil, awakens in Harry the realization that even now as he lies in this antiseptic white fog tangled in tubes and ties of blood and marriage *he is just like the people he felt so sorry for, falling from the burst-open airplane: he too is falling, helplessly falling, toward death. . . .* What met them was no more than what awaits him. Reality broke upon those passengers . . . and that same icy black reality has broken upon him; death is not a domesticated pet of life but a beast that swallowed baby Amber and baby Becky and *all those Syracuse students* and returning soldiers and will swallow him, it is truly there under him, vast as a planet at night, gigantic and totally his. His death. . . . [H]e feels all but suffocated by terror. (176; emphasis added)

It takes some knowledge of what the media were writing and saying to appreciate how much Updike's text grows out of the heat of history. When Nelson tells Rabbit that "they think they know now exactly what kind of bomb it was—there's a kind with a barometric device that activates a timer when a certain altitude is reached" (175–76), he is repeating almost word for word the *New York Times*. Like his father and the other characters in the novel, Nelson, too, has been historicized. Although Rabbit's appropriation of the accident is more explicitly a way of dealing with his private fear of death, he also, like most Americans, politicizes the issue and blames the "damn Arabs" for the accident. In fact, by December 31 it had already been established that a bomb had caused the explosion. On December 30, Sheila Rule reported for the *New York Times* that again "an unidentified caller claiming to represent a Pro-Iranian group . . . took responsibility for the Pan Am bombing" (A16). Rabbit's mistaking Iranians for Arabs should not surprise us. His confusion is also that of his two Jewish friends earlier in the novel. In the context of the Arab-Israeli conflict, as in the context of the novel, because of Iran's historical anti-Israel and America's historical pro-Israel stand, the mix-up is probably deliberate.

Almost at the end of the novel, although Rabbit cannot fail to notice the large number of accidents occurring, he seems to be less concerned, as if after the explosion of Pan Am flight 103 all the rest is anticlimactic, as if it were after all only another boring television show: "Like everything else on the news, you get bored, it gets to seem a gimmick" (501). Yet it is a mistake to assume that Rabbit has simply become bored. At stake here are the forces of his ideological setup. Rabbit's nationalism naturally leads him to view an attack by foreign terrorists as an attack targeted at the heart of America, his heart. But an attack by the same foreign terrorists who, "in the name of Allah," shoot down a French plane with 171 people aboard, he doesn't mind that much, not as much as "the Lockerbie Pan Am bomb" (501). Rabbit's declaration of boredom is then not as political as one might be led to believe. His nationalism has grown beyond politics—it has become religious faith. It has placed the rest of the world into otherness, restricting the extension of his sympathies. He will acknowledge that 171 persons were killed, but they were not Americans, they were not exactly *his* people, and therefore their death is void of meaning.

This behavior would also explain why the shooting down of a civilian Iranian jet by the USS *Vincennes* (456),[3] although mentioned in the text, does not occupy Rabbit's mind for very long. Similarly, one wonders why the crash of a Cuban airplane on September 4, 1989, within the chronological time of the novel, has been completely neglected. It is quite clear that the necessary ideologically oriented historical preferences are not only Rabbit's—they are also Updike's, who needs them to portray middleness. If we consider that the accident involving the Cuban airplane barely made the news, we cannot fail to notice that the "forgetfulness" of the historical scene matches that of the novel. It is as much a strategic "forgetfulness" for the country as it is for *Rabbit at Rest*.

The Death of an Era

In the same way that terrorist bombs are causing the death of many Americans and developing in Rabbit an acute consciousness of death's ominous presence, the end of the cold war has Rabbit thinking that America has lost a major part of its identity. He asks himself, "Without the cold war, what's the point of being an American?" (442–443). The question is extremely meaningful when we consider that Rabbit is somebody who had anticommunism as a major goal in life and who in essence, throughout the 1980s, along with Reagan, pushed the world toward a new cold war. For him the end of the cold war is less a goal achieved than the loss of purpose in life: "The cold war. It gave you a reason to get up in the morning" (353).

This "bizarre nostalgia for the Cold War," as Peter Tarnoff (A14) calls it, is not only Rabbit's. On September 19, 1989, Tarnoff complains that, strangely enough, top Bush administration officials seem to sanction the idea that the cold war was not such a bad thing after all and that its end could be harmful to American interests, especially in Europe, now that world power relations are no longer clearly defined. The power that was once concentrated in Washington and Moscow has now become diffused among a large number of states, forcing the administration to define a new agenda with a multitude of low-profile engagements.

As with Reagan and the anticommunist ideology of the 1950s, Rabbit's time is passed, although the Chinese and the Nicaraguan communists and a few others are still around and deserve his attention. Since the novel's chronology matches perfectly the chronology of the corresponding historical events, it is interesting to notice that Rabbit's increasing concern over China and Eastern Europe matches that of the newspapers. China and Poland gain greater and greater attention in the media and in the novel as the Moscow-Washington talks seem to show promising results, suggesting that perhaps the emphasis on China was the establishment's way of cushioning Middle America's landing in the post–cold war era. The crackdown on the pro-democracy protesters on June 4, 1989, when thousands of troops retook Tiananmen Square, firing on unarmed civilians and killing about five hundred of them, shows that Rabbit sees China also as "the other side." For him the crackdown is not surprising. What surprises him is that "kids were allowed to run the show for a month and nobody knew what to do about it! It's like nobody's in charge of the other side any more" (353). Strange as it may seem, Rabbit is pressed quietly and perversely to condone the Chinese government's determination. The end of the war with the Soviets seems to require that he find a new "reason to get up in the morning." It demands a new enemy, and the Chinese may well gain that status as long as they do what the "other side" is supposed to do.

In a way "Reagan's reign" provided a fertile soil for Rabbit's ideology to flourish. Reagan's "America is standing tall again" policy and his belligerent anti-Soviet, anticommunist, anti-Arab determination made Carter's crisis of confidence a thing of the past. He very successfully managed to restore national pride, despite some obvious disasters on the military, social, and economic fronts. Although Rabbit has ambiguous feelings about Reagan, he has to admit that he liked him:

> He liked the foggy voice, the smile, the big shoulders, the way he kept his head wagging during the long pauses, the way he floated above facts,

knowing there was more to government than facts, and the way he could change direction while saying he was going straight ahead, pulling out of Beirut, getting cozy with Gorby, running up the national debt. The strange thing was, except for the hopeless down-and-outers, the world became a better place under him. The Communists fell apart, except for in Nicaragua, and even there he put them on the defensive. The guy had a magic touch. He was a dream man. Harry dares say, "Under Reagan, you know, it was like anesthesia." (62)

Reagan's "magic touch," however, seems to have come less from his foggy voice, his statesman's posture, and long pauses than from his inextricable identification with widespread cold war values. His magic touch is in fact an intimate part of the new cold war that characterized his presidency, and which can be especially perceived in Reagan's attempt to characterize the Soviet Union as the "evil empire." The sense of America being pushed around by Iran, Nicaragua, the Arabs, and others, so noticeable during the Carter era, disappeared under Reagan, so that "pulling out of Beirut,"[4] instead of being regarded as a political defeat, was actually and quickly perceived by Middle America as a victory, transformed as it was into another anticommunist military action—the invasion of Grenada.[5]

The speed with which Reagan managed to divert the attention of the media is, in retrospect, astonishing, so much so that the impression is that the casualties of Beirut are actually the toll to be paid for the victory over the communists in the tiny island of Grenada. Rabbit carries with him the Beirut experience as something not fully explained and attributes Reagan's getting away with it to his "magic touch." Had he connected Beirut to Grenada, his explanation would certainly have been different. But, much as we saw earlier, a more refined and politically polished understanding is strategically denied him, for it would obviously remove him from middleness.

But, in *Rabbit at Rest* we meet Rabbit at the end of one presidency and at the beginning of another. "Reagan's reign" is coming to an end, and George Bush is about to be inaugurated. The official beginning of Bush's presidency was on January 20, 1989, so most of the action in the novel takes place during the first year of Bush's administration. The effects of Reaganomics are beginning to be felt, and Bush does not seem to be quite the president Rabbit wanted. Although he was the only one among his Florida friends who actually voted for Bush, certainly because Bush represented continuity rather than change, he begins to realize that America is awakening from the Reagan anesthesia, and, as his friend Bernie had predicted, "when you come out of anesthesia, it hurts like hell" (62).

Bernie's remark seems to have come straight out of Anthony Lewis's article "The Cost of Reagan," published in the *New York Times* of September 7, 1989. Lewis reminds us that the self-indulgent policy of the eight years under Reagan has led to the S&L and HUD scandals, which are a constant presence in the news Rabbit reads or hears, and which will cost taxpayers billions of dollars. All these scandals, argues Lewis, have created "hostility to the role of government" (A27), diminishing the common citizen's faith in political institutions.

Rabbit, however, has certainly not lost faith in political institutions, although he does realize that foreign and national debt have increased and that scandals of all sorts can be seen in many institutions—in Washington, D.C., in state and local governments, on Wall Street and in the financial world, in police departments, in prestigious nationwide religious organizations. In short, scandals are as visible with politicians as with ministers of the church. His conservatism and nationalism are, however, much too strong for him to distrust these American institutions per se. That kind of behavior belongs to another color band of the ideological spectrum. For him, America is "the happiest fucking country the world has ever seen" (371), no matter what some greedy, no-good Americans do.

Instead, Rabbit's anxiety has to do with his uncertainty about Bush's capacity to match Reagan's leadership. His feelings are ambiguous. He respects the president but cannot hide his disappointment at hearing his name on television, robbed of its dignity. It hurts him, for example, to hear that Bush and his wife "take showers with their dog Millie" (295). This behavior makes the president too human—or perhaps less than human—and is, therefore, inappropriate for someone in charge of running the country. Rabbit cannot help missing Reagan. Why? Because "at least he was dignified, and had that dream distance; the powerful thing about him as President was that you never knew how much he knew, nothing or everything, *he was like God that way*. . . . With this new one you know he knows something, but it seems a small something. Rabbit doesn't want to have to picture the President and middle-aged wife taking showers naked with their dog. Reagan and Nancy had their dignity" (295; emphasis added).

Rabbit's feeling is that under Bush the country is losing strength. He comments, "Now that Bush is in . . . we are kind of on the sidelines . . . we're sort of like a big Canada, and what we do doesn't much matter to anybody else. . . . It's a kind of relief, I guess, not to be the big cheese" (358). Rabbit makes this observation at the lot on June 19, 1989, five months after Bush's inauguration. The comment is made to Elvira, a salesperson Nelson hired.

Elvira's reaction to Rabbit's comment deserves our attention, for she quickly nationalizes Rabbit, as if aware that not only will he parade as Uncle Sam in the coming Fourth of July festivities but that he already feels he is Uncle Sam. Elvira promptly realizes that Rabbit's discourse has a meaning that Rabbit himself is not aware of. He is not talking about Bush at all, she correctly observes, but about himself: "You matter to everybody, Harry," she says, "if that's what you're hinting at" (358).

In fact, Elvira's insight is just another suggestion to the reader to look at Rabbit as more than an individuality. He *is*, in many ways, the Uncle Sam who paraded down the streets of Mt. Judge. More than the right physical build, he has the ideological setup that makes him adequate for the occasion. In this sense, then, he is transmuted into the collective, and, like the collectivity to which he belongs, he has already, through his exceptional capacity for adaptation, slowly begun to appropriate the life of his new president: Bush's difficulty to run the country becomes his difficulty to run his home; Bush's difficulty to pay the foreign debt becomes his difficulty to pay what Springer Motors owes the Japanese; and neither of them is at the moment "the big cheese." Under the circumstances, Rabbit cannot help thinking, "Well, . . . doing nothing works for Bush, why not for [me]?" (476). The process of appropriation is on its way.

Waking up from the Reagan anesthesia means waking up, among other things, to the reality of foreign debt. As Rabbit appropriates Bush's plight, America is emblematized in the Springer Motors Concessionary or, as Rabbit calls it, "the lot." The lot becomes a microcosm of America, plagued by debt to foreigners, completely at their mercy, and administered by "scatterbrains" who, like Janice and Nelson, "will just drift along deeper and deeper into debt like the rest of the world" (431).

Although Nelson insists that what they owe is relatively little money and that in fact Springer Motors has been underfinanced for years, Rabbit cannot, as a good American, help expressing his fears that the country has been taken over by foreigners and that Americans are losing control: "We're drowning in debt! We don't even own our own country any more" (417). Earlier in the novel, Nelson predicted that, in ten years, the Japanese will "have bought the whole country. Some television show I was watching, they already own all of Hawaii and half of L.A. and Nevada. They're buying up thousands of acres of desert in Nevada!" (37). Rabbit also gets to see a similar scare documentary, so that his and Nelson's fear can be in part explained by the fact that America, throughout the decade, as Vinod Goyal explains, was the country in the world with by far the highest rate of foreign investment. However, as

David H. Blake and Robert S. Walters (92) tell us, the major part of the foreign money invested in the United States was not Japanese, but British and Dutch. As can be seen, this does not match Rabbit's perception, which clearly comes less from the statistical evidence of foreign presence than from the way this foreign presence threatens the stability of his world. And in this respect, considering Rabbit's white Anglo-Saxon Protestant tradition, it is easy to understand why he would perceive non-Europeans as posing a greater threat. The Japanese, not the British or the Dutch, are the true foreigners, the others.

As Stacey Olster correctly observes, whereas in *Rabbit, Run* and *Rabbit Redux* communism was regarded as the major threat to America, in *Rabbit Is Rich* the threat is represented by the Arab control of large oil resources, and in *Rabbit at Rest* the major threat has become the possession by the Japanese of technological advantage over the United States. This comparative advantage has been translated by the Japanese into financial resources, which have been translated into investments. And investments are made where return proves most profitable. Olster points out that the Japanese financial invasion can be seen in RCA's example: "Considering the fact that the black-and-white box first invented by RCA had become, by 1976, a commodity ninety-eight percent of which was imported from Japan, this growth in television's power epitomizes the shift from American to Japanese power that *Rabbit at Rest* assumes as a given" ("Rabbit Rerun" 46).

The lot as a parallel of America operates in Rabbit's mind as a prefiguring of national economic disaster—a disaster to be caused by increasing national and international debt and by reckless spending. Springer Motors's losing of the Toyota franchise due to debt and poor administration is but an ominous warning of what Rabbit perceives might happen to his country.

Mr. Shimada, the Toyota representative, not only *informs* Rabbit about the cancellation of the franchise, he also *lectures* him about the proper ways to conduct business. But, as we can see, Mr. Shimada is not lecturing to Rabbit, the individual; he is lecturing to the American nation, using Rabbit as a token audience: "In recent times big brother act rike rittle brother, always cry and comprain. Want many favors in trade, saying Japanese unfair competition. . . . American way in old times. But in new times America make nothing, just do mergers, do acquisitions, rower taxes, raise national debt. Nothing comes out, all goes in—foreign goods, foreign capital. America take everything, give nothing. Rike big brack hole" (390). What Mr. Shimada is saying can be read as the Japanese version, with a Japanese accent, of what concerned the Reagan and Bush administrations in relation to foreign trade throughout the decade. Japanese trade restrictions were the main topic of many high-level meetings between officials of the two countries. Both the American trade deficit and budget deficits were the concern also of the International Monetary Fund, which actually registered a complaint in April 1989.

Mr. Shimada's speech is then a construed Japanese answer to well-known problems that Americans are facing at the time. Although he blames poor administration for America's present predicament, he tries to find a deeper, more meaningful explanation for this evil. As he continues with his lecture, he identifies as the ultimate cause of America's difficulties the imbalance between Americans' discipline and freedom. For him, America is failing because there is too little *giri* (order) and too much *ninjō* (freedom). In America these two forces are said to have lost their balance, and that is why Toyota sees it as its role to create "ireands of order in oceans of freedom" (392). While blaming national attitudes, Shimada is also blaming Nelson and especially Nelson's father, who spends half the year "in Frorida, enjoying sunshine and tennis, while young boy plays games with autos" (393). Again, Rabbit and America are regarded as one.

Rabbit's humiliating experience with Mr. Shimada, and his disappointment at losing the Toyota franchise and finding out that they owe the Japanese over $200,000, is for a moment replaced by optimism when Janice suggests that they could reopen the lot as a family business, as it used to be before the Japanese came in: the idea of "rebuilding the lot from scratch . . . excites him" (398). In another demonstration that he sees himself as sharing the problems and concerns of the nation, he appropriates the hegemonic national attitude: "So they owe a few hundred thousand—the government owes trillions and nobody cares" (398).

What could be a solution for the lot could also be a solution for the country. But the idea of the whole world in debt and nobody paying is troubling and difficult to follow. International relations work in mysterious ways, and business has become so complex for Rabbit that he does not trust himself to analyze the books of Springer Motors, especially now that Lyle has their accounts on computer diskettes. Somehow the global economy, with its intricate national and international net of operations, plays tricks that are brought right into his home. When Rabbit complains that everybody owes and nobody seems to have to pay, Nelson explains that the debt of the lot with Toyota has already been settled. How?

"A second mortgage on the lot property, it's worth at least half a million. A hundred forty-five, and they consolidated it with the seventy-five for Slim's five cars, which will be coming back to us pretty much as credit on the rolling inventory we were maintaining with Mid-Atlantic Motors. As soon as they took our inventory over to Rudy's lot, don't forget, they started owing *us.*"

"And you're somehow going to pay back Brewer Trust selling water scooters?"

"You don't have to pay a loan back, they don't *want* you to pay it back; they just want you to keep up the installments. Meanwhile, the value of the dollar goes down and you get to tax-deduct all the interest. We were underfinanced, in fact, before." (418)

To Rabbit's despair, Nelson, the former drug addict turned Billy Graham, seems to have it all worked out, very much in tune with the creditors of third world debtor countries. How much further into debt will Nelson drive them? Rabbit's feeling is that there is already a second mortgage on the country—a country that, like the lot, he realizes, is no longer his. Foreigners are everywhere—Japanese, Koreans, Italians, Mexicans, Cubans, Africans—all of them placing demands, giving orders, complaining. And they all seem to get on his nerves. In Miami, Rabbit realizes that not even in hospitals can he get rid of them. He gets extremely irritated at Dr. Olman, an Australian this time, who, according to him, "keeps attacking America. If he doesn't like the food here, why doesn't he go back where he came from and eat kangaroos?" (172). The irony of it all is that, with Rabbit's nationalism turned into xenophobia, a foreigner is taking care of his very heart, his "typical American heart" (166).

The end of the cold war, then, coincides with a time of increasing foreign presence in the country, especially in the economy, so that besides being robbed of his political motives, Rabbit is being robbed of his economic national stability. On December 27, 1988, Dimitri K. Simes, in an interesting article in the *New York Times* called "If the Cold War Is Over, Then What?" states: "For more than 40 years, America's international strategy has been subordinated to one overriding concern—deterring Soviet global designs against the West." And he concludes that the "one-dimensional fixation on the East-West rivalry is no longer a credible option" (A12), suggesting a new, pragmatic approach to redefine America's role in the world. The same day, in the same paper, James M. Markham writes an article entitled "Unpredictable Russians Boggle West's Brains," where he tries to determine the next moves of President Gorbachev. The end of the cold war thus brought with it great uncertainty. A national revision of American ways and goals became necessary, and Rabbit's difficulties are largely those of his country.

Simes's and Markham's interpretation of America coincides with Updike's portrayal of Harry Angstrom. Updike reminds us that, although the collapse of communism in Eastern Europe happened late in 1989 (the novel ends around September 23), Rabbit knows it is coming. In "Why Rabbit Had to Go," Updike writes: "Like me, he has lived his life in the context of the cold war . . . and in some sense [was] always justified, at the back of his mind, by a concept of freedom, of America, that took sharpness from contrast with Communism. If that contrast is gone, then that's another reason to put him, regretfully, to rest in 1990" (1).

All these concerns, which point to the death of an era and the birth of a new one, find Rabbit also unprepared. His mind, like the minds of other Middle Americans, is perplexed by what is happening to the world and especially to America. He, too, finds it hard to understand the beginning of the end of communism, the end of the cold war, the extensive internationalization of the American economy with all these "scare documentar[ies] about foreigners buying up American businesses" (114). Somehow the death of the era is also the portentous foreshadowing of his own death, on its way to get him. But Rabbit is still moving, walking to "forbidden" places in the country that once was his, asserting his right, insisting that he is not quite dead yet.

Rabbit's life in *Rabbit at Rest* is, thus, an enactment of the major concerns of America in the 1980s through the mind of the man in the middle. His world, however, is not only plagued by communists, Arabs, Iranians, Mexicans, and Japanese. These we could call the external enemies. Internally, Rabbit also finds himself besieged by major destabilizing "enemies"—feminism, AIDS, and drugs, to name three. These three "enemies" trouble Rabbit with great intensity, and his life, like the lives of Americans in general in the 1980s, does not remain unaffected.

The Threat of Feminism

From the beginning of the novel, we sense that the forces of feminism have acted upon Rabbit and his wife. Janice is clearly more in control of things. She participates in women's group meetings, attends to the family's problems, runs Springer Motors during the time of crisis, and studies to become a real estate agent.

Her group meetings are clearly changing her behavior toward Rabbit and toward life. Harry sees her as more aggressive, more condescending, less herself, speaking with gestures that are not her own and using words that are not part of her or Rabbit's vocabulary. Early in the novel she comes back from a women's group meeting and tells him how awful men have been to women: "Oh, Harry, you men have been so awful! Not only were we considered chattel, but all those patriarchal religions tried to make us feel guilty about menstruating. They said we were un*clean*" (79).

This seems to be the beginning of Janice's independence, following the general trend of her old friends—Doris Kaufmann, Peggy Fosnacht, and Cindy Murkett—all of whom hold or have held jobs, as "the women her age almost all do something now" (188). But it is clear that the movie *Working Girl*, which Rabbit cannot watch to the end, also had a great influence on her decision to join the workforce. To Harry's disbelief, Janice has barely come out of the movie theater when she announces, "I think I need a job. Wouldn't you like me better, Harry, if I was a working girl?" (107). Thus the historical scene once again becomes an inseparable part of the story, and Janice, like Rabbit, will have to be read as an emblem, as meaning always more than just Janice.

From his macho perspective, Rabbit makes it clear from the beginning that he hates it all, quietly "blaming [women] for the world as it is" (98) and suppressing his impulse to help Janice with the household chores. He resents the food she prepares, the courses she is taking, her liking of the television show *Roseanne,* her not having time for him (throughout the story, we should remember, Janice spends twenty weeks taking courses), her going out with her classmates, her going out with their friend Charlie "to process" (although it was Harry who suggested that Charlie talk things over with Janice). In short, Rabbit is afraid. He prefers Janice incompetent, unable to leave; he prefers her as she always was—his.

Profoundly troubled by the direction things are taking, Rabbit adds to his uncontrollable sexism his also uncontrollable, almost genetic, anticommunism: "They have jobs, money, even the young ones that used to be home making babies. If you look, more and more, you see women driving the buses, the delivery trucks. It's getting as bad as Russia; next thing we'll have women coalminers. Maybe we already do" (352).

In "Why Rabbit Had to Go," Updike points out that Rabbit's "sense of being useless, of being pushed to one side by his wife and son" (1) has a dimension similar to the political dimension of the end of the cold war. Indeed, this seems to be the frame of mind that determines Rabbit's actions. His reasoning is much like that of the president: if Reagan can "get cozy with Gorby"—if capitalist America can talk to its archenemies—why can't this war between women and men come to an end as well? This is what, at moments, he tries to do—never, however, overcoming the feeling that recognizing the other's equal rights violates his very nature.

During his first visit to the lot, he is surprised to discover that Nelson has hired Elvira Ollenbach as a salesperson. He immediately feels the need to "control his face, so his chauvinism doesn't show" (209), knowing as he does that hiring women and minority employees has become Toyota's policy. Later in the book, to strike up a conversation, Rabbit makes reference to the abortion issue so prevalent in the papers. He refers to a story about four men chaining themselves to a car in front of an abortion clinic.[6] He does it because "he knows where she stands: pro-choice. All these independent bimbos are. He takes a pro-life tilt to gall her but his heart isn't really in it" (353).

In fact, the discussion brings back his pro-life stand of the 1950s, when he begged his mistress, Ruth, to have their baby. Although Ruth wants to make him believe she had an abortion, he still thinks she had the baby, and that he is the father of Annabelle Byer, a young woman Harry meets at the dealership. Reagan and Bush and their followers stand with him on the abortion issue, but as time passes he is more and more confused, not so much because he is convinced by any of Elvira's arguments but because he perceives that the war will lead him nowhere.

It should be remembered that on April 9, 1989, an estimated 300,000 people marched in a pro-choice rally in Washington, D.C., and since that event, more than ever before, abortion had become a crucial issue for the feminist movement. Although a *New York Times*/CBS poll on April 26, 1989, pointed out that the nation was sharply divided, it became clear that feminists felt stronger than ever after the April 9 march. As Gloria Steinem, one of the feminist leaders of the march, declared, "We are marching here to ask, is the Supreme Court going to affirm that women are full citizens and not a property, or is the Supreme Court the captive of the extreme right wing?" (*New York Times* 10 Apr. 1989: A1). Judging from the news, the April 9 march was among the most important feminist events of the decade.

The march did not, however, settle the matter. As expected, counterdemonstrators also showed their presence, chanting "Life! Life! Life!" They also made their presence felt in other parts of the country, especially in Ocala, Florida, where two abortion clinics were destroyed by arson the same day. These anti-abortion attacks on clinics reached their height around June 20, 1989, when the *New York Times* reported in Connecticut militant abortion protesters literally clogged the state's jails. In just one incident that day, 261 protesters were arrested for disrupting normal activities, breaking in, and damaging equipment.

It is within this context of national conflict that Rabbit and Elvira have their discussion on abortion on Monday, June 19, 1989. Rabbit thinks that perhaps an "alliance with this female" would be better than war. He is, however, "torn between a desire to strike an alliance . . . and an itch to conquer her, to put her in her place." He prefers the alliance because it will not "rock the agency worse than it was being rocked" (352). In other words, Rabbit is not convinced by the pro-choice view—he just realizes that learning how to deal with the issue is a matter of convenience and, perhaps, survival. The fact is that the feminism of the 1980s has spread its roots all over America and, in one way or another, has touched everybody.

What we know for sure is that Harry's relative indifference precludes his participation in the April 9 march in Washington, but that he would otherwise have been among those few hundreds shouting "Life!" rather than among the hundreds of thousands shouting "Choice!" The pro-choice perspective on the abortion issue, a feminist issue par excellence, is a destabilizing factor, something for women who cherish their independence, and Rabbit, a lover of old order and stability, sees it as a threat to masculine dominance. Whereas Janice is trying, in her own confused and prejudiced way, to find out how the world works, Rabbit is stuck. And stuck because his view of women as objects of sexual pleasure has become old-fashioned. The 1950s are over, but Rabbit, having absorbed and commercialized the 1960s and cleverly survived the 1970s, finds it hard to believe that he has to change. But, then, why should he change if he, with all the others who think like him, can still elect the president of the country? Middleness is not dead yet.

The Threat of Drugs and AIDS

Drugs and AIDS have become Rabbit's disgrace. They have ruined his business, thrown him into debt, affected his sex life, interfered with his family life, scared away some of his employees, and put him to shame with the Japanese. The 1980s being the decade of the AIDS epidemic, it is only natural to expect that it would serve as an action-generating factor in a story as scene-centered as Rabbit's. Having been immersed in the world of AIDS, the major characters of *Rabbit at Rest* have their whole lives affected by it: Pru refuses to have sex with Nelson, and Harry is afraid to make love with Thelma, after ten years of their secret affair; Rabbit now sees sex as a "willing slide down into death" (202).

Aware of the danger and unwilling to risk her life, Pru conscientiously has a condom handy when having sex with Harry, and tells Nelson she won't have sex with him again until he proves to her that he is HIV negative. To have sex without such precautions would be suicidal. As Pru says to Nelson, "Why should I risk my life sleeping with you, you addict, you think I want to get AIDS from your dirty needles when you're speedballing or from some cheap coke whore you screw when you're gone until two in the morning?" (160).

One can better appreciate how much the AIDS issue makes *Rabbit at Rest* a book of the 1980s when one remembers how nonexistent these fears were in books such as *Couples* and *Rabbit Redux,* books of the 1960s, or in *Rabbit Is Rich,* a book of the 1970s. One can also perceive more clearly history's contribution to the making of the novel when one is aware that all-pervading AIDS became one of the major issues even in the mayoral election in New York City during 1989. There is hardly a day during the second half of 1989 in which AIDS did not produce major reports in the *New York Times.* Concern and fear of death were everywhere, and it is no surprise that this same concern and fear are present with such emphasis in a novel that has Middle America in its cast of characters.

Nelson's drug problem becomes extremely serious. Not only does he owe drug dealers a lot of money, but his addiction is making him aggressive to the point of physically attacking his wife and children. Pushed to the edge of despair, Pru, one night in April, at 2:00 A.M., calls Janice and Rabbit for help. After this incident, Nelson is sent to a rehabilitation clinic.

It is not surprising then to find that the story incorporates not only the mood of the times, but also the vocabulary and topical events. Bush's war on drugs and all that led to it become part of what Updike likes to call "the daily doings of ordinary people" (qtd. in Plath 37). Pru and the children seem to have learned all the slang words associated with drugs, and Rabbit, in talk after talk, brings up the subject.

While having lunch with Charlie, the topic shifts from female sexuality to punk girls and to the change in values that seems to be occurring. For punks, Charlie argues, "ugly is beautiful" (240), to which Rabbit adds his observations on another visible change in the local mores. He mentions his drive around Brewer early in April when he saw that "some of these Hispanics were practically screwing on the street" (240). From this point on, the discussion shifts to drugs, for Charlie sees drugs as responsible for this behavior. Rabbit's contribution comes immediately and, as expected, out of the papers:

> "Did you see in the *Standard,* some spic truck driver from West Miami was caught over near Maiden Springs with they estimate seventy-five mil-

lion dollars' worth of cocaine, five hundred kilos packed in orange crates marked 'Fragile'?"

"They can't stop dope," Charlie says, . . . "as long as people are willing to pay for it."

"The guy was a Cuban refugee evidently, one of those we let in."

"These countries go communist, they let us have all their crooks and crackpots." . . .

"That's the other thing preying on my mind. I think Nelson is into cocaine."

Charlie nods and says, "So I hear." (240–41)

The passage is a rich example of history writing itself into fiction, ceasing to be mere background for the story. No longer is the story merely immersed in history or set upon a historical background—it actually grows out of, or from, history. Again, as with all the previous cases, not all history serves the story. It has to be the kind of history that helps to portray the predominant ideological construct of the characters, especially Rabbit's.

It is, thus, possible to observe once more how Rabbit sees foreigners as responsible for the disruption of established mores, how he treats Hispanics derogatorily, and how the drug problem is easily transformed into a possible international communist plot to destabilize the country. If we recall how this dialogue started, we may add sexism to his blatant nationalism, anticommunism, and racism.

At times we are led to believe that Rabbit is not aware of the history he verbalizes and appropriates. An instance of this may be found in the following dialogue, which takes place during the night Pru calls Harry and Janice for help:

"Nelson, when will it end?" Janice asks, tears making her voice crack, just from looking at him. . . . "You must get off this stuff."

"I am, Mom. I am off. Starting tonight."

"Ha," Harry says.

Nelson insists to her, "I can handle it. I'm no addict. I'm a recreational user."

"Yeah," Harry says, *"like Hitler was a recreational killer."* It must be the mustache made him think of Hitler. (260; emphasis added)

Rabbit's analogy comparing Nelson to Hitler is certainly remarkable. Rabbit himself is startled by his analogy. He can't understand why he thought of Hitler. He thinks the explanation is that his son's mustache reminds him of Hitler. Knowing, however, the way Rabbit's mind operates, readers know better. A quick look at the newspaper will tell us that throughout the week Rabbit's mind has been bombarded by news of America's now ancient enemy—Adolf Hitler. Why? Quite simply, because throughout that week neo-Nazis everywhere were celebrating the hundredth anniversary of the dictator's birth. Being aware, then, of what nourished Rabbit's mind during those days brings into the interpretation much more than a possible similarity between Nelson's and Hitler's mustaches.

The drug problem was raised to an unprecedented prominence during the last year of the decade. Not only was it considered the most important domestic issue, but it was also, according to a CBS poll, the most important international issue for almost 50 percent of the respondents, surpassing terrorism and arms control. Waltraud Queiser Morales claims that during those days the "war on drugs" became America's new national security doctrine, accompanied as it was by a "conscious effort by the government to convince the American public and the US Congress of the intimate linkage between drug traffickers and leftist guerrillas" (167). According to Morales, the drug war in 1989 can be read as a natural consequence of major foreign policy setbacks in Latin America. Considering that many parts of the plan remain as classified information, this might very well have been the case. With the cold war gone, the war on drugs could perhaps fill, during the period of transition, the vacuum created by the absence of the need to fight communism. Morales points out, "The average American citizen, whether he has accepted the official ideological linkage of drugs with terrorism as a global communist conspiracy or as a valid national security threat in its own right, is mobilized against international drug trafficking" (167). Rabbit's examples indeed seem to confirm that he associates drug trafficking with communism. Although a poor substitute for the ever-present forces of the cold war, it does give him literally something to worry about and very literally a reason to get up in the morning. Rabbit has experienced the destructive effects of drugs in his own home.

These are, then, some of the major forces at work in the novel. Charged with Middle America's ideology, such forces incessantly bombard both story and history, reader and narrator, and, through their affirmations and denials, create a focus, a point and a horizon of attention, around which and through which life and death circulate. The frontiers of history and story, fact and fiction, background and foreground, become more and more tenuous as we realize that the total Rabbit is as much one as the other. *Without* this understanding Rabbit is dead when the novel starts; *with* this understanding he will remain alive, a celebration of the paradoxical "glory of the daily," a living memory of American history. Or story.

Notes

1. All references to the Rabbit novels are to the Knopf editions.

2. On December 22, 1988, the *New York Times* reported that "aviation authorities thought that since the jet disappeared from ground controllers' radar screens without an emergency call from the cockpit, whatever brought it down must have happened instantaneously" (A16).

3. A U.S. Navy warship downed a civilian Iranian airliner in the Persian Gulf on July 4, 1988, killing all 290 persons on board. The airliner was said to have been mistaken for an F-14.

4. Rabbit's reference to Beirut goes back to October 23, 1983, when 216 American marines were killed when a suicide terrorist drove a truck loaded with explosives into the headquarters of an American marine unit.

5. The United States invaded Grenada on October 26, 1983, only three days after the disaster in Beirut. The invasion was intended, according to President Reagan, "to protect American citizens and to help restore democratic institutions on the Caribbean island." Reagan also declared to the press that the United States "had no choice but to act strongly and decisively [to oppose] a brutal gang of leftist thugs" (*New York Times* 26 Oct. 1983: A1).

6. News on abortion made the papers during most of the days in which the action in the novel takes place.

5

Edward Vargo

Corn Chips, Catheters, Toyotas
The Making of History in *Rabbit at Rest*

All characters, localities, and business establishments represented in this book are fictional, and any resemblance to actual
places or to persons living or dead is purely coincidental.

Rabbit at Rest, copyright page

My fiction about the daily doings of ordinary people has more
history in it than history books.

Updike, Picked-Up Pieces *(501)*

Many *things* went into the making of *Rabbit at Rest*—notes, manuscripts, discarded fragments, galleys, foldout postcards of Sarasota's Jungle Gardens,
newspaper clippings, real estate flyers, medical pamphlets, car ads, and still
more. Among these personal papers gathered in Harvard's Houghton Library, two items stand out as icons of a culture. The first is a blue and yellow Planter's Peanuts wrapper. The second, many layers later, is a red and
yellowish-orange Keystone Snacks Corn Chips bag. Both are torn open,
empty, pressed flat.[1]

Transposed into the fictional discourse of *Rabbit at Rest,* these castoffs
of a consumer society become nuclei around which other artifacts and discourses revolve to form scenes. On a scrap of newspaper found elsewhere in
his leavings, Updike wrote: "Whenever Harry's death becomes real to him,
he has impulse to eat." This note is activated in the first pages of the final
text, where Harry tries to suppress a personal "sense of doom" by eating a
"Planter's Original Peanut Bar." Unsuccessful in shaking off the mood, he
proceeds to think of the death and disaster reported in recent newspapers,
even of the nation's infrastructure "falling apart" during the sanctimonious,
money-hustling, debt-accumulating Reagan years (7–9).[2] Out of a junk-food
wrapper, a scribbled idea, carefully selected newspaper items, and some political editorializing there emerges a specific scene.[3] Disparate elements mesh
seamlessly into a fictional narrative with some historical texture.

The corn chips bag serves as referent for a similar narrative transposi-
tion. On the day that Harry leaves the hospital after the angioplasty, he walks
around the neighborhood of the old Springer house. To counter a sadness

that settles upon him, he "buys a ninety-nine-cent bag of Corn Chips." Information on the preserved bag is reinscribed directly into the fictional discourse for a kind of verisimilitude: "*Manufactured by Keystone Food Prod., Inc., Easton, Pa. 18042 U.S.A. Ingredients: Corn, vegetable oil (contains one or more of the following oils: peanut, cottonseed, corn, partially hydrogenated soybean), salt.* Doesn't sound so bad. KEEP ON KRUNCHIN', the crinkly pumpkin-colored bag advises him" (327). Harry savors the feel of each flake in his mouth, and his mood changes. Later, alone in Florida, Harry gobbles bowl after bowl of Keystone Corn Chips while watching television until his heart rebels once again (471, 490).

When I came upon these empty bags in my dig through the Houghton papers, I could imagine Updike himself munching away as Rabbit's arteries slowly clogged up with all the junk food *he* was consuming. As I shifted back and forth between these traces of 1980s consumables, jottings for their use in the story, and their appropriation in various versions of the text, I could experience how precisely this fiction is rooted in quotidian "fact," in the material world in which the author lived even as he wrote. Data originally provided for consumers or information already processed by journalists for a mass audience leads to narrative event and multilayered interpretation: by the author; by the narrator, whose voice often meshes with Rabbit's; and by Harry and the other characters.

In counterpoint to historians Carl Becker and Simon Schama, who have used fictional accounts to write history, Updike has constructed his fiction out of an active, daily engagement with facts and current events. This intersection of the larger world's "present-ness" (White, *Tropics* 48) with his writing of *Rabbit at Rest* forced him on occasion "to stop to let real time catch up with my fictional time. The private events are the main thing, of course, but you don't want some public event . . . [to] make everything anachronistic" ("Why Rabbit" 25). One might conclude that the con/text of society is producing the text, but the text is also producing a unique kind of historical record for society. Facts are displaced "onto the ground of literary fictions," and the novel's plot structure is projected "onto the facts" (White, *Content* 47).

Yet the enterprise is not so simply dualistic. The context of *Rabbit at Rest* is composed of a tremendous interweaving of contradictory phenomena, multiple perspectives, and heterogeneous interpretations. In the next section I will explore how these broad discontinuities serve the purposes of history in *Rabbit at Rest.* Then I will focus upon the interplay of fact and fiction in scenes from *Rabbit at Rest* related to two specific "cultures" within the complex American context. These are the medical culture of repairing clogged arteries and the business culture of selling Toyotas. On the basis of these considerations, I will conclude with a few remarks about the kind of realism (or history) *Rabbit at Rest* represents.

First, however, I want to indicate why I am concentrating on the last of the four novels. One reason is that Updike's writing strategies have remained consistent from the first to the last. For instance, in each novel there is the placement of narrative within a specific decade, the same kind of omniscient narrator, the use of the present tense, the cataloging of mundane details. Then, even a first reading of *Rabbit at Rest* makes clear that it is an elegiac reprise of the previous three novels. My discussion to come will demonstrate that Updike consciously returned to these novels and even to some of their sources during his writing of *Rabbit at Rest*. Focus upon this one novel allows me to illustrate in greater detail the manner in which the author fused history with fiction in all of the novels. In short, *Rabbit at Rest* is a paradigm of the methods used to create all four novels.

Multiple Cultures: Multiple Perspectives

Historian Fred Weinstein has written: "No one lives or acts—even in the course of a day—in a single structural reality" (9). In other words, one's context is not a monolithic entity but is composed of many interacting contexts. Each of these can be identified with a (sub)culture that operates somewhat autonomously, with a special world that has its own in-group and out-group. These multiple circles of influence overlap, stand contiguously, coalesce, or contend with each other in different configurations at different times in the life of an individual, group, or nation. Cumulatively, they often produce in the text of society or novel a scatter-effect, a sense of dislocation.[4]

One can easily make a list of the heterogeneous "worlds" or "cultures" of 1980s America that function actively in significant portions of *Rabbit at Rest*. Perhaps most obvious are the contrasting, geographically circumscribed cultures of Florida and Pennsylvania. Constantly present within these settings are the interlocking worlds of infotainment (newspapers, television, radio, film) and of sports vicariously tracked through the media (Mike Schmidt, Deion Sanders, Michael Jordan) or actively pursued (golf, basketball). The concerns of various characters with open-heart surgery, lupus, or AIDS, with junk food or low-fat diets and physical fitness, tap into the decade's health and medical cultures. Intimately linked to this is the drug culture that Nelson enters—and leaves. Punk and yuppie cultures relate in various ways to the culture of consumerism, with its fads and fashions (rattails, Nikes, body gloves, males wearing earrings). Also connected to consumerism are the world of auto dealerships and America's road culture; the world of air travel with its special dangers from terrorism; the culture of tourist attractions set up to educate, entertain, and make money; and the culture built on Reaganomics, out of which emerges a new culture of the homeless. Then there is the women's movement, which leads Janice into the circle of night school culture, which in turn prepares her to move into the world of business as an independent real estate agent. Nor does this exhaust the list.

Multiple "histories" interact with each other in *Rabbit at Rest* in much the same way as do multiple "cultures" or "worlds." Through the intrusion into the home of news items in daily newspapers and on the television screen, the neat demarcation of inside/outside breaks down. Current events that will get into the history books enter into the characters' ordinary activities as topics of conversation, distractions from confrontation, pivots for reflection, or handy explanations for one's actions. The American family becomes the micro-setting for the macro-world. Updike himself has spoken of the presence of the television set in Harry's house (in *Rabbit Redux*) as making him "the middle class man whose living room becomes the scene of atrocities and teach-ins and all those things" (*Picked-Up Pieces* 286). Moreover, Harry's hobby of reading history brings *formal* historical discourse into *Rabbit at Rest,* in the form of extensive quotations from *The First Salute,* Barbara Tuchman's book on the American Revolution. Stacey Olster has argued convincingly that this juxtaposition of historical discourse with present narrative sets "eventual decline in America" within the context of "the inevitability of imperial decline in general" ("Rabbit Rerun" 47).[5]

Multiple histories exist for individual human beings as well. Rabbit has a "recent medical history" and an "ancient history of high-school athletics" (351). During the eulogy at Thelma's funeral, Harry thinks "of the wanton naked Thelma he knew, how little she had to do with the woman the minister described; but maybe the minister's Thelma was as real as Harry's" (374). Then, on the day before Harry's massive myocardial infarction, one of the boys on the basketball court mocks him with the words, "you're history!" (491). Unwittingly, this adolescent forecasts what will soon come true for Harry.

As Weinstein has argued, the intermixing of multiple worlds, cultures, and histories spawns "competing perspectives" and "discontinuous bases for action" (3). The ability of individuals and societies to construct imaginative "versions of the world in terms of their own needs and interests" intensifies this fragmentation (9). Weinstein has isolated "ideology, authority, property, and money" as the most important ways in which people and societies have tried to contain "the potentially or actually threatening effects of heterogeneity and discontinuity." He has also maintained that, as people have moved toward "a more independent course of action in a heterogeneous world," especially in democratic societies, property and money have tended to replace ideology and authority as the "objects of support" (10).

A case can be made for the unfolding of such a dynamic in the course of the Rabbit novels. While ideology and authority were the major systems of meaning production for the author, narrator, and characters in *Rabbit, Run* and *Rabbit Redux,* property and money have tended to become the dominant "objects of support" in *Rabbit Is Rich* and *Rabbit at Rest.* The evolution of Harry's own responses to the "outside" world has followed a similar pattern. Like Updike himself, Rabbit has lived his adult life coterminously with the cold war and was "in some sense always justified, at the back of his mind, by a concept of freedom, of America, that took sharpness from contrast with Communism" ("Why Rabbit" 25). What looked like rebellion against society and authority in *Rabbit, Run* developed into patriotic defense of the Vietnam War in *Rabbit Redux* and, in *Rabbit Is Rich,* into a cozy acceptance of the capitalist system and a nominal support of family and religion.

Harry's understanding of what it means to be an American has also led him from the start into what we now call politically incorrect behavior. In offhand comments and in the vulgar language Rabbit uses to describe people, male chauvinism is already evident in *Rabbit, Run.* Out-and-out bias or ambivalence toward ethnic groups (African Americans, Italians, Hispanics) comes to the surface with *Rabbit Redux.* Harry's homophobia becomes most explicit in his response to the minister at Nelson and Pru's wedding in *Rabbit Is Rich.* All of this locates Harry somewhere among political certainties to the right of center.

Yet Harry continues to live in dis-ease. The "usable" pasts that he has tried to appropriate over the decades seem to crumble in *Rabbit at Rest.* He is still caught between "competing perspectives," and no single ideology or complex of ideologies has the power to anchor his present life. The feeling of disorientation caused by the end of the cold war resonates, as Updike has remarked, with Rabbit's "sense of being useless, of being pushed to one side by his wife and son" ("Why Rabbit" 25). When Harry is driving through Virginia on his flight from home, the many military bases make him think of this key ideology in his life, but his comfort lies in the past: "War is a relief in many ways. Without the cold war, what's the point of being an American? Still, we held out. We held off the oafs for forty years. History will remember that" (442–43).

Earlier in the novel, when Rabbit's Jewish golf buddies in Florida share perspectives diverging from his own on the Bush/Dukakis presidential campaign, the Reagan style of governance, and the Arab-Israeli conflict, the clarity of vision Rabbit hopes to gain from these friends eludes him (69). Later, when he tries to respond to Pru's depression on the day Nelson leaves for detox, he feels obliged to tell her, " 'Nobody's trash.' But even as he says it he knows this is an old-fashioned idea he would have trouble defending. We're all trash, really. Without God to lift us up and make us into angels we're all trash" (344). Though not entirely emptied of religious belief, Harry realizes how the present social context has weakened its power.

Most of all, Harry's faith in the consumer society into which he burrowed so comfortably in *Rabbit Is Rich* is increasingly shaken. It is almost as if he is coming full circle to his dissatisfactions in *Rabbit, Run,* but without the drive to revolt. More and more, he realizes, latter-day capitalism is undermining or marginalizing values that he is trying to uphold, however inchoately— love of country, old-fashioned ethics, respect for authority, and religious notions of human worth (*Rest* 263; Holland 55). He now perceives that he lives in a throw-it-away economy where *everything* is disposable, even human beings (*Rest* 460). As Harry (and the narrator articulating his thoughts) come to see it, money has become the primary support in the capitalist system. It has the power to control all of life—business, the legal and financial systems, religion (461).[6]

Harry's ongoing scuffles with Nelson bolster this conclusion. Early on, where Harry champions a "God Bless America," Uncle Sam type of nation, his son is more cynical: "It's easy to be rich, that's what this country is all about" (40). Later, Nelson characterizes Harry's call for financial discipline as an outgrowth of his 1950s blue-collar work ethic and argues that in today's consumer society one takes what one wants (417).

Rabbit's exasperation at the actions of his son is often conflated with his "political indignation," with his protest against certain perspectives of the complex culture within which he lives. Waiting for the Toyota representative to lower the boom on Springer Motors, he projects his anger at Nelson's cheating onto the climate of corruption in the world at large (Pete Rose, Ollie North, drug dealers) (384). His interwoven indignations move between family and state, fusing the private with the public: he resents the family attention given to the rehabilitated Nelson, Janice's growing independence from him, the reneging on debts of Mexico, Brazil, and the "sleazy S and L banks" (400).

Rabbit at Rest, like the earlier novels, is both a record and a subversive critique of the American politico-economic system of its decade. The diverse ideologies converging or warring with each other are part of the discontinuous scene in all four novels. Each character has his or her own way of trying to meet a society composed of many complex cultures and heterogeneities. The narrator sometimes mirrors, sometimes elaborates upon these multiple perspectives and interpretations.[7] As for Updike, his orchestration of these disparate elements in the four novels has as its by-product a record and interpretation of forty years of history.[8] He obviously loves the American society that he reconstructs in his ongoing story, even as he quarrels with many of its manifestations.

The above discussion underscores political and economic issues usually linked to the making or interpretation of history. In the next two sections, I will argue for a less obvious, yet perhaps even more significant, way in which history is made in the Rabbit novels. As Stacey Olster has written in "Rabbit Rerun: Updike's Replay of Popular Culture in *Rabbit at Rest*": "For all his ranting about global events and crises in American foreign policy, the concerns that touch him personally are contained more in the popular than in the political" (46). In other words, the consumption of junk food, the couch potato habits of a televiewing culture, and the fascination with material products (from MagiPeelers to Toyotas) determine Harry's life more than all the facts about world events he gathers from the media.

Scenes related to Harry's angioplasty and Nelson's demolition of the Toyota franchise at Springer Motors are the sites for my synchronous reading of Updike's working papers and the final text of *Rabbit at Rest*. The discontinuities between disparate elements that might be erased by finished narrative stand exposed when going through the working papers. This synchronous reading involves a jumpy, disconnected series of scattered items on the one hand and a smooth, continuous narrative on the other. By oscillating between these texts, I hope to provide a reconstruction of the writing process. Moreover, such a reading will reveal how some of the heterogeneities, multiple perspectives, and differing interpretations considered above are interwoven into scenes that at first blush appear to be ahistorical. This Janus-like reading should also uncover the various interactions that produce a kind of historical discourse within the fictional discourse of the novel.

Hospital Culture: Angioplasty or Bypass?

Charles Berryman, in his earlier essay in this volume, has already shown how Updike's care for his mother in her final sickness and death coincided with his writing and completion of the first draft for *Rabbit at Rest*. Updike made this link himself in prepublication remarks to the American Booksellers Association; he returned to this enfolding of his mother's sickness and death into Harry's own in "*A special message for the first edition from John Updike*," which I found among the layers of notes, drafts, and leavings: "Her decline . . . contributed to the hospital scenes of this book and to its overall mortal mood."

Building upon this personal experience, Updike actively engaged America's high-tech health care culture in other ways as well. Interspersed with the manuscripts for *Rabbit at Rest* at Houghton are a half-dozen letters from Dr. Barry Meyers of Littleton, Colorado, dated between April 17 and August 3.[9] There are several articles from medical journals and newspapers sent by the doctor, as well as galleys returned with comments on the fictional Dr. Olman's angioplasty/bypass lecture and the angioplasty episode. One could conjecture that Updike was consulting the doctor with questions coming out of his mother's (real) and Harry's (imaginary) experiences. A few layers below the newspaper items (one of them deals with abuses of angioplasty—overpricing, unqualified practitioners) are photocopied sheets on topics like cardiovascular disorders, symptoms, treatments, and medications. At least some of this information comes from a nontechnical book called *Physicians Manual for Patients*.

Three of the articles sent on April 17, all published within the previous twelve months, present the pros and cons of angioplasty versus bypass surgery. A major point in Mark S. Hochberg et al.'s "Coronary Angioplasty versus Coronary Bypass" is that after three years, only 63 percent of the patients in the angioplasty group were alive, in contrast to 92 percent of the patients who had undergone surgery. Two passages are highlighted in John L. Ochsner's "The Interaction between Percutaneous Transluminal Coronary Angioplasty [PTCA] and Coronary Bypass Surgery." The first passage discusses complications to the femoral artery and potential catastrophes for the heart—arrhythmias, occlusion of the coronary artery, and ventricular fibrillation (20). The second mentions the likelihood of the failure of angioplasty under particular conditions, such as long lesions (22). The bias tends to favor surgery. The third article, written by Michael B. Mock et al. for the *New England Journal of Medicine*, calls for a randomized trial of the benefits and effects of PTCA versus coronary artery bypass.

Updike works information and attitudes from these various sources into the narrative in different ways. These appropriations are especially apparent in the following scenes: (1) Dr. Olman's explanation to Janice of Harry's condition in the Deleon hospital (164–72); (2) Rabbit's search for medical advice from Charlie Stavros over lunch at the Salad Binge (236–39); (3) the angioplasty procedure (269–75); and (4) Dr. Breit's discussion with Harry the following Sunday (283–86). In what follows, I will focus primarily upon the angioplasty episode, taking it as emblematic of the ways in which medical discourse becomes inextricably bound up with that of other cultures in the writing of this fictional discourse.

In the first two scenes, Dr. Olman and Charlie Stavros both argue for bypass surgery, in line with the drift of the technical articles introduced above. Harry cannot get himself to agree. On the day of the angioplasty itself, while he waits for the procedure to begin, Harry recalls the video on bypass operations and the articles given to him to read at the Deleon hospital. These are similar to the materials culled from the *Physicians Manual for Patients*. Calling up the details of the bloody operation revives his revulsion for all intrusions into his body, and the information takes on the color of cinematic, sexual, and homely images. The narrator likens the high-tech machines of cardiac surgery to those in the "old Frankenstein movies with Boris Karloff" (269). The entire process is like a rape: "The surgeons' hands in their con-domlike latex gloves fiddle and slice and knit away" (270). Just as repulsive to Harry is "the idea of a catheter being inserted at the top of his right leg, and being pushed along steered with a little flexible tip like some eyeless worm you find wriggling out of an apple where you just bit" (269). All this leads to a sense of dislocation between his self-identity and its material basis, ex-pressed in the warring elemental images of fire and water: "Harry has trouble believing how his life is tied to all this mechanics. . . . How could the flame of him ever have ignited out of such wet straw?" (270).

Dr. Meyers of Littleton entered into dialogue with the draft for this epi-sode at four points. In a flashback to Dr. Breit's explanation of the angio-plasty Harry had opted for against the doctor's preference, Harry now re-members Dr. Breit's warning that "twenty per cent of PTCA patients wind up having a CABG eventually anyway. Sorry—that's percutaneous translu-minal coronary angioplasty versus coronary artery bypass graft" (270). Dr. Meyers agrees to these statistics with a qualification: "True in the long run; only about 5% acutely (i.e. same day as PTCA)." When Dr. Breit notices his patient's incomprehension at his use of acronyms familiar to the professional, Updike reinscribes terms from the articles Dr. Meyers had sent him. The lan-guage, however, does not fully become the layperson's until Harry's response: "Still, let's do the balloon first, and save the knives for later" (270). Harry's persistent choice of this option despite everyone's arguments to the contrary—doctors with author and characters with Harry—makes the outcome of his early death all the more likely.

During the operation itself, conversations between the doctors or explanations given to Harry along the way weave in and out of the actual procedures. There is also an oscillation between the "real" and the "imaged." Next to the operating room there is "a monitoring room with several TV screens that translate him into jerking bright lines, vital signs: the Rabbit Angstrom Show, with a fluctuating audience" of staff (271). Off and on, Harry himself watches this show—observer and observed, participant and spectator. This view "of the procedure as a television program" (Olster, "Rabbit Rerun" 57), springing from the double vision of Harry and the narrator who enters his mind, effects an alienation of the participant from the actual experience. The world of home television penetrates the world of the operating room; Dr. Breit's running commentary uses a technology familiar to the patient to distract him during this incursion into his body.

When Harry turns at one point to look at this show, what Dr. Meyers of Littleton saw with him was "the shadow of his heart on an X-ray monitor screen, . . . webbed by its chambered structure and *whitened* in snaky streaks and bulbous oblongs by injections of the opacifying dye" (272–73; emphasis added). He comments to Updike that the "dye shows up *dark* on monitor screens as it is injected—shows up white only on final developed films." The author accepts the correction for accuracy of detail and changes *whitened* to *darkened* in his final text.

The one emendation Dr. Meyers suggested in the galleys relates to another action of the dye. He indicated that the large amount of dye injected "into the left ventricle for a 'ventriculogram' causes a mild sensation of warmth or flushing over most of the body but nothing nearly so severe or localized to the chest as this passage suggests." In this case, Updike does not eliminate sensation localized to the chest in the final text: "But then there's no pain, just an agony of mounting urinary pressure as the dyes build up in his system, injected repeatedly with a hot surge like his chest is being cooked in a microwave" (272). He ever so gently stretches accuracy of detail, perhaps to communicate Rabbit's sense of being assaulted by modern machines through the microwave simile.

As the dyes begin to take their effect, Harry tries to pray, "but it feels like a wrong occasion, there is too much crowding in, of the actual material world. No old wispy Biblical God would dare interfere." He also thinks of the nuns who used to run this hospital when his two children were born. They are no longer visible: "Vocations drying up, nobody wants to be selfless any more, everybody wants their fun." That was the end of the paragraph in the first draft. In a revision, Updike added further comments that expanded this remark on changing religious attitudes into a critique of a scientistic, profit-oriented culture: "No more nuns, no more rabbis. No more good people. Just technology, and the profit motive, and getting all you can while you can." Updike continued to mull over this text in further revisions; in the final text three more lines introduce the breakup of Soviet Russia and the rise of Japan: "No more nuns, no more rabbis. No more good people, *waiting to have their fun in the afterlife. The thing about the afterlife, it kept this life within bounds somehow, like the Russians. Now there's* just *Japan, and* technology, and the profit motive, and getting all you can while you can" (272; emphasis added). The end result is a multilayered sequence that draws upon several clashing cultures to convey the prostrate Harry's sense of history, residual faith, nostalgia for lost moral restraints, and America's move to an unabashedly secularist ideology in the course of his lifetime. Updike captures a complex moment in history which at the same time he interprets from a particular perspective.

Two times in the text Dr. Meyers observes a "hissing" sound made by the inflating balloon. He indicates that this is not so, but if the author wants to bring in sounds of the operation, that "occasionally the ciné camera makes a humming sound." In the final text given to us, there are neither "hissing" nor "humming" sounds. Instead, on the second inflation of the balloon, we read: "The tense insufflation repeats, and so do the images on the TV screen, silent like the bumping of molecules under the microscope on a nature program" (274). The factual correction is made and related to the action on Harry's private television show, then intensified by a simile from science viewed on public television.

The most interesting interchange between writer and doctor, however, involves another correction of fact that leads to both a more accurate and a more figurative expression of the catheter's operation. In describing the first inflation of the balloon within the artery—to press the plaque against the sides so that the blood may flow freely once again—Updike had written: "He sees, on the monitor, . . . a segment of the *wire* thicken and swell, . . . and stay inflated, pressing, filling" (emphasis added). Here the doctor/reader noted that "technically the balloon catheter and the guide wire are independent units; . . . so actually the catheter and built in balloon would 'thicken and swell' and not the 'segment of the wire.'" To correct this inaccuracy, Updike incorporated the technical understanding without using the literal discourse about catheter, balloon, and guide wire. He took his cue from the word *segment* and transformed the wire into a worm. Now, we and Harry see "a segment of the *worm* thicken and swell" on the screen (274; emphasis added).

Of course this now recalls the likening of the catheter's action to a worm wriggling out of an apple (269). It also reprises the narrator's metaphoric description of the moment when the catheter makes its crucial entry into the heart: "The mechanically precise dark ghost of the catheter is the worm of death within him. Godless technology is fucking the pulsing wet tubes we inherited from the squid, the boneless sea-cunts" (274). With no offense to scientific discourse though bucking at scientific culture's secular attitudes, the fiction stitches together statements and interpretation that incorporate the literal, the synecdochic, and the metaphoric. While accenting the physical details of the procedure, the figurative language also intensifies the reader's entry into the mind-set, instinctive beliefs, and emotions of the patient in whom the worm turns. A richly layered scene from 1980s medicine becomes a historical record of more than the action in the operating room.[10]

On Sunday morning Dr. Breit gives Harry a hard sell on going for bypass surgery within a few months because "a lesion is developing at the bifurcation of the circumflex and the LAD" that will be hard to treat further with angioplasty (283). In a marginal note to the galleys, Dr. Meyers writes that he and other doctors who had read it considered this entire scene (283–86) "very technical—quite accurate but still—quite *technical*." The implication is that their patients—and Updike's lay readers—might find this scene too difficult unless the language is changed into a more broadly accessible discourse. It is as if the specialized information is being pasted into the text with insufficient assimilation, a criticism brought against Updike's method in many of his novels since *Rabbit Is Rich*. Updike did not bend much to this observation. It *is* heavy going, but Dr. Breit's talk is not any more jargon-laden than ordinary 1980s conversations of many elderly heart patients comparing notes on medical procedures and medications. Neither does the fictional doctor's discourse simply parrot professional language: in arguing for the bypass over further angioplasty, for example, he earthily says, "It's the difference between scrubbing out your toilet bowl with a long brush and actually replacing the pipes" (285).

The medical scenes presented above, with all their heterogeneous elements, approximate the experiences and responses of many Americans in the 1980s. Updike's dialogues with specialists, his appropriation of technical information (whether in professional or lay language), and his correction of inaccuracies reveal his ever-present interest in what we call the world of history. At the same time, Updike's ability to attend to accuracy in figurative ways, his adaptations of medical discourse for purposes other than literal exactitude, and the commentaries and interpretations of his narrator and characters (often in opposition to the prevailing culture) take the "history" that he is writing beyond any simple notion of one-to-one correspondences. As in the earlier novels, the discourse of *Rabbit at Rest* both reflects and acts upon the complex cultures that are its referents.

Company Culture: Nelson's Scam

Among the materials together with the manuscripts and galleys for *Rabbit at Rest* are Toyota publications: the annual reports for 1987 and 1988 as well as booklets introducing the company and the 1989 Corolla and Camry. In addition, there are things like the Special Automotive Issue of the *Boston Sunday Globe* for October 1, 1988; other newspaper ads for Toyota; notes and clippings that evaluate new features, drawbacks, or mechanical failures in various 1989 models of Honda and Toyota; and information on car agencies.

These advertisements and reports collected by Updike become part of Harry's world, too. Left alone when the women and children go down to the pool at the Florida condo, Harry and Nelson "try to be friends" through small talk over beers. With his only knowledge of the new 1989 Toyotas coming from advance brochures, Rabbit is especially fascinated by a photo of a Corolla in the mountains with no car tracks in the snow: "How many millions you think those ad agencies get for making up those brochures?" (35–36).

All the publications mentioned above can be considered update information, for Updike had already accumulated much material and knowledge on the business of selling Toyotas when he wrote *Rabbit Is Rich*. Next to a box with the final fair copy of *Rabbit at Rest* at Houghton, there is a manila folder marked "Includes some Toyota research from RIII," that is, *Rabbit Is Rich*.[11] The key artifact I would like to consider from this collection of twice-used materials is a photocopy of selected pages from Martin H. Bury's *The Automobile Dealer*, a manual for owners and managers of car dealerships. These pages include marginal notes, summary comments, and markings by Updike. Many of these comments are relevant to the creation of *Rabbit Is Rich*; here I will try to isolate a few that I consider significant for the making of *Rabbit at Rest*.

This time around, much of the writer's energy went into exploring the feasibility of various legal and financial aspects of Nelson's scam. Going through Bury's manual, Updike noticed various reasons for dealers to quit, especially "for not conforming to their selling agreement" (Bury 9). He noted various "methods of financing" (113). Apparently, Updike was also reading this business manual with emplotting in mind. Next to a paragraph that addresses the drop in the number of "franchised domestic-car dealers" in the United States, he wrote: "Rabbit worries they can lose the franchise and they call in Charlie to save" (218). On the top of an earlier page, he had written: " 'loss reserve' scam//possible source of funds for Nelson" (116). As Nelson's scam is finally developed in the novel, it seems partially inspired by an example found under this note. There Bury had described the situation of "a prominent new car dealer in a medium-size Pennsylvania city" whose greed had ultimately destroyed his profitable business. "He started pocketing an ever-increasing portion of payments [in the margin Updike asked, "what payments?"], instead of clearing that money through his business as income." Finally, a routine IRS audit "revealed that the dealer's finance income was far below the normal average of other dealers." The dealer lost everything and landed in jail "for tax evasion" (116–17).

Updike's evolution of Nelson's scam also involved dialogues through the mail with lawyers and salesmen and the gathering of information from newspapers. An article in the *Boston Sunday Globe* for February 19, 1989, for example, suggests a motivation for Nelson's scam in the emplotting of his situation at the dealership. In "Drugs: Silent Killer of Profits," Barbara Carton discusses the prevalence of drug abuse in the American workplace. She speaks in particular of the low self-esteem of these substance abusers and of the need to confront them.

Many of these newspaper items refer to unsavory practices or court cases against car dealerships. Among two articles on the problems of new-car dealerships from the *Wall Street Journal* of December 11, 1989, sent to Updike well after his first draft was completed, the second is entitled "Rags-to-Riches Dealer Leaves Behind Big Losses and Allegations of Fraud." Highlighted passages outline illegal activities, notably, failing to pay back loans after cars were sold and taking out loans beyond the ability to repay. One highlighted passage reads: "out-of-trust—that is, customers had bought the cars, but he never had repaid the loans he took out to buy the cars from the factory."

These are only a small part of the materials that went into selecting, clarifying, and focusing the plot elements of Nelson's scam. Out of all the possible options suggested by this documentation, a few words scribbled on a filecard crystallize the idea settled upon: "the scam—tells them he has sold one less car than he has; they send 4 instead of 3, he transfers money to self and his account with Mid-Atlantic goes up."

The elaboration of this outline comes to its full disclosure when Janice reports to the hospitalized Harry that an accountant has discovered what has been going on at Springer Motors. To pay for Nelson's drug habits and for Lyle's illegal AIDS medication, Nelson first "got the idea of offering people a discount on the used cars if they paid in cash or with a check written directly out to him" (*Rest* 296). Then he and Lyle worked out a scheme that involved giving false information to Toyota headquarters in California, much as outlined on the filecard: "So every month we'd owe this TMCC [Toyota Motors Credit Corporation] for one or two more cars than were actually on the lot and our debt to them kept getting bigger and our actual inventory was getting smaller" (298).

At least one more scene in the novel germinated during the rereading of the business manual. On the top of a page in Bury's final chapter, "The Score: Profit or Loss," Updike wrote: "factory representative / scene—Japanese visits his dealership?" (368). In August, such "a representative of the Toyota Corporation, a Mr. Natsume Shimada," does visit Springer Motors to deal with the exposed scam (*Rest* 381). He announces that there will be no court case if Springer Motors pays up its debt by the end of the month. In any case, it will lose its Toyota franchise. But before handing down this judgment, Mr. Shimada lectures Harry about America's degeneration from an admired "big brother" into a whiner about "Japanese unfair competition." In the new America, "Nothing comes out, all goes in—foreign goods, foreign capital. America take everything, give nothing. Rike big brack hole" (390). Toyota is trying to counterbalance this lack of discipline and abuse of freedom with its company culture: "In U.S., Toyota company hope to make ireands of order in ocean of freedom" (392).

Earlier versions of this scene were written in a more standard English than seen above. Certain changes with an ear to Japanese mispronunciations of English enter into the galleys. Over several pages, many *l*'s in the dialogue are now changed into *r*'s to mimic a difficulty many Asians have with discriminating between these two sounds. To accentuate the same difficulty, the word "small" is changed to "rittle," and the phrase "can quickly buy" into "before too rate should buy." While these modifications reflect a common error, even in persons as competent in English as Mr. Shimada, I believe they would have been more difficult to make in a different social climate. Many of Updike's readers have fed on "flied lice" jokes in high school; at least a segment of his reading public must still accept such language as humorous for the scene to be fully effective. This is yet another example of how society is writing the text—and my comments.

Is Realism Possible after Posthistoricism?

In *Rabbit at Rest,* Updike continues to follow the standard he set in *Rabbit, Run* "of fidelity to the present world of information" (Falsey 15). Not everyone, however, regards this as doing the work of history. Judie Newman, for one, explains Harry's "tendency to catalogue his environment in excessive detail" in *Rabbit Is Rich* "less as a documentary approach to Middle America in all its facticity than as an expression of the relentless desire to collect, store up and incorporate information" (64). Yet, I would argue, Harry does have a particular view of history, one that has its roots in nineteenth-century realism and correspondence theory, hardly a postmodern mind-set.

While in the hospital for his angioplasty, Harry finds that he is hungry for "facts, not fantasies." In the large doses of television that he swallows, he wants only "the truth" transmitted in news programs or in documentaries on nature or historical events like World War II (294). Harry trusts in the factual, the real, the true. Concomitantly, Harry distrusts interpretations that ignore what *he* sees as fact. In family therapy he resents the therapist's questions to the others about how his statements make them feel, "as if what he's saying isn't a description of facts but a set of noises to be rolled into some general mishmash. All this 'talking through' and 'processing' therapists like to do cheapens the world's facts" (348). His perspective excludes the possibility of reading facts in any way other than his own. Harry firmly believes that *his* "immediate consciousness" accurately re-presents the "real" world "outside" (Flores 29). As far as he is concerned, his "telling is an accounting for—a re-counting of—events" and is to be taken at face value (11).

Of course, Harry Angstrom is not John Updike. No easy correlation should conflate a single character with the orchestrator of the entire novel; the assemblage of multiple perspectives and heterogeneous interpretations within the novel speaks to that. Still, it is clear that factual accuracy and "objective consistency" are no small matters for Updike. From the beginning, he has reveled in a knowledge of the material world and sensed blessing in details.

To borrow the words of Robert Detweiler, Updike's "presentational, heavily metaphorical language" shows a concern to reflect "the referents of the 'real' historical, natural, cultural world" (*Breaking the Fall* 19). In 1974, Joseph Waldmeir had already argued that Updike's intention in *Rabbit, Run* "is to reveal the thing itself—scene, situation, character, even argument—as perceived, with no revelation beyond the perception" (16). Since *Rabbit, Run* set the tone for subsequent Rabbit novels, it should be no surprise to find traces of its 1950s empiricist trust in "thing-ness" continuing to emerge from postmodern erasures of its problematization.

Yet what kind of reality do referents have? In this posthistoricist age, the facts that we used to consider solid and permanent are regarded as fragile and unstable; they shimmer and change as different observers respond to or construct them. Moreover, in the thirty years from the first to the last Rabbit novel, the dominant critical theory has become skeptical about the universal, the timeless, and the transcendent. From this perspective, nineteenth-century realism's claim to present "life as it really is" depended "on a specifically narrative mode of discourse" that "substitute[d] surreptitiously a conceptual content . . . for a referent that it pretended merely to describe" (White, *Content* 37).

Critics have often noted that Updike writes out of this tradition. His writing certainly upholds many features linked to traditional realism, but it is not a naive realism. As strong as is the pull of verisimilitude in the Rabbit novels, the creation of a highly figurative discourse is just as important. Likewise, while Updike does employ national = personal equations like "Natl deficit = Nelson's debts" (on a piece of paper found among notes for "Florida"), he is not trying to turn Harry, Janice, Nelson, and Pru into dehistoricized, universal types. Harry and his family are deeply rooted in their own time and place. They are products and, in some minuscule way, makers or resisters of the many cultures and worlds within which they live and move.

Awareness of the larger historical context becomes more and more explicit in the progression from *Rabbit, Run* to *Rabbit at Rest*. With the clashing and coalescing of contradictory phenomena, multiple perspectives, interpretations, and theories, the novels serve a function of history beyond simple representation. They invite "the reader to see with new clarity materials to which he has become oblivious through sustained association, or which he has repressed in response to social imperatives" (White, *Tropics* 45). In addition, Updike's sensitivity to "a language complicit with shaping reality and making meaning" (Detweiler, *Breaking the Fall* 19) results in a rich fictional history that cuts across the boundaries of many different discourses.

Louis de Berniéres has written in *Corelli's Mandolin* that history should consist "only of the anecdotes of the little people who are caught up in it." One of his reviewers, W. S. Di Piero, characterizes the presentation of history in that novel as "composed of sufferings large and small, of national catastrophes and household agonies" (7). The same can be said of the Rabbit novels. Around three generations of Angstroms, Updike has constructed a fictional history that intertwines complex social contexts with the story of one family. These richly textured tales promise to be a multilayered source for students of our age in generations to come.

Elég. Talán elég.

Notes

1. Preliminary versions, manuscripts, galleys, and any materials that are identified as used in writing *Rabbit at Rest* can be found in MS Stor 279 (1 of 4), John Updike Papers, Houghton Library, Harvard University, Cambridge. Here I would like to express my deep appreciation to John Updike for his gracious permission to quote from these materials. I would also like to thank Fu Jen University and the National Science Council, Taiwan, Republic of China, for their support of this research.

2. All references to the Rabbit novels are to the Knopf editions.

3. Throughout this essay, I use the term *scene* much as Dilvo I. Ristoff does in *Updike's America*, the first book-length critical study to examine the Rabbit novels through the lens of new historicism. For Ristoff, "the scene works as . . . a finger pointing to segments of history and to segments of America which are believed to be, when put together, a recognizable picture of the impossible-to-grasp totality" (5). Moreover, "scene" not only "parallels the social, political, economic, and cultural scene of the" relevant decades, but also "acts upon the characters as forces which generate actions, thoughts, judgments, and emotions" (8–9). Central to Ristoff's approach is the "need to restore referentiality," the "generative power of the referents," and the "inseparableness of fiction and history" (xviii). Though I find Ristoff's reading of Rabbit's character too deterministic, *Updike's America* led me to Houghton and, in many ways, undergirds this essay.

4. What I am here designating as *cultures* or *worlds*, A. Leigh DeNeef calls *histories:* "Old historicism assumed that history could be recognized and summarized in a stable, coherent, collective, and 'monolithic' world picture. . . . The new historicism follows Frank Lentricchia in positing any number of histories, each of which is characterized by 'forces of heterogeneity, contradiction, fragmentation, and difference' " (501).

5. For an extensive treatment of the uses of Tuchman's discourse in *Rabbit at Rest,* see Olster, "Rabbit Is Redundant." Also see Judie Newman's essay in this collection for a discussion of Updike's use of Tuchman's book.

6. For a discussion of Harry's broken faith in capitalism, see Judie Newman's essay in this collection.

7. Genevieve Later has addressed a persistent question of some critics upon the publication of each new Rabbit novel: "Why the metaphoric ornateness of the

narrative voice in contrast to the mundaneness of small-town lives in Pennsylvania?" (15–16). In Later's opinion, one in which I concur, the narrator's metaphors primarily contribute neither clarity nor objectivity to our picture of Rabbit. Rather, "the distance between the narrative voice and the other voices" provides "density." In this way, "Updike tries to capture the infinitude of unseen thoughts, gestures, and moments that exist in the silences between people, people so inarticulate (by virtue of class or personality) that without Updike, they would be silent altogether" (17).

8. In *Rabbit, Run*, the pacesetter for the entire tetralogy, Genevieve Later notes the construction of "a very strong, omniscient narrator, often identified with Updike himself," to supplement the relative inarticulateness of Rabbit and the other characters created within this fictional world (5). But the voices of author and narrator are not to be confused. A recognition that Updike is "conducting the narrative voice along with all the others, controlling the wide range of dialogues in the work," keeps us from becoming "fixated . . . on this unitary third-person voice as the primary voice in the novel" (6). In the orchestration of the novel's discourse, Later identifies "hybrid constructions," " 'pure' dialogues," and "dialogized languages" (9). Expanding upon Bakhtin's concept of "double-voice discourse," she suggests the operation of a triple-voice discourse that weaves together "the triple threads of Updike's intention, the narrative voice, and whatever character is forming an intention" (11).

9. Any letters referred to in this essay are interspersed with other papers directly related to the making of this novel, but I do not have access to their content. I conclude that these letters of Dr. Meyers are all from 1989, the year of composition of the first draft, except for the letter of May 2. This must be from the following year, since it was sent to Updike with pages 269–75 of the galleys for the final text.

10. For another discussion of the use of images during Harry's angioplasty, see Judie Newman's essay in this collection.

11. These older materials can be found especially in the following places among the John Updike Papers in the Houghton Library:

*81M-51 (689) Updike, John. Rabbit is Rich: research and notes. 13 folders.
*81M-51 (691) Updike, John. Rabbit is Rich. A.MS., TS. with A.MS. revisions, MS. in the hand of Martha (Bernhard) Updike; [Georgetown, 1979–1980]. 222s. 282p. 9 folders.

On December 5, 1988, Updike borrowed *81M-51 (689) (486) (304) (594) (512) for his work on *Rabbit at Rest*. Martin Bury's *The Automobile Dealer* was in (689). Some of these materials relate to the first two Rabbit novels.

6

Matthew Wilson
The Rabbit Tetralogy
From Solitude to Society to Solitude Again

Frederick R. Karl, in his exhaustive survey of postwar American fiction, has little to say about novel sequences because, he claims, in comparison to Britain, there is a "paucity of sequential novels" in America.[1] Our "social expectations" and "our need for movement and escape" militate against novel sequences, which, of necessity, imply "limited options." The relative scarcity of this form in America, Karl argues, is "tied to our optimism, our desire to break from predetermined forms, to free ourselves from the historical past, emerging into that purer atmosphere of pastoral, which promises liberation" (252). The predominant "predetermined form" from which American writers have attempted to liberate their characters has always been that of society, which, as Richard Poirier pointed out in discussing *Huck Finn,* has been pervasively conceived of as "nothing but artifice, tricks, games, and disguise" (194). Poirier concludes that *Huck Finn* "discovers that the consciousness it values most cannot expand within the environment it provides, that the self cannot come to fuller life through social drama" (195). All that self can do is to escape, and like so many other American male protagonists, Huck flees society, women, and history. Twain's inability late in his career to imagine a subsequent life for Huck is evidence, as Fitzgerald claimed, that in America there are no second acts. Having escaped, there is no imaginable social milieu within which the characters can continue to exist.

Against Karl's model of interpretation, I am going to offer John Updike's Rabbit tetralogy as a paradigm of how American novel sequences in the postwar years[2] embrace rather than reject "predetermined forms"—in particular, familial and social connections—and of how Updike's main character, Harry "Rabbit" Angstrom, comes to "fuller life through social drama." Over the course of these four novels, Updike transforms Rabbit from the traditional solitary American male character fleeing society (and women as representatives of that society) to a man integrated into society and surrounded, almost comically, by women. The final novel, *Rabbit at Rest,* does transform him again into a man isolated from his family and society, but his isolation is not a return to an earlier mode of being because Harry has developed an almost acute historical consciousness.

In these novels, Updike has been exploring a long-term tension in American experience, the kind of tension that Emerson articulated in "Solitude and Society": "Nature delights to put us between extreme antagonisms, and our safety is in the skill with which we keep the diagonal line. Solitude is impracticable, and society fatal. We must keep our head in the one and our hands in the other. The conditions are met, if we keep our independence, yet do not lose our sympathy" (*Complete Works* 7: 15). The tetralogy executes, I will argue, a complicated interplay between these "extreme antagonisms." Moving from the solitude of the fleeing young man to the solitude of the death-saturated older man, the sequence tacks between solitude and society. A momentary balance is achieved in *Rabbit Is Rich*, only to be inevitably destroyed by Rabbit's dwindling toward death. Within this interplay, the sequence also reveals an increasing awareness of history, which becomes a subject, almost obsessively, in the guise of contemporary events, and which is transformed in the final novel into a historical consciousness within Harry Angstrom.

In broad national terms, the first novel, *Rabbit, Run*, is the least impinged upon by contemporary history and "takes . . . little account of the public terms of life in its time" (Edwards 94). Although Rabbit was in the army during the Korean War, he served stateside, and apart from the dim memory of his army service, his world is largely innocent of anything outside of Brewer, Pennsylvania, the somewhat insulated setting of the series. That very limitation, however, makes the novel typical of what Robert Lowell called the "tranquilized *Fifties*" (85), a time of conformity and of national somnolence in small cities like Brewer. It was also a time that experienced the beginnings of a more urban revolt against that conformity, as seen in the Beat movement, but Rabbit (like the country, one could almost say) is so self-involved that he is not aware (as he is in later novels) of participating in or reflecting any national trends. As Updike has written, this novel was a "product of the 50's" but was not "really in a conscious way about the 50's" ("Why Rabbit" 24). Like the novel itself, Harry is not conscious of his place in time and history; all he knows is his primary emotion—a feeling of being trapped and enclosed.

Crucially, Rabbit is a former high school basketball star, aware enough to realize that his life offers him only diminishment. As he says, "I once did something right. I played first-rate basketball. I really did. And after you're first-rate at something, no matter what, it kind of takes the kick out of being second-rate" (*Run* 101).³ His dissatisfaction with himself and with his "second-rate" marriage drives him to leave his wife, Janice; he takes up with Ruth, a part-time prostitute, whom he abandons in turn when Janice goes into labor with their second child. He returns to his wife, whom he abandons again for Ruth, and the final sentences of the novel find him in ecstatic escape once again: "His hands lift of their own and he feels the wind on his ears even before, his heels hitting heavily on the pavement at first but with an effortless gathering out of a kind of sweet panic growing lighter and quicker and quieter, he runs. Ah: runs. Runs" (284).

All of Rabbit's improvised escapes, all of his bouncing back and forth, demonstrate the impossibility of any flight except the most provisional. His improvisations are based on his insistence on the primacy of his own feelings: "All I know is what's inside *me*. That's all I have" (102). Or as he says to Ruth late in the novel: "All I know is what feels right. You feel right to me. Sometimes Janice used to. Sometimes nothing does" (281). His instincts tell him his marriage has gone wrong; he is tired of holding "this mess together" (100), tired of domestic responsibilities, all of which is compounded by the failure of sex between him and his wife. This is a central failure because it has been through basketball and through sex that he has defined himself. He thinks of the first girl he had sex with in high school, one with a "touch of timidity." "As if she wasn't sure but he was much bigger, a winner. He came to her as a winner and that's the feeling he's missed since. In the same way she was the best of them all because she was the one he brought most to." The triumphs of basketball and sex "were united in his mind" (184). Once his basketball career was over, he inevitably "brought" less to sex because he could find no public role and, consequently, no way of conceiving of himself as a "winner."⁴ In this diminishment, however, sex became the sole expression of the ecstatic in his life, and much of the connection between him and Ruth is sexual. Sex with her returns him to a kind of physical freedom, makes him feel like a winner again, free of all traps, momentarily "out of all dimension" (78). When at the end of the novel, however, she demands that he turn the solitude of the ecstatic into the social and public, divorce his wife, and marry her, Rabbit runs again. In these novels, consequently, sex is the promise of the possibility of escape, but it is also always the enactment of the impossibility of escape.

In running to and from women, Rabbit leaves unhappiness and eventually death in his wake, but there is something admirable in his struggle against the inadequacy and deadness around him. Ruth says she likes him " 'Cause you haven't given up. In your stupid way you're still fighting" (89).

This is a struggle, however, with no object. Inevitably, sex seems to become institutionalized, and escape is another trap, a widening enclosure. The one time he actually tries to leave town, resolving to drive south, he sees himself entangled. He looks at a map and "the names melt away and he sees . . . [it] whole, a net,[5] all those red lines and blue lines and stars, a net he is somewhere caught in" (39). In *Rabbit, Run* the only escape, the only liberation, is provisional—in sex or in the first moments of running.

Obviously, Rabbit shares the impulse to "break from predetermined forms" that Karl discusses, but the novel demonstrates the constant bafflement of that impulse. In his desire to evade social constraints, Rabbit is allied to the Huck Finn who stated, "I reckon I got to light out for the Territory ahead of the rest" (321). What Rabbit enacts in this novel, however, is the state of belatedness. There is no "Territory" to flee to, and, as Jeff Campbell explains earlier in this collection, even Kerouac's protagonists, Rabbit's fictional contemporaries, have only the object of the open road itself. Rabbit cannot attain even the freedom of the road, and although the final sentences of the novel seem to promise escape, the structure of the novel leaves no doubt that the effort to "find an opening" (249) is a futile one. In Updike's depiction of Rabbit's world, either there are no openings, or any seeming opening inevitably closes to become a trap. Rabbit runs in circles.

In both of his escapes, sex and running, Rabbit is fleeing his wife, and in referring to the "yes, but" quality of Updike's fiction, Campbell rightly suggests the connection between fleeing women and the social circumstances of 1950s America that creates the moral debate of these novels. The moral dilemma that Updike is framing is, in part, that the women get hurt; women are desired and feared; and women are, centrally, the representatives of society in the constraints of marriage, the entanglements of which the protagonist seeks to cut through. In cutting through, Rabbit badly damages two women: we do not see the results for Ruth until twenty years later in *Rabbit Is Rich*, but the consequences for Janice constitute a large part of both *Rabbit, Run* and *Rabbit Redux*. One indirect result of Rabbit's attempts to escape is the death of their baby;[6] a direct result of these escapes and returns is Janice exacting her revenge by leaving Rabbit for another man in *Rabbit Redux*.

Rabbit, Run is, according to Updike, an enactment of the inevitable bafflement of "Harry's search for infinite freedom" (*Picked-Up Pieces* 510), and the author's decision to write a sequel, *Rabbit Redux*, means that Harry is being "led back," obliquely, to the "diagonal line" of society and contemporary history. Updike has reported that after *Rabbit, Run* he was asked what happened to Rabbit, and his decision to write a sequel meant confronting "all the oppressive, distressing, overstimulating developments of the most dissentious American decade since the Civil War" (*Hugging the Shore* 858). This dissentiousness meant that the 1960s "were much more self conscious, much more conscious of themselves as a decade" than were the 1950s ("Why Rabbit" 24). In contrast to the earlier novel, *Rabbit Redux* is a "political novel of a particular historical moment" (Edwards 96), that of the embattled 1960s, where the contentious public issues of Vietnam and civil unrest are unavoidable even in Brewer, Pennsylvania. Although Rabbit combatively claims that he does not "*think* about politics" (*Redux* 47), politics are inescapable in this era, and his are, predictably, intuitive. He has a fervent, almost religious belief in America. While the younger Rabbit ignored politics, the older one identifies himself with what he perceives as the beleaguered America of the Vietnam era: "Rabbit is locked into his intuition that to describe any of America's actions as a 'power play' is to miss the point. America is beyond power, it acts as in a dream, as a face of God. Wherever America is, there is freedom, and wherever America is not, madness rules with chains, darkness strangles millions. Beneath her patient bombers, paradise is possible" (49). This passage is astonishing both for its visionary quality and for its unreflecting provinciality, and whatever else is changed, Rabbit is still the man who relies on his instincts, which have changed him from a passive to an active patriot, one who sees America as "the city on the hill," a place beyond traditional moral and political considerations. In the tranquilized 1950s, Rabbit's politics were invisible; in the rebellious 1960s, his politics are to mystify and apotheosize America.

Although in *Rabbit, Run* Harry was the complete outsider, he is still in *Rabbit Redux* an outsider, but one who defends conventional values, yet who enjoys confronting and testing those values. Janice, for instance, sees that his anticlimactic final return (between novels) means he has, in fact, bought into the values of the society he once so eagerly fled. As she says, "Maybe he came back to me, to Nelson and me, for the old-fashioned reasons, and wants to live an old-fashioned life, but nobody does that any more, and he feels it. He put his life into rules he feels melting away now" (54). As the rules come under greater attack, Harry's defense of them tends to be complicated by his perception of himself as an outsider, as one who has earlier attempted to escape.

In the first of the Rabbit novels, Harry found most of his energy in the rebellion of flight; in the second, however, he expresses his rebellion in less

energetic, more social ways. As the novel opens, Rabbit and Janice have virtually exchanged roles. He has become passive, his desire to flee all but bled out
of him by ten years of working nine to five, and his passivity is connected, in
part, to the failure of sex as a mode of escape. After giving up running in
order to return, he finds himself increasingly incapable of having sex with his
wife, and he refuses to let her conceive again: "It had all seemed like a pit to
him then, her womb and the grave, sex and death, he had fled her cunt as a
tiger's mouth" (33). Sex "with her had become too dark, too *serious,* too kindred to death" (41) for him to be able to find escape or even much physical
release in it. Sex has become the memory of death, the death of their baby
girl. Because he associates sex with Janice with death, he is quick to try to
reestablish the ecstatic in his life, once she has left him, by taking up with
someone else who from the first is identified as a "girl." This relationship creates the possibility of sex unshadowed by death, but sex with Jill lacks intensity, and his desire for her is ambiguous from the start. The first time she
strips for him, Harry sees: "The horns of her pelvis like starved cheekbones.
Her belly a child's, childless. Her breasts in some lights as she turns scarcely
exist" (129). He sees her as "childless," and also as slightly androgynous. He
walks into the bathroom and sees her bending over: "From behind she seems
a boy's slim back wedged into the upside-down valentine of a woman's satin
rear" (130). It is as if in having sex with her, Rabbit is more aroused by this
hint of androgyny and her age (eighteen) and her upper-class background
than by her physical appeal. Sex with Jill is not, however, a complete failure
as it was with Janice, because it is transgressive, a crossing of boundaries invisible until personified in her.

Soon after Jill begins living with him, Rabbit also takes in Skeeter, a
crazed black Vietnam vet, and his relationship with Skeeter also has erotic
overtones: "Physically, Skeeter fascinates Rabbit. The lustrous pallor of the
tongue and palms and the soles of the feet, left out of the sun. . . . The curious greased grace of his gestures, rapid and watchful as a lizard's motions,
free of mammalian fat. Skeeter in his house feels like a finely made electric
toy; Harry wants to touch him but is afraid he will get a shock" (221).

He is tempted to touch, to experience that shock in a scene in which
Skeeter, Rabbit, and Jill, stoned, role-play in the dark. Skeeter directs a scene
out of slavery, but one in which he reverses the roles: he plays the white master while Jill and Rabbit play the black slaves. He extends his role to having
sex with Jill while Rabbit watches, powerless to intervene. Although Rabbit is
supposed to be powerless in his role as a slave, he insists on the power of the
gaze. He wants to see more, and he turns on a light:

"Hey man, what's with that? Cut that light."

"You're beautiful," Rabbit says.

"O.K., strip and get into it, she's full of holes, right?"

"I'm scared to," Rabbit confesses: it is true, they seem not only beautiful but in the same vision an interlocked machine that might pull him apart. (260)

The ambiguity of Rabbit's statement, "You're beautiful," emphasizes his desire for them both, something Skeeter seems unaware of, but the beauty of the vision is predicated on his position as voyeur, on his awareness of difference, both social and racial. Rabbit senses that to cross over from vision to touch would mean a kind of self-destruction; he would be inserting himself into an "interlocked machine" that would rend him, tear at him in directions powerfully opposed. He is saved from his temptation and fear by the appearance of yet another voyeur, this one looking in through the living room window, who breaks up the scene.

The next night Rabbit makes love to Peggy, a woman his own age, and he sees a parallel to the evening before; she is "kneeling to him in the pose of Jill to Skeeter, so he has glided across a gulf, and stands last night where he stared." His sense of a gulf crossed points to a devastation avoided, and this encounter ends up being "a fuck innocent of madness" (273), an act that confirms his identity rather than one that would have destroyed it. "Pulled apart," he would no longer have recognized himself. And one reason why sex with Peggy confirms his identity rests on the fact that she is of Rabbit's generation, a representative of society for him, and thus she confirms a sense of their shared values.

In Jill and Skeeter, by contrast, he constantly confronts his social and generational fears. For a time, they, with his son, Nelson, constitute a marginal community—sharing meals, smoking dope, and having what used to be called "consciousness-raising sessions"—but this community can be only precarious and provisional, serving the same function as did sex and running in the earlier novel. The very existence of this interracial, intergenerational community in Harry's white suburb, however, emphasizes how marginalized he has become—his wife has left him; he has lost his job; he smokes dope—but as a marginalized defender of the status quo, he is compromised by Jill and Skeeter. They belong to a generation rejecting the values he so ardently defends, and they are from class backgrounds he finds troubling. For instance, Jill has fled her affluent parents in a Porsche, which she ruins by forgetting to check the oil. While Rabbit mourns her "waste" and "carelessness" (237), he has no scruples about taking advantage of her carelessness about her own life. Once he is having sex regularly with her, he can take her and her class background for granted because he has imprinted himself on her in a way he never can with Skeeter. What he thinks about Peggy is relevant here: "A blank check. A woman is blank until you fuck her. . . . Us and Vietnam, fucking and being fucked, blood is wisdom" (270). Jill is no longer blank to him; he imagines his semen as corrosive, leaving marks on her body like "acid burn[s]," and "he has the vision of her entire slender fair flexible body being eventually covered in these invisible burns, like a napalmed child in the newspapers" (142). The imagery is clearly destructive, and the topical allusion alerts the reader to the political implications of Harry's vision. Sex with him is burning her away, just as Skeeter is burning her out by hooking her on drugs again; the two of them unite to burn out her class and her gender and her life.

With Skeeter, on the other hand, color and class lines cannot be crossed, and Rabbit finds himself both terrified by and drawn to the black man. As Skeeter says of all blacks: "We fascinate you, white man. We are in your dreams. . . . Why else you so scared of me, Rabbit?" Rabbit's answer, "Because you're a spook" (208), while dismissive, is also quite accurate. He does fear blacks—for their obvious differences and for their sudden prominence in the 1960s with the civil rights movement and, during the action of the novel, with riots in the streets of nearby Pennsylvania cities. On a more personal level, he is fascinated by Skeeter because he still feels the attraction of disruptive energies, an electricity in Skeeter, and because the black man represents an eruption of the demonic in what Rabbit calls "this stale peace" (16). Indeed, Rabbit sees him as a reflection of his own abortive revolt ten years before; he says, "I once took that inner light trip and all I did was bruise my surroundings. Revolution, or whatever, is just a way of saying a mess is fun. Well, it *is* fun, for a while, as long as somebody else has laid in the supplies. A mess is a luxury" (154). In his passive mode, Rabbit is ambivalent; by allowing things to happen, he is creating a "mess," so he is both revolutionary outsider and defender of the status quo, but his revolution in this novel is social, moving beyond the boundaries of his immediate surroundings and incorporating troubling and troubled outsiders.

This little community of outsiders becomes the last expression of his revolt, and the degree to which he has somewhat unwittingly marginalized himself is made clear when Rabbit is taken aside by two neighbors who tell him he is sullying "a decent white neighborhood" (252) by allowing Jill and Skeeter to be together, and they demand that he throw Skeeter out. He ignores their warning, but his failure to ask Skeeter to leave comes not out of any conviction about integration or even personal freedom, but out of instinct. He can still claim, late in the novel, "I did what felt right" (311), but as Jill points out, there is now a kind of nihilism in him: "Your thought is frozen because the first moment your instincts failed, you raced to the conclusion that everything is nothing, that zero is the real answer" (203). His nihilism and passivity combine, and he is drawn to, sucked into, disaster: his house is firebombed, Jill burns to death, and Skeeter goes on the run.

At the end of the novel, Rabbit is almost completely bereft, but as his sister points out, that in itself, for him, is a kind of freedom: "You like any kind of disaster that might spring you free" (318). Now that Rabbit is sprung free from society, his freedom liberates him into nothing, into the impracticability of solitude, and he retreats into the social, back into domesticity and marriage; in the final scene, he and Janice reconcile. With his little community shattered and Jill's death on his conscience—a death balancing that of their daughter in *Rabbit, Run*—he opts for the shelter of his marriage, and this retreat is "a return to the past" (Uphaus 89). This second return to his marriage is, of course, different from the first. The intersections of the public and personal in his experience have made him more aware of his place in the world, more aware of the threat that the world outside the marriage can bring with it. In that sense, this "return to the past" is in itself a kind of escape, a refuge from a series of bruising confrontations with an antagonistic world.

By the time of *Rabbit Is Rich*, the world is no less threatening, but Harry seems to have learned how to ride the threat and profit by it. The novel begins with Harry's heightened social and historical awareness: "Running out of gas, Rabbit Angstrom thinks . . . The fucking world is running out of gas" (1). In the middle of the gas shortage of 1979 Harry is, surprisingly, doing well as the manager of his wife and mother-in-law's Toyota franchise. As a businessman selling Japanese products, he is, perforce, more aware than he has been in the previous two novels of what is happening in the nation and the world at large, and in this sense the novel could be called "a story of the economic life" (Edwards 100). Since his modest success, Rabbit has become something of a model citizen, a man of consequence in his town: "He likes the nod he gets from the community, that overlooked him like dirt ever since high school" (3). Ironically and inadvertently, he has gone back to being "the star and spearpoint" (2), "the man up front" (3), and again he has the qualified approval of his community. In the earlier novels, there had been no way for him to integrate himself socially; he could find no public equivalent of

being, as his sister says in *Rabbit Redux,* the "showboat" (314) of the basketball team. In the absence of that adulation, he cultivated the solitude of a
lone wolf, constantly affronting and confronting his society.

Enjoying the "nod" of recognition and approval from his town, Rabbit
entirely relinquishes his status as outsider. He not only has a position within
society, but he has also become resolutely social, part of a circle of friends
and acquaintances. This is the most radical change in the Rabbit novels, for
in the previous two he has been the solitary American hero, seeking to evade
the constraints of a society that offered him no place for his disruptive energies. He now realizes that "the stifled terror that always made him restless has
dulled down. He wants less. Freedom, that he always thought was outward
motion, turns out to be this inner dwindling" (*Rich* 89). Giving up outward
motion, his energies begin to fail, and he plants himself in society. He belongs
to a country club, the Flying Eagle, where he plays golf; with his country club
friends, he attends a constant round of parties and even takes a Caribbean
vacation.

Harry's new affluence and his social choices bring his world closer to
that of Updike's other novels—those of the upper-middle-class suburban
marriages in *Couples,* for example—but Updike's depiction of that affluence
and Harry's social world clearly has a satirical edge. That satire is balanced,
however, by what Edwards has identified as Rabbit's "almost saintly capacity
for sympathy and concern" (101), a sympathy that alerts us that Rabbit, in
this novel, balances between "extreme antagonisms," his "safety . . . in the
skill with which [he] keep[s] the diagonal line." Moreover, this is also, in
Emerson's terms, a novel in which Rabbit manages to keep his independence
while developing his "sympathy." Rabbit has invested, however, so much in
his image of himself as outsider that his diminished energies threaten his
idea of himself. He has to find ways not to bloat and degenerate in the smug
satisfactions of his success. As Updike himself remarked in an interview, "A
person who has what he wants, a satisfied person, a content person ceases to
be a person. Unfallen Adam is an ape" (*Picked-Up Pieces* 504). What keeps
Harry fallen and unsatisfied in *Rabbit Is Rich* is sex and paternity.

Since Janice is unable to have any more children, sex with her is no
longer serious; it has been deprived of an edge, especially since it seems no
longer "kindred to death" (*Redux* 41). It seems to Harry just sad, a "blurred
burrowing of two old bodies, one drowsy and one drunk" (*Rich* 47). To
arouse himself, Rabbit thinks of Ruth from *Rabbit, Run* and of a girl he remembers from ninth grade, her "wisps of armpit hair" and the "thin cotton
of her blouse . . . against the elastic trusswork of her bra" (48). Sex is not a

mode of revolt or escape in the novel; it is a regression into fantasy. He also thinks of Cindy, the young, sexy wife of one of his golf partners, as "a plump brown-backed honey still smelling of high school" (52). The reference to high school suggests that Rabbit is unconsciously in search of the kind of frisson of sex and success he knew then, and his lust for her is so persistent that it becomes, at times, comic. When, during an episode of wife-swapping on a Caribbean vacation, Rabbit's fantasy of Cindy seems as if it is going to be fulfilled, he ironically and comically gets the wrong wife. This "wrong" wife, Thelma, has been obsessed with Rabbit much as he has been with Cindy, but Thelma is Rabbit's age and is dying of lupus. She says, "I want to do something for you so you won't forget me, something you've never had with anyone else" (390). She suggests anal sex, which Harry has never experienced, and it has the nature of a negative revelation: "The grip is tight at the base but beyond, where a cunt is all velvety suction and caress, there is no sensation: a void, a pure black box, a casket of perfect nothingness" (390–91). Afterwards, he "can't take his mind from what he's discovered, that nothingness seen by his single eye" (392). Instead of the frisson of sex and success he expected, a reconnection to his past, Rabbit experiences a frisson of sex and death, an intimation of a future "nothingness." Rather than offering the kind of inhibitory pressure death placed on sex in *Rabbit Redux*, this vision presages the conclusion of the novel and is an unexpected revelation in the only Rabbit novel where no one dies and where, as Edwards has pointed out, "disasters [are] averted" (100).

Since sexuality is not a venue of revolt or escape, and since the central sexual action in the novel is such a negative revelation, family is what keeps Harry unsatisfied, discontent, and fallen. Early in the novel, he begins to count his family dead who have been "multiplying, and they look up begging you to join them, promising it is all right, it is very soft down here. Pop, Mom, old man Springer, Jill, the baby called Becky for her little time. Tothero. Even John Wayne, the other day" (7). In reaction to his awareness of all these deaths, he fantasizes about having had a daughter by Ruth, and he worries over Nelson, who, a coworker reminds him, is "all you've got" (24). His obsession with his could-be daughter is played out when he finds the courage to confront Ruth, who denies the girl is his. In seeing Ruth again, Rabbit experiences her anger at him, and he measures the consequences, for this woman, of his running twenty years before. The reason he is ready to face Ruth is that his relationship with Nelson is so bad that he unconsciously wants another child. Nelson, he tells Ruth, is "enough . . . bad news" (416). The deep antagonism between Nelson and his father clearly dates from the night their house was firebombed and Jill burned to death. Nelson's grievance against his father, however, is not so much Jill's death, but that Harry seems to have come to terms with the past, that he will not allow past disasters to disrupt his present success. Nelson, on the other hand, cannot relinquish, and throughout the book he acts out against his father: by dropping out of college, and by smashing up, one by one, Harry's cars. In holding onto the past, Nelson seems almost suffocated by his father. Nelson says: "He's forgotten everything he ever did to us. . . . He's so smug and *satisfied*, is what gets me" (297). Rabbit, for all his distress over Nelson, takes an almost perverse delight in Nelson's opposition; as he says to Janice, "I like having Nelson in the house. . . . It's great to have an enemy. Sharpens your senses" (116). Nelson functions much as Skeeter did in *Rabbit Redux;* he constantly threatens his father, and part of Rabbit takes sustenance from this antagonism.

If Nelson's role is similar to Skeeter's, Harry's has changed dramatically; no longer is he any kind of outsider. He is the one to have "laid in the supplies" (*Redux* 154), and because he has laid them in, *he* is the one being rebelled against. What Harry does not understand is Nelson's revolt against him, his father. When he was younger, Harry's flight from his wife signaled a kind of perverse maturity. As he says to Nelson, "In my day kids *wanted* to get out in the world. We were scared but not so scared we kept running back to Mama. And Grandmama. What're you going to do when you run out of women to tell you what to do?" (*Rich* 193). Although Harry is himself surrounded by women, he can speak from the authority of all his abortive flights, and in his "inward dwindling" he can gauge his life. Not only can he see the difference between his experience and Nelson's, but he can also see, worrisomely, patterns about to repeat themselves. Nelson now faces the same choice Rabbit did when he was younger: whether to marry a woman he has made pregnant. Apparently, for Rabbit, there was no choice, but he now tells Nelson:

> "You could just . . . disappear for a while. I'd give you the money for that."
> "Money, you're always offering me money to stay away."
> "Maybe because when I was your age I wanted to get away and I couldn't. I didn't have the money. I didn't have the sense." (193)

Even though Nelson acts out against him throughout the novel, Harry is still willing to provide the money for flight, and although his desire for Nelson to go away is certainly self-serving, he does see his son, as himself, diminished:

"I just don't like seeing you caught," he blurts out to Nelson. "You're too much me."

Nelson gets loud. "I'm not you! I'm not caught."

"Nellie, you're caught. They've got you and you didn't even squeak. I hate to see it, is all. All I'm trying to say is, as far as I'm concerned you don't have to go through with it. If you want to get out of it, I'll help you." (194)

Nelson refuses all help from his father and goes through with the wedding. When Rabbit sees him step outside the church a few minutes before the service, his magical word springs to mind: "*Run,* Harry wants to call out, but nothing comes" (223). Although he does not flee at the wedding, Nelson eventually does run, deserting his new wife even before the birth of their child; but unlike his father, he does not run in circles, he runs *to* something—back to college, where Rabbit must pay the bills.

At the end of the novel, Harry is in his newly bought house, in society and surrounded by the women of this family, watching the Super Bowl on his new Japanese television, and the halftime show helps to locate Harry and his domestic drama even more firmly in contemporary history: " 'Energy is people,' they sing. 'People are en-er-gy!' Who needs Khomeini and his oil! Who needs Afghanistan? Fuck the Russkis. Fuck the Japs. . . . We'll go it alone, from sea to shining sea" (436). Harry's combative jingoism is simply a reflex that recalls the Rabbit of ten years before. His television and his Japanese car dealership demonstrate, however, the comic fall into interdependency and prosperity of the traditional solitary male American hero. He cannot—the country cannot—"go it alone," and his prosperity depends on a fortuitous combination of family circumstances and international relations. Dependent on the vagaries of family (Janice inheriting her father's Toyota dealership) and on those of international relations (the oil crisis), Harry watches the Super Bowl, surrounded by women: mother-in-law, wife, daughter-in-law, and in the last, marvelous sentences of the novel, one more: "In his lap, his hands, a real presence hardly weighing anything but alive. Fortune's hostage, heart's desire, a granddaughter. His. Another nail in his coffin. His" (437). The "His" here shifts Harry's acquisitiveness throughout the novel into another key, and it also reminds us of the central sexual, negative revelation of the novel. Harry is dwindling toward death, but he has also found a kind of freedom in social drama, the drama of "the skill with which we keep the diagonal line."

The final novel of the tetralogy, *Rabbit at Rest,* is death-saturated from the first sentence: "Rabbit Angstrom has a funny sudden feeling that what he's come to meet . . . is not his son Nelson and daughter-in-law Pru and their two children but something more ominous and intimately his: his own death" (3). Physically, Harry has deteriorated—he has become a junk-food addict; he is seriously overweight, and in the course of the novel he has two heart attacks, the second of which kills him. Harry's physical degeneration, however, is only one sign among many of how he has been thrown back, almost without understanding how it has happened, into a solitude even more isolating than the one he experienced as a young man in *Rabbit, Run*. In *Rabbit at Rest,* Harry's sexual energy has almost completely disappeared, depriving him of one of his primary modes of self-definition, and he is semiretired, living half the year in Florida, depriving him of the milieu of work and the social circle at his country club. Marginalized, again an outsider, seemingly less a child of history than he has ever been, Harry becomes, unexpectedly, a kind of historian, replete with a historical consciousness of personal, regional, and national pasts.

Since the end of *Rabbit Is Rich,* Nelson has taken over management of Springer Motors, taking away from Harry his inadvertent position as "the man up front" (*Rich* 3), leaving him with a diminished social identity. As he confesses to Thelma, the woman with whom he has carried on a ten-year affair, "The reason I never left Janice and never can . . . is, without her, I'm shit. I'm unemployable. I'm too old. All I can be from here on in is her husband" (*Rest* 207). At least when he was managing Springer Motors, he had a kind of sustaining male social interaction, in particular with Charlie Stavros. Harry remembers how "the two of them used to stand by the display window over at the lot on dull mornings and rehash the day's news" (232). Now that Stavros is retired and Harry lives half the year in Florida, they rarely see each other; he meets the group from the Flying Eagle even more infrequently. He nostalgically recalls "those boozy late afternoons at his old club back in Diamond County, the Flying Eagle, before Buddy Inglefinger married that lanky crazy hippie Valerie and moved to Royersford and Thelma Harrison got too sick with lupus ever to show up and Cindy Murkett got fat and Webb divorced her so you never saw anybody any more" (70).

His social world having dissolved, Harry feebly attempts to reconstruct it in Florida by playing golf, only to have his status as outsider underlined. He feels that everyone in Florida is "so cautious, as if on two beers they might fall down and break a hip" (70), a caution due to age, but also among his golf partners a caution due to cultural difference. Harry's three partners are Jewish; with them, he feels, "he is a big Swede, they call him Angstrom, a comical pet gentile, a big uncircumcised hunk of the American dream. He in turn treasures their perspective; it seems more manly than his, sadder and wiser and less shaky. Their long history has put all that suffering in its pocket and strides on" (57–58). Although he craves, as he did with Stavros, a perspective that he feels is more linked to a kind of history he has no access to, that very lack of access means that he is never quite sure, as he was with the Flying Eagle crowd, where the boundaries are. His bringing up the bombing of Pan Am flight 103 over Scotland makes them, he feels, "uneasy." "With Jews," he thinks, "everything in the papers comes back to Israel" (69), to a place and to a history.

If he is, among these Jewish men, a "pet gentile," unanchored in time and place, he is also in Florida an outsider among the women. He envies the "solid domestic arrangements" (73) and the "sexy elderly wives" (71) of his golf partners, but late in the novel when an older woman is friendly to him he feels that she has been "invading him [so] he takes two Nitrostats to quell his heart" (489). In a sense, this fear of invasion typifies Harry's social relations, and even he realizes that his present feelings are almost a complete contradiction of what he has desired throughout most of his life: "There was a time, when he was younger, when the thought of any change, even a disaster, gladdened his heart with the possibility of a shake-up, of his world made new. But at present he is aware mostly of a fluttering, binding physical resistance within him to the idea of being uprooted" (429). Harry cannot even contemplate anymore the provisional transcendence of sex; it is as if the distinction between the promise of escape in sex and the enactment of the impossibility of escape had collapsed, and all Harry can see is its sad futility. As Janice thinks, "Poor Harry, until he began to slow down, he hopped into bed every night expecting wonders" (146). Having diminished expectations in general, Harry rarely makes love to his wife (as she notes wryly during the novel), and after his first heart attack he breaks off his affair with Thelma, in part because he is feeling physically fragile, "his heart as an unwilling captive inside his chest" (204), and in part because he simply no longer has the energy for sex or for an affair. Early in the novel, he thinks, momentarily, of buying a "skin mag," only to realize that "he will not be enough aroused, boredom will be his main feeling. . . . How disgusting we are, when you think about it—disposable meat" (18).

As Brooke Horvath (87–88) has argued about the first three Rabbit novels, *Rabbit at Rest* enacts the consequences of Harry's failure as an erotic quester. Like a superannuated roué, he is now disgusted by the "wonders" he expected throughout his life. Horvath would probably argue that this failure is an inevitable one because of how Harry imagines the connection between sex and the world. She quotes from an early review of Updike's where he discusses, through personification, the Western love-myth: "Her concern is not with the possession, through love, of another person but with the prolongation of the lover's state of mind. Eros is allied with Thanatos rather than Agape; love becomes not a way of accepting and entering the world but a way of defying and escaping it" (*Assorted Prose* 222). One could argue that for Harry, eros has always been allied to thanatos; he remembers in *Rabbit at Rest*, for instance, Ruth calling him, thirty years before, "Mr. Death" (*Rest* 60), and clearly, eros has also always been, as I have been arguing through this essay, a way of "escaping" the world.

In addition to putting Harry's eroticism into perspective, this passage from the review also helps to illuminate the most troubling moment in the whole novel: when Harry returns from the hospital after having an angioplasty, he and his daughter-in-law, Pru, have sex: "Pru says '*Shit*,' jumps from the bed, slams shut the window, pulls down the shade, tears open her bathrobe and sheds it, and, reaching down, pulls her nightie up over her head. Her tall pale wide-hipped nakedness in the dimmed room is lovely much as those pear trees in blossom along that block in Brewer last month were lovely, all his it had seemed, a piece of paradise blundered upon, incredible" (346). Any sense of transgression in this incident is almost completely denied by the visionary quality of Harry's perception of Pru's nakedness. For him, this moment, as "a piece of paradise blundered upon, incredible," is unparalleled; it is almost as if by not attempting to escape, he has finally achieved a kind of transcendence. This is, I would offer, the only instance of eros in the Rabbit novels where sex is *not* a mode of escape; rather, Harry is "accepting and entering" the world, a change signaled by his reference to the "pear trees in blossom." Before his angioplasty, driving around the Brewer area, "freshening his memory and hurting himself with the pieces of his old self that cling to almost every corner" (181), Harry comes upon, unexpectedly, a vision of spring: "Rabbit is suddenly driving in a white tunnel, trees on both sides of the street in white blossoms, the trees young and oval in shape and blending one into the other like clouds. . . . [H]e is moved enough to pull the Celica to the curb and park and get out and pull off a single leaf to study, as if it will be a clue to all this glory" (187). When he tells Janice about this vision, she remarks, " 'You see differently now.' Since his heart attack, she means" (188). His new angle of vision and his new receptivity allow him to enter and accept, whether that acceptance means the sight of trees in flower or sex with his daughter-in-law. Although he thinks of their encounter afterwards in a slightly diminished way—"A certain matter-of-fact shamelessness about Pru reduced a bit the poetry of his first sight of her" (354)—he never feels shame or remorse.

Even when Pru reveals their encounter, Harry seems unaware of the transgressive nature of this sexual experience. Janice lists all of his infidelities and says, " 'Now you've done something truly unforgivable.' 'Really?' The word comes out with an unintended hopeful lilt" (433). Janice's reaction is that having sex with Pru was "perverted" and "*mon*strous" (434), and the collision between his vision of Pru as naked "paradise" and his wife's reaction of moral outrage drives him back to his elementary, intuitive response—he runs. One last time he flees his family and society, but this time he runs from one home to another. He drives south to Florida, completing the abortive journey he began thirty years earlier in *Rabbit, Run.* Ending his life in almost complete social isolation in their condominium in Florida, he takes solitary walks around Deleon, where, twice, he plays basketball. These scenes are clearly meant as echoes of the shooting of basketballs early in *Rabbit, Run,* and, fittingly, Harry has his final massive heart attack during the second game.

This isolation would seem an unexpectedly sour ending to this tetralogy, and would be except for an unanticipated change in Harry. As one of the basketball players says: "Hey man, . . . you're history!" (491). He *is,* in the sense of that taunt, history: he is superannuated, he is the past, he is irrelevant, contemptuously to be dismissed. On the other hand, as history he should not be so easily seen as valueless, the novel insists, and the most revealing sign of this is his marching in the Mt. Judge Fourth of July parade as Uncle Sam: "They wave ironically, calling 'Yaaaay' at the idea of Uncle Sam, this walking flag, this incorrigible taxer and frisky international mischief-maker. . . . The crowd as it thickens calls out more and more his name, 'Harry,' or 'Rabbit'— 'Hey, Rabbit! Hey, hotshot!' They remember him. He hasn't heard his old nick-name so often in many years; nobody in Florida uses it, and his grandchildren would be puzzled to hear it" (368). As the figurative embodiment of America, Harry can, through the reaction of the crowd, recall a part of himself he thought irrecoverable: his public identity. Momentarily, he experiences people's recognition of him as Rabbit, as "hotshot," as former basketball player. And at the end of the parade, his personal and mythic identities fuse: "Harry's eyes burn and the impression giddily—as if he has been lifted up to survey all human history—grows upon him, making his heart thump worse and worse, that all in all this is the happiest fucking country the world has ever seen" (371). Even though he knows this is a "sort of foolish revelation" (371), he increasingly has been "lifted up to survey" history, both as an embodiment of American history and in his own experience. Although his development of a historical consciousness might seem to be at odds with his social isolation throughout the novel, it may be that he finds a kind of consolation for his isolation and approaching death in the contemplation of history, a contemplation that is also a logical extension of his growing awareness in the novels of being in history. As Dilvo Ristoff writes, Harry is " 'the man in the middle,' pressed between life and death, past and future, an object of the cosmos, an object of history" (28).[7] Although I find this formulation a little hyperbolic, I do agree that Updike wants us to see Harry as an object of history, but as one who becomes increasingly aware of his status as an object over the course of thirty years. Harry may be as isolated and as much of an outsider in *Rabbit at Rest* as he was in *Rabbit, Run,* but in the later novels he is aware of having, as Nathan Zuckerman says in Philip Roth's *The Counterlife,* "a role in history without its having to be obvious," aware of "standing in time and culture" (146).

As an example of his knowledge of standing in time and culture, consider what Harry sees from his hospital bed when he is recovering from his angioplasty. Looking out his window, he can see, across the street, the tops of three buildings with "festive patterns of recess and protrusion, diagonal and upright, casting shadows in different ways at different times of the day" (*Rest* 293). He wonders whether the bricklayers "of another century" who made these designs were Pennsylvania Dutch or immigrant Italians. Out of this moment of historical awareness, he creates a metaphor for his own place in history: "He tries to view his life as a brick of sorts, set in place with a slap in 1933 and hardening ever since, just one life in rows and walls and blocks of lives. There is a satisfaction in such an overview, a faint far-off communal thrill, but hard to sustain over against his original and continuing impression that Brewer and all the world beyond are just frills on himself . . . himself the heart of the universe" (293–94). This is a variant of the Emersonian dilemma I discussed earlier, except that his version pits the "communal thrill" against an Emersonian sense of the individual as center. As Emerson wrote in his journals, "I have taught one doctrine, namely, the infinitude of the private man" (*Selections* 139), and as a corollary of that belief Emerson was rather dismissive of history, which he scorned as "a shallow village tale" (*Complete Works* 2: 40). In "Self-Reliance," he is even more explicit about the proper function of history: "History is an impertinence and an injury if it be anything more than a cheerful apologue or parable of my being and becoming" (*Complete Works* 2: 66). In the passage above, Harry is contesting versions of history and Emersonian individualism, one asserting that he is just another brick in the wall, the other trying to hold onto a sense of the centrality and "infinitude" of the individual, a position that reduces history to a parable of that ever "becoming" infinitude.

If there are moments when Harry insists on his centrality in the novel, he is incessantly pulled back by his historical consciousness, by his awareness of having been marginalized. When he comes back to manage Springer Motors for a few weeks while Nelson is in treatment, he realizes that in "terms of Springer Motors he has become a historian" (*Rest* 213). His is the institutional memory, and this memory is allied to a sense of the history of the region where he grew up. Lovingly, he registers the details and the changes, much as Updike himself did in the first chapter of his autobiography, *Self-Consciousness,* "A Soft Spring Night in Shillington." Harry's historical awareness is so extensive, however, that he realizes that even the land to which he longed to escape, the South, is replete with its own history; in Florida, "all feels virgin, though in fact there is a history too, of Indians and conquistadores and barefoot mailmen who served the mosquito-plagued coastal settlements" (*Rest* 120).

But the most amazing sign of Harry's historical consciousness is his reading of history. The only previous reading he has ever done in the novels is of *Consumer Reports,* but throughout *Rabbit at Rest* Harry reads history: "In his semi-retirement he has taken to reading history. It has always vaguely interested him, that sinister mulch of facts our little lives grow out of before joining the mulch themselves, the fragile brown rotting layer of previous deaths." Reading in bed, he leans "back against its padded satiny headboard with a book, staring dimily down into the past as if high in a jade-green treehouse" (44).[8] Late in the novel, when his doctor asks him if he has any hobbies, Harry says, "I read a lot of history. I'm a kind of buff" (476). His reading and his awareness of current history, as Updike himself has pointed out in "Why Rabbit Had to Go," make him even more aware of his marginalization. As Harry thinks in the novel, "If there's no Cold War, what's the point of being an American?" (442–43). Updike's gloss on this sentence is quite illuminating:

> His sense of being useless, of being pushed to one side by his wife and son, has this political dimension, then. Like me, he has lived his adult life in the context of the cold war. He was in the Army, ready to go to Korea, hawkish on Vietnam, proud of the moon shot, and in some sense always justified, at the back of his mind, by a concept of freedom, of America, that took sharpness from contrast with Communism. If that contrast is gone, then

that's another reason to put him, regretfully, to rest in 1990. ("Why Rabbit" 25)

These sentences make quite clear how solidly the Rabbit tetralogy has been anchored by the cold war, by the history of the last thirty years. Even though Harry was quite unaware of contemporary history in *Rabbit, Run,* he was a product of that historical moment, as Updike has pointed unmistakably to that postwar consensus (see *Run* 34, 61). As Harry says nostalgically, "The cold war. It gave you a reason to get up in the morning" (*Rest* 353).

Having no reason to get up in the morning, Harry has but one option, to die, and the novel could be seen as a long suicide on his part. Even though he has grandchildren—one of whom he saves from drowning, thus balancing the death of his daughter in *Rabbit, Run*—the grandchildren are not enough to sustain him. Janice and Nelson change in the course of the novel, but Harry cannot adapt, "reared in a world where war was not strange but change was" (*Rest* 461). Comprehending the provisionality of the world, Harry tries to escape, only to circle back into social drama, tacking, in Emerson's terms, between the impracticability of solitude and the fatality of society. Because he understands provisionality, he also begins to see himself as a historical creature in a nexus of social and familial drama, a nexus out of which only one escape is possible—in Karl's terms, the final "limited" option—that of death. But the Rabbit tetralogy has demonstrated how the desire to "break from predetermined forms" (Karl 252) is defeated by the "historical past," and how in these novels, one is drawn back, even on the verge of death, into history and social drama.

Notes

I would like to thank the members of the English Institute of the University of Łódź, and in particular Agnieszka Salska, for giving me the opportunity to read a much earlier draft of this paper. I would also like to thank Marjan van Schaik for her encouragement, over these ten years, of this project.
    1. See Jack Moore's essay in this volume for a discussion of Farrell's *Studs Lonigan* trilogy and Cooper's *Leatherstocking* novels. In my essay, I assume that there is a fundamental difference between novel sequences, which are limited in scope and ambition, and novelistic universes, such as Balzac's *Comédie Humaine* or Faulkner's Yoknapatawpha, which are potentially limitless.
    2. There actually seems to have been an explosion of novel sequences in the postwar period. To name only some: Philip Roth's Zuckerman novels; John Edgar Wideman's *Homewood Trilogy;* John Nichols's *The New Mexico Trilogy;* Thomas

Berger's Reinhart novels; David Plante's *The Francoeur Novels;* Mary Lee Settle's Beulah quintet; Paul Auster's *The New York Trilogy;* R. M. Koster's *The Tinieblas Trilogy;* and Frederick Buechner's *The Book of Bebb.* Very little critical attention has been paid to this development.

3. I use the following editions: *Rabbit, Run* (1960; New York: Fawcett Crest, 1983); *Rabbit, Redux* (New York: Fawcett Crest, 1971); *Rabbit Is Rich* (New York: Fawcett Crest, 1981); *Rabbit at Rest* (New York: Knopf, 1990); *Assorted Prose* (New York: Fawcett, 1966); *Hugging the Shore* (New York: Vintage, 1983).

4. For a more thorough examination of this subject, see Jack Moore's essay in this volume.

5. Net and web imagery constitutes one of the tetralogy's major unifying motifs, relating Harry's early sports experience with later adult entanglements.

6. In the first two Rabbit novels, females die. Possibly in the bafflement of escape, a kind of reversal takes place: instead of men escaping, women die, since they are representative of the constraints of society.

7. The first phrase is from *Rabbit Redux.* Obviously, one could easily do a Luckácsian reading of the Rabbit tetralogy with Harry as "the man in the middle." As Lukács writes of the typical central figure of a Walter Scott novel, he is "always a more or less mediocre, average English gentleman"; this figure is a "middling, merely correct and never heroic 'hero' " (33). Ristoff comes close to an analysis like this; he argues that the emphasis in the novels on "social entrapment" makes "Harry a creature of his time and place, a representative man rather than an eccentric freak" (145). I want to resist claims that make Harry into a "representative man"; I am more interested in his historical specificity, in the politics of his location, and the ways in which he becomes aware of his position as the man in the middle, aware of his being in history.

8. Rabbit's increasing awareness of being in history is signaled by Updike's metaphors of ascension. While reading history, Harry stares "dizzily down into the past" (*Rest* 44), and when he is Uncle Sam at the Fourth of July parade, it is "as if he has been lifted up to survey all human history" (371). In the second ascension, though, Harry concludes that the United States is "the happiest fucking country the world has ever seen" (371), and clearly, despite his interest in history, he is still the unreflecting patriot of *Rabbit Redux.* In writing about the tetralogy, Raymond Mazurek finds this saturation in the national imaginary most problematic. He claims that "Updike's use of language seeks to mystify, to make the reader feel the power of the cultural myths his characters live within" (147). Indeed. I can think of no other American novel sequence that immerses one in the power of the national imaginary in the way that the Rabbit novels do. Mazurek argues that the tetralogy is fundamentally flawed because it fails to provide "an authorial or other perspective that is very convincing in analyzing . . . [the] social alienation" (144) found in the novels. He criticizes Updike for a failure of his social analysis: "He has never found a sustained and convincing alternative to Rabbit's point of view . . . and Rabbit's con-

sciousness . . . is almost by definition unreflective and incapable of such evaluation" (159). I would probably want to contest that assertion in the novels following *Rabbit, Run;* I see an increasing awareness on Rabbit's part of his participation in the larger currents of American and even international history. But I also suspect that this assertion would not satisfy Mazurek, because he objects to the very cultural saturation that accounts, in my view, for the power of the tetralogy.

7

Joseph J. Waldmeir
Rabbit Redux Reduced
Rededicated? Redeemed?

In 1974, I published as essay on *Rabbit, Run*[1] in which I argued that it was John Updike's intention in that novel to delineate and examine the forces in conflict that both constitute and direct the quest for order and value upon which most contemporary American fiction is built. I tried to show that Updike casts the conflict in terms of the two idealisms—one pragmatic, the other transcendental—that have dominated American intellectual life since colonial days. But, I argued further, Updike does not intend to resolve the conflict in the direction of either idealism—nor, indeed, in the direction of any other intellectual/philosophical construct—for he does not believe it is resolvable.

He dismisses vulgar pragmatism out of hand, but he also rejects the social-reform aspects of applied pragmatic idealism, on the grounds primarily of its sterility; for, despite its righteousness, its busyness, it is far too smugly sure of itself, too shortsighted to fix or improve anything, let alone what it aims at. Likewise, though he implicitly sympathizes with transcendental idealism, with belief in and profession of absolute, essential value, he rejects it too, as vague in its credo and direction, and as impotent in its struggle with pragmatic reality. The only viable alternative, organized Christianity, is ultimately unworthy.[2]

Thus, because he cannot in all honesty resolve this conflict, Updike focuses his own and the reader's attention upon the conflict itself, in all its twists and turns and ramifications. In my earlier essay I pointed out the artistic problems he faced in fulfilling this intention—problems entailing the maintenance of distance from his characters, of strict uninvolvement, on his and the reader's part, with his characters, and not the least, the problem of a necessarily inconclusive ending. And I tried to show that his main method of dealing with the problems was through an appeal to irony. But Updike did let himself become involved with the Harry Angstrom of *Rabbit, Run,* did care what happened to him, relinquishing his and our precious detachment to such an extent that no appeal to the ironic mode could reestablish it for him.

And consequently, as I concluded in that essay, *Rabbit, Run* is both his best and his most flawed work.

In all of the novels since *Rabbit, Run*, however, as in *Poorhouse Fair* which preceded it, Updike has scrupulously detached himself from his people, making possible that at once intense and dispassionate examination of the conflict that lies at the heart of his work, and which, inconclusive and irresolvable though it may be, is the principal reason for the work's existence. Any of the later novels amply illustrates these points; however, partly at least because it is an announced sequel to *Rabbit, Run*, I have chosen *Rabbit Redux*[3] for extended discussion here. If the deck seems to be stacked by my choice, I beg the reader to keep in mind that, while I have done the choosing, John Updike has done the stacking.

Superficially, the novels are very closely related. The locales are the same; the cast of major characters, with the significant exception of Tothero and Eccles and the equally significant promotion of Mim to majority status, is the same; the vulgarity of the American scene is the same. There is even a similarity in the plots—someone runs, sexually motivated; someone stays behind and, due to irresponsible self-indulgence, causes the death of a daughter. But, largely because Harry Angstrom and Updike's attitude toward him are vastly different, *Rabbit Redux* more closely resembles the other previous novels in the Updike canon than its namesake.

While the former Rabbit was an intuitive transcendentalist joined in fruitless battle with the forces of social pragmatism, this Rabbit is truly committed to neither idealism. He consciously rejects his former transcendentalism in pragmatic terms, telling Jill, "I once took that inner light trip and all I did was bruise my surroundings. Revolution, or whatever, is just a way of saying a mess is fun. Well, it *is* fun, for a while, as long as somebody else has laid in the supplies. A mess is a luxury, is all I mean" (172). But he unconsciously reasserts its basic tenet at the end of the novel, saying to Janice, "Confusion is just a local view of things working out in general" (405); it would seem to be hardly accidental that at this point he is impotent, that "lately he has lost the ability to masturbate; nothing brings him up" (403), including, as it turns out, a very willing Janice.

In a turnabout reminiscent of the Peter Caldwell–Joey Robinson switch in that other, disguised, original and sequel, *The Centaur* and *Of the Farm*, Rabbit seems to have shifted toward pragmatism. Jill accuses him of it, calling his cynicism "tired pragmatism" (228), and Skeeter, meaning very much the same thing, tells him, "You still cluttered up with common sense. Common sense is bullshit, man" (262). But at best, Rabbit is a pragmatist manqué.

In the first place, his pragmatic conclusions are built either on faulty evidence or faulty interpretation of the evidence. Janice puts it succinctly, saying to Stavros, "Maybe he came back to me, to Nelson and me, for the old-fashioned reasons, and wants to live an old-fashioned life, but nobody does that any more, and he feels it. He put his life into rules he feels melting away now. I mean, I know he thinks he's missing something, he's always reading the paper and watching the news" (53). Those news reports, liberally sprinkled throughout the novel ("the papers and television are full of the colored riots in New York, snipers wounding innocent firemen, simple men on the street, what is the world coming to?" [57]) along with the expressed attitudes of his elders, Pop and Mr. Springer, buttress his fear not only of blacks who have turned Brewer into a ghetto through which a man is afraid to walk at night with a white girl (137–38), but of rebellious youth in general: "I guess I don't much believe in college kids or the Viet Cong," he says to Babe, an all-knowing, pot-smoking, piano-playing black regular at Jimbo's Friendly Lounge, inside which "all the people are black" (114). "I don't think they have any answers. I think they're minorities trying to bring down everything that halfway works. Halfway isn't all the way but it's better than no way" (131). And his patriotic support of the Vietnam War, expressed most vehemently (for reasons that partially lie outside the discussion) to Charlie Stavros—"It really burns me up to listen to hotshot crap-car salesmen dripping with Vitalis sitting on their plumped-up asses bitching about a country that's been stuffing goodies into their mouth ever since they were born" (44)—is based on the outmoded belief that America is "his garden. Rabbit knows it's his garden and that's why he's put a flag decal on the back window of the Falcon even though Janice says it's corny and fascist" (13); that "wherever America is, there is freedom, and wherever America is not, madness rules with chains, darkness strangles millions" (47). And the belief is reinforced as Rabbit takes the familiar path of an Updike protagonist, into his sports-loving youth. At the baseball game with Nelson and Mr. Springer, he muses: "There was a beauty here bigger than the hurtling beauty of basketball, a beauty refined from country pastures, a game of solitariness, of waiting, waiting for the pitcher to complete his gaze toward first base and throw his lightning, a game whose very taste, of spit and dust and grass and sweat and leather and sun, *was America*" (83; emphasis added).

In the second place, Rabbit's instinctive pragmatism is weakened by his hesitant, dimly understood awareness that his conclusions are given the lie by the evidence. He senses that "something is wrong" at the baseball game. The crowd is "sparse, loud, hard . . . their catcalls are coarse and unkind . . . Rabbit yearns to protect the game" from them (83). But there isn't any game to protect anymore; "The eight-team leagues of his boyhood have vanished with the forty-eight-star flag. The shortstops never chew tobacco anymore. The game drags on" (84). He is reminded constantly that his old-fashioned reasons and rules no longer apply. He is surrounded by the slick, the superficial, the artificial. Downtown Brewer, besides being black, is garish and cheap. His house sits over a broken sewer line and

> the furniture that frames his life looks Martian in the morning light: an armchair covered in synthetic fabric enlivened by a silver thread, a sofa of airfoam slabs, a low table hacked to imitate an antique cobbler's bench, a piece of driftwood that is a lamp, nothing shaped directly for its purpose, gadgets designed to repel repair, nothing straight from a human hand, furniture Rabbit has lived among but has never known, made of substances he cannot name, that has aged as in a department store window, worn out without once conforming to his body. The orange juice tastes acid; it is not even frozen orange juice but some chemical mix tinted orange. (71–72)

Likewise, like Piet Hanema of *Couples,* he is a craftsman; and like Piet he is shunted aside, offset by slicker mechanical methods. He sees his mother's pain eased by L-Dopa, a drug that offers no cure, only relief; and his father, "whittled by the great American glare, squinting in the manna of blessings that come down from the government, shuffling from side to side in nervous happiness that his day's work is done, that a beer is inside him, that Armstrong is above him, that the U.S. is the crown and stupefaction of human history" (11). The Armstrong reference is to the moon landing, which takes place during the time of the novel—"this unique summer, this summer of the moon" (201)—and is the overriding image of American technological ascendancy. But ironically, the moon is dust: arid, lifeless, empty. Reaching it is the supreme achievement of pragmatic know-how; but it is useless, except as a sign of that ascendancy. "The moon is cold, baby," Rabbit tells Jill during an argument. "Cold and ugly. If you don't want it, the Commies do. They're not so fucking proud" (170). And significantly, Rabbit lives on Vista Crescent, and at one point sees Jill and himself as "moonchild and earthman" (202).

Rabbit's lack of commitment to either idealism leads to his depressive self-awareness—"Let's face it," he says to his mother, "as a human being I'm about C minus. As a husband I'm about zilch. When Verity folds I'll fold with it and have to go on Welfare. Some life" (97)—and both in turn account for his aggressive fears—of communism, blacks, the youth culture—even of the former Rabbit. He tells Charlie Stavros, "You know, you're just like me, the way I used to be. Everybody now is like the way I used to be" (182). But in an Updikean apparent paradox, this complex of fears and self-pity leads him to accept Jill and Skeeter into his home. It is his one truly pragmatic action in the novel. He does it, or Updike makes him do it, in order that he might be exposed to, might experience in a sort of controlled learning situation, those ideas, points of view, and attitudes that Jill and Skeeter represent and which Rabbit hitherto has feared and despised. And most importantly, that he might observe, and Updike might report on, the most complex conflict between the two idealisms present in any of the novels. For, beyond all else, Jill and Skeeter represent the warring factions—Skeeter as revolutionary pragmatist, Jill as transcendentalist whose sole essential value is love. Furthermore, the conflict rages within each of them as well, so that Skeeter's pragmatism is corrupted by his transcendent apocalyptic vision, and Jill's essentialism is corrupted by her pragmatic need for drugs. However, to complicate matters still further, Skeeter's vision of apocalypse is dependent upon the pragmatic necessity of war, and the practical fulfillment of Jill's need induces her awareness of essential value: she sees God while under the influence of drugs.

And Rabbit? Rabbit is simply observer, dispassionate, uninvolved, nonresponsible, a participant only on his terms and only when he feels like it. He is closer to being a representative of Updike than any of the author's other protagonists. He is a very unsympathetic character, far more unsympathetic than his namesake; he has to be, if Updike is to avoid the trap that caught him in *Rabbit, Run* and concentrate his and the reader's attention on the conflict. He keeps Skeeter on in the house despite the veiled threats of his neighbors, despite the pleas of Jill and Nelson to send him away, despite his own foreshadowing foreboding at the outset of the novel that he had better hurry home "in case it's burned down. In case a madman has moved in" (9). He knows that Skeeter has hooked Jill on drugs, but he neither protests nor does anything for her. At the climax of the struggle, as the two idealisms merge, each driven by its own necessity, Rabbit is invited to participate; and out of fear, he refuses (298). He fears involvement, responsibility, commitment. Later that night, in bed with Jill, he relents, offering to get her a doctor for her drug habit, to take her back to her mother, get her car out of hock. " 'It's too late,' Jill tells him. 'It's too late for you to try to love me' " (301). And, despite knowing that he has exposed them all to serious danger, the next day he leaves to indulge himself sexually with Peggy Fosnacht.

Neither idealism is equipped to cope with hard pragmatic reality, vulgar though it may be. Skeeter, in his evangelical fervor, eschews politics and revolutionary activism, though he foresees chaos as the first step toward a new social order. Vietnam is both sign and symbol of chaos for him; hence like Rabbit, though for obviously opposite reasons, he defends the war. But even as he defends it, he sees it abstractly, comparing it to a black hole in space that promises not only infinite contraction but infinite expansion as well—incidentally making clear the references early and late in the novel to Stanley Kubrick's *2001*—thus promising the chaos out of which may come a new beginning. But violence per se does not interest him: "That it's gonna blow up we can as*sume*" (245). Nor does the politics of violence: "People talk revolution all the time but revolution's not interesting, right?" (245), he says; and again, "I confess that politics being part of this boring power thing do not much turn me on" (295); and yet again, "As to Robert Seale, any black man who has John Kennel Badbreath and Leonard Birdbrain giving him fund-raising cocktail parties is one house nigger in my book" (275). Thus, for all his surface toughness, Skeeter is more mouth than muscle, more Skeeter than guided missile. And of course, he is incapable of defending himself and Jill against the forces of social righteousness. Jill, flower child, love child, moonchild, is even more defenseless. She cannot even defend herself against Rabbit and Skeeter, who are at least as guilty of her death as those who set the fire—the one because he rejected his responsibility to defend her, the other because he is responsible for her unrousable narcotic stupor. Nelson adores her, is converted by her, and is her only mourner—indeed, Nelson's main function in the novel appears to be to express Updike's sympathetic approval of Jill, yet another of his admirable though impotent essentialists, this one gentle and unselfish, a wounded bird and, inevitably, a victim. When Rabbit asks her why she has sex with Skeeter though she doesn't like it, she replies, "Because whatever men ask of me, I must give, I'm not interested in holding anything for myself. It all melts together anyway, you see" (214). The statement is remarkable not only because of the transcendentalism inherent in the last sentence, but also because of the Christianity implicit in what goes before.

This Rabbit's day is as "bothered by God" as was the Rabbit's of *Rabbit, Run*. Skeeter's evangelism is, as I have said, apocalyptic. The Four Horsemen ride in Vietnam; the black hole "is where God is pushing through" (261), and "chaos is God's body. Order is the Devil's chains" (275). The millennium will bring "the new Jesus [who] will liberate the new money-changers. The old Jesus brought a sword, right? The new Jesus will also bring a sword. He will be a living flame of love" (275). " 'And you're the black Jesus going to bring it in,' Rabbit mocks. 'From A. D. to A. S. After Skeeter. I should live so long. All Praise Be Skeeter's Name' " (245). But for Skeeter, the metaphor is serious.

The North Vietnamese are merely "one more facet of the confusion of false prophecy by which you may recognize My coming in this the fullness of time" (295).

However, it is Jill who truly opens both Rabbit and Nelson to an awareness of God and Christianity—and as is usual in Updike, it is a nonreligious (in terms of churches and organization) awareness. Rabbit has no Bible, "we've kind of let all that go" (142); he feels he "ought to go to church but he can't get himself up to believe it" (148). He asks Jill to describe God as she perceived him in her narcotic-inspired mysticism or intuitionism. "Oh, God," she says. "He changed. He was different every time. But you always knew it was Him. Once I remember something like the inside of a big lily, only magnified a thousand times, a sort of glossy shining funnel that went down and down. I can't talk about it" (146). But she can talk about it to Nelson, more abstractly and about as foggily as most transcendentalists. "Anything that is good is in ecstasy," she says. "The world is what God made and it doesn't stink of money, it's never tired, too much or too little, it's always exactly full." She goes on to describe the order of the universe in terms of Pythagorean music of the spheres, and asserts that our egos make us deaf to the notes—"it's like putting a piece of dirt in our eye," for "without our egos the universe would be absolutely clean." When Rabbit the cynic asks why God simply does not clean up the universe, she answers, "I'm not sure He's noticed us yet. The cosmos is so large and our portion of it so small." When she proceeds to argue that the planets need not be *used* for anything, that they may exist only to teach man to count or to give him an awareness of the third dimension, the cynic responds, "Pretty thoughtful of God . . . if we're just some specks in His mirror"; and the intuitive essentialist rejoins, "He does everything . . . by the way. Not because it's what he has to do" (159–61, *passim*).

Jill's arguments are insubstantial—even, as I say, foggy; but they are also convincing. At the end of her section, before Skeeter comes on the scene, Rabbit prays unselfishly: "*Make the L-Dopa work, give her pleasanter dreams, keep Nelson more or less pure, don't let Stavros turn too hard on Janice, help Jill find her way home. Keep Pop healthy. Me Too. Amen*" (199; Updike's emphasis).

But the Christian religious level of *Rabbit Redux* is handled quite differently from the way it is handled in most of Updike's other novels. There are no organized churches here or men of the cloth for him to snipe at or side with—no Eccles or Kruppenbach, no church with a golden cock on its steeple and a Reverend Pedrick in its pulpit. Instead, Christianity functions metaphorically here, and is intended to clarify the relationship of the three characters, to establish the distinction between Jill and Skeeter, and to affirm as well Jill's ascendancy over Skeeter. Jill's "Beatitudes of Skeeter" about halfway through his section playfully reinforce both the distinction and the ascendancy:

> Power is bullshit.
> Love is bullshit.
> Common sense is bullshit
> Confusion is God's very face.
> Nothing is interesting save eternal sameness.
> There is no salvation, 'cepting through Me. (264)

And in a remarkable exchange at the end of Skeeter's section, the religious metaphor sets forth once and for all the complex set of relationships upon which the action has thus far been built. Rabbit spirits Skeeter out of town; "a wooden arrow at the intersection" where he drops him off says "Galilee 2. Otherwise it could be nowhere." He gives Skeeter thirty dollars, and "wonders now what would be proper. A Judas kiss?" Skeeter spits solemnly into the palm of Rabbit's proffered hand, and Rabbit, choosing "to take the gesture as a blessing . . . wipes his palm dry on his pants." As they part, Skeeter says, "Never did figure your angle"; and when Rabbit answers "Probably wasn't one," Skeeter "cackles" his final line: "Just waiting for the word, right?" (336).

Not uncommonly in Updike, the passage is fraught with ambiguity and apparent paradox. The one truly consistent identity is Jill, the "word" that Skeeter recognizes Rabbit had been waiting for. But the identities of Skeeter and Rabbit shift and squirm and float interchangeably. "Galilee 2" is an obvious reference to the Second Coming that Skeeter prophesies; and Skeeter assumes the role of Jesus, blessing Rabbit with his spit as Jesus has blessed the blind man to restore his sight.[4] But just as obviously, Skeeter is Judas here, accepting the thirty dollars as his due for turning Jill over to the mob. And Rabbit, who may see himself as Judas, giving rather than accepting the kiss (one recalls that it was he who turned on the light and identified Jill for the mob), is more nearly a Pilate figure, Judas's paymaster. This identity fits better his characterization as an objective observer, uncommitted, who washes his hands of responsibility in Skeeter's spit. What seems most paradoxical in the scene is the sympathetic treatment of both figures that Updike extends even into the dual identification of Skeeter as Jesus and as Judas. But even this is consistent in terms of that portion of the Christian legend alluded to. Paradoxically, the falls of Judas and Pilate were indeed fortunate, for without their betrayals the sacrifice of Jesus could not have been consummated. Nor could Jill's, without the falls of Skeeter and Rabbit.

But what purpose does the sacrifice of Jill serve? It is a disturbing question. One might argue that it enables Rabbit to distinguish and choose between the forces in conflict that Jill and Skeeter represent. Updike prepares us for such an interpretation when he tempts Rabbit with the naked, black, masturbating Skeeter, then sends him running to Jill instead, "up the varnished stairs, into the white realm where an overhead frosted fixture burns on the landing. His heart skips. He has escaped. Narrowly" (283). Rabbit has made the distinction, but he rejects the choice. Even with Jill, he finds "nothing to breathe but a sour gas bottled in empty churches, nothing to rise by" (284), and he turns his back to her. Later, of course, he refuses to partake of her even as Skeeter does; and immediately after this, as I pointed out above in a slightly different connection, Jill tells him that it is too late for him to try to love her.

But despite Jill's sacrifice, Updike does not let Rabbit choose between the conflicting forces—though he does let him lean, as do all Updike protagonists, toward the essentialism that Jill represents. He cannot let him choose and still remain true to his intention: the portrayal of the conflict in all its inconclusiveness. The sterility of Skeeter's pragmatism must be matched by the impotence of Jill's transcendentalism; neither the spit of the one nor the death of the other can be permitted to give Rabbit sight or to redeem him, any more than the sacrifice of Rebecca could identify him or give direction to his running in *Rabbit, Run*.

Thus, one might conclude that the purpose of Jill's death is to clear the air and the stage, suggesting the return to greater reader sympathy for Harry in *Rabbit at Rest*. Updike appears to reestablish whatever distance we may have lost by our involvement with the characters and with the somewhat bizarre nature of the action thus far, and to prepare us for the reconstruction of the battle lines of the philosophic conflict that is the subject of the last section of the novel. Updike establishes the distance and points up the conclusion by first alienating us from Jill with narcotics, then, unlike Rebecca, sacrificing her offstage, so that even if we care, our caring, like his own and even like Rabbit's, is more intellectual than emotional, the hysterics of Nelson the convert notwithstanding; and by the ironic intellectual gamesmanship of the religious metaphor itself. As we finish Skeeter's section, we are ready to move onto the plane where conclusions may be drawn, where resolutions may be proposed.

We are ready for Mim, deus ex machina from the dark side of the moon, sexual machine and uncompromising pragmatist from Las Vegas, the gambler's moon crater, epitome of artificiality and sterility. We never get to know Mim, never get inside of her or become involved with her in any way. We know only that she is an unphilosophical social meddler, determined to put matters right as she sees the right. Furthermore, because she functions on a strict day-to-day basis, Mim is, more than most Updikean pragmatists, prone to wrongheaded oversimplification; and, like Conner or Eccles or the switching couples, she can achieve little more than the merely superficial, little more than stopping Janice's running and keeping Rabbit from starting off again—little more, that is, than a landing on the moon. Thus, she is ideally suited both to reconstitute the battle lines of the philosophic conflict and to justify half of Updike's unwavering conviction that any resolution of the conflict is necessarily inconclusive. The other half of the justification is borne by Rabbit—but only after Mim has worked him into position.

She conducts Rabbit back through his guilt. Referring to Jill, she says:

> "She let herself die. Speaking of that, that's what I do like about these kids: they're trying to kill it. Even if they kill themselves in the process."
> "Kill what?" Rabbit asks.
> "The softness. Sex, love; me, mine. They're doing it in. I have no playmates under thirty, believe it. They're burning it out with dope. They're going to make themselves hard clean through. Like, oh, cockroaches." (361)

Her generalization may be accurate, but any application of it to Jill is simply wrong. And Rabbit doesn't argue, even though he must know better; the statement neatly reinforces his prior belief and excuses his irresponsibility.

Mim takes him back to his belief in the war, the belief that Jill and Skeeter had shaken. He learned from them, he says at one point, that "the country isn't perfect." But "even as he says this he realizes he doesn't believe it, any more than he believes at heart that he will die" (358). And shortly thereafter, he can reaffirm that "anybody with any sense at all is for the damn war. They want to fight, we *got* to fight. What's the alternative? What?" (366). And Mim, prompted by Charlie Stavros, interprets this commitment precisely opposite to the way Janice had interpreted it earlier. Janice had told Charlie that Rabbit had "put his life into rules he feels melting away now" (53); but, according to Mim, Charlie's "theory is . . . you like any disaster that might spring you free. You liked it when Janice left, you liked it when your house burned down" (366). That is to say, both Mim and Charlie see Rabbit as he was ten years earlier. And when he offers no demurrer, Mim is free to pursue her oversimplified course, to negate specifically Janice's argument, and in effect, by conducting him even further back, to reconstruct him as the original Rabbit:

> "Why don't you tend your own garden instead of hopping around nibbling at other people's?" Mim asks. . . .
> "I have no garden," he says.
> "Because you didn't tend it at all. Everybody else has a life they try to fence in with some rules. You just do what you feel like and then when it blows up or runs down you sit there and pout."
> "Christ," he says, "I went to work day after day for ten years."
> Mim tosses this off. "You felt like it. It was the easiest thing to do." (370)

That Janice is right and Mim is wrong is attested to by everything Rabbit does in the novel. It is true that he has rejected commitment and that he accepts only minimal responsibility for any of the "disasters" that strike; but the fact remains that he did give shelter to Jill and Skeeter, and to Nelson. "Black, white, I said Hop aboard. Irregardless of color or creed, Hop aboard. Free eats. I was the fucking Statue of Liberty," he says to Mim; and adds, "I did what felt right" (358). And the further fact remains that he groped persistently for whatever answers, whatever rules, Jill and Skeeter might have given him. However, he allows himself to be placed unprotestingly into that semblance of his former identity that Mim marks off for him. And once she has him there, Mim effectively gets rid of Charlie Stavros by overstimulating his heart (significantly, his weakest organ), thus making possible Janice's return. Then she remounts her machine and returns, pragmatic god that she is, to the never-never moonscape of Las Vegas.

She leaves behind a Rabbit Angstrom who is "still pretty screwed up" (403), a Rabbit whose idealistic vacuum she has helped inadvertently to refill with transcendent value—whose belief, cited earlier, that "confusion is just a local view of things working out in general," is only slightly less transcendentally muddy than his namesake's belief that "there's something out there that wants me to find it." She leaves him, that is, right where Updike wants him: inconclusive, uncertain, leaning toward an essentialism that is both intellectually and physically impotent.

Right where Updike wants him, for now. Having maintained his distance throughout the novel by his characterization of Rabbit as dispassionate observer—indeed, having taken a further step away from involvement with his people by permitting the intervention of Mim—at the end Updike focuses our attention where it remains until the surprising existential shift in *Rabbit at Rest*. That is, Updike reaffirms both the conflict that has been at the heart of the novel, and its inconclusiveness. And he leaves the reader in a familiar void, an emptiness filled with Hook's unaskable question, with Peter Caldwell's unsayable thing, with the questioning sounds of the first Rabbit's running feet. He leaves us with a Rabbit cured of incipient pragmatism, purified of the cynicism that startles the ending of *Couples*. He leaves us with as many fears and as much hope as we can reasonably expect. He leaves us with a human being. O.K.?

Some Notes toward an Essay on *Rabbit Is Rich* and *Rabbit at Rest*

But when we come to *Rabbit Is Rich*, it is no longer O.K.—at least, not in the same sense as it was in the first two novels. Oh, Rabbit is still haunted by a combination of his and the nation's past and his and the nation's present, as well as apprehensive about the futures of each. His exploitative relationships with women trouble him as well—with Melanie, Pru, Cindy Murkett, Ruth's daughter, and, not the least, Thelma Harrison. His days are still bothered by God: "he really believes there is a God he is the apple of the eye of" (325); and he is bothered once again, albeit briefly, by an Episcopal minister—not an Eccles, who was a seriously agnostic social uplifter, but "Soupy" Campbell, an effeminate accommodationist whose principles collapse easily before compromise: "The new prayer book," he says, "omits the fear of God" (201).

But Rabbit is no longer a 1950s rebel antihero as he was in *Rabbit, Run*, nor is he any longer the eager victim of a variety of 1960s rebels—Skeeter on Vietnam and civil rights, Jill on drugs, even Janice on sex and a sort of foggy feminism—as he was in *Rabbit Redux*. Nor does he any longer attempt to resolve the external conflict between society and rebellion by confronting the internal religio-philosophic conflict that, in my reading, dominates the first two novels. Indeed, in the face of Rabbit's richness, which results from Janice's inheritance of her father's Toyota dealership, coupled with the Me-ness of the 1970s, the conflict dissipates. While Harry's materialism accents the philosophical dualism even more sharply, the transcendental resolution which I would argue concludes the first two novels is no longer an option. Rabbit has become the ultimate American pragmatist: an automobile dealer in non-American toy cars (at the time of the novel, the full-sized Toyota has not yet emerged) who makes most of his profit from the sale of used cars.

Harry wonders what his father, who never earned more than forty dollars a week, "would think if he could see him now, rich" (29).

Updike guides the reader toward the conclusion that Rabbit has opted for the pragmatic by a device similar to though far more subtle than the index at the end of *The Centaur:* he precedes *Rabbit Is Rich* with an inscription from *Babbitt,* Sinclair Lewis's quintessential novel of the American pragmatic businessman—in real estate, by the way, a calling second only to used-car salesman in the American lexicon of businessman shysterism. But at the same time, the comparison of Babbitt and Rabbit is ironic; the 1970s were not the 1920s, after all. While Rabbit, like Babbitt, might be inclined to "whoop the ante" a little for profit, he is by no means as hypocritically unethical as George F. And Babbitt's wife, Myra, remains faithful while Babbitt strays, led by the booze-and-sex rebellion of the 1920s. And most importantly, there is a bonding between Babbitt and his son that climaxes his story, while there is increasing alienation between the Angstrom men.

In response to Rabbit's anger after Nelson has smashed up Rabbit's car, he says, "Dad, it's just a *thing*" (107); and a little later, "All you think about is money and *things*" (119). And still later, on the subject of selling, "People don't *care* that much about money anymore, it's all shit anyway. Money is shit" (169). This transcendental anti-thingness is a recurring refrain throughout the novel, driving father and son further apart and establishing Nelson as a sort of mini-rebel in the old Rabbit sense while, more importantly, letting him identify Rabbit's pragmatic materialism.

The wonderfully comic episode of the Krugerrands wherein Janice and Harry reenact the famous scene from *McTeague* (the movie version of which was called *Greed*), rolling about on and having sex upon a bed covered with the golden coins, serves to lock in this identification. The comic absurdity of the episode is reinforced later as Rabbit and Janice trade the gold coins for silver, which is much heavier because there are so many more coins, then stagger across downtown Brewer looking for a safety deposit box big enough to hold the treasure.

The superficiality, the emptiness of 1970s/1920s values as set forth in these scenes is the theme of *Rabbit Is Rich,* a theme fittingly clarified in the broadly comic climax of the novel: the wife-swapping episode on the Caribbean holiday. The decision to swap is made by the women. Rabbit acquiesces, hoping to get voluptuous Cindy Murkett. Instead, Ronnie gets her while Webb gets Janice, and Rabbit winds up with "yellowy, stringy" (410) Thelma, who, in disappointing addition, is menstruating. But he also gets an exciting, totally new experience—sodomy; Thelma gives him her anus, "a void, a pure black box, a casket of perfect nothingness" (417). And his climax there, "in that void, past her tight ring of muscle" is also the climax of the novel, what all the 1970s materialistic to-do has added up to: Up yours.

Immediately after this episode, as if keyed to it, a secondary climax occurs: Nelson runs, sending Harry and Janice scurrying guiltily back to Brewer and starting the novel descending good-naturedly toward a threefold denouement: Harry finds that Nelson, no Rabbit, has simply run back to Kent State and shacked up with Melanie, while Pru gives birth to a daughter (Judy); Rabbit visits Ruth to see if her Annabelle is *his* daughter, and Ruth, after cutting him up badly as a Babbitt ("A regular Brewer sharpie," she calls him. "A dealer. The kind of person you used to hate, remember?" [443]), denies he is the father while teasingly hinting that he might be. And the Angstroms buy a house in upper-middle-class Penn Park estates, a rabbit hutch "tucked in off a macadamized dead end" (451) with room for a garden. The cul-de-sac is numbered 14½, but it has no name; they think of calling it Angstrom Way.

The novel ends with Rabbit buried in this dead end as he had been buried into Thelma's "casket of perfect nothingness," her dead end, comfortably surrounded by Janice, Pru, Ma Springer: his women. And Pru's girl child deposited into his lap, "Another nail in his coffin. His" (467).

These final two sentences of this novel—indeed, the whole denouement—serve as a neat transition into *Rabbit at Rest*, at the ending of which, Rabbit seems to die. But whether he does or not—and I maintain that the ending of the novel is inconclusive—there is no question that *Rabbit at Rest* is about dying, the preparation for it, the inescapability of it. At the same time, it is about having lived, about why and how Rabbit has become what he is now, at the end. It is at once the most existential of the four novels and the one in which Updike permits the distancing, the detachment between himself and Rabbit, and the reader and Rabbit, to dissipate. We become emotionally involved with Rabbit even more than we had been in *Rabbit, Run*, and as a consequence we understand him better, and sympathize with him more fully, than we ever have before.

Updike succeeds in attaching us to Rabbit by detaching him from Babbittry and restoring him to Rabbitry. His occupation is gone; just as Updike installed Rabbit in the Toyota dealership and gave him his riches in *Rabbit Is Rich*, he allows Janice and Ma Springer to take the dealership from him and give it to Nelson in *Rabbit at Rest*. Gone too is his body; he is fat and out of shape, and from the outset of the novel he suffers the chest pains that ulti-mately result in a heart attack. His geographical and social roots are gone as well, or at least they are split. He begins and ends the novel in a retirement condo in Deleon, Florida, without a garden or a view, playing golf daily with three Jewish men who would never have been accepted in his country club in Brewer.

Rabbit is loose, open-ended. He is no longer the 1950s rebel, nor beset by 1960s rebels. Nor is he the 1970s pragmatic businessman. In fact, the whole pragmatism/transcendentalism dilemma has been subordinated in *Rabbit at Rest* to Rabbit's existential search for authenticity—a search through the 1980s, with "everything falling apart, airplanes, bridges, eight years under Reagan of nobody minding the store, making money out of nothing, run-ning up debt, trusting in God" (9).

His days bothered by an awareness of his own mortality, as well as still bothered by God, and ensconced now, along with other ancients, in a city named ironically for the explorer who sought eternal youth, Harry longs to seek answers to ultimate questions from the Jewish trinity with whom he golfs. "He has an unaskable question for these wise Jewish men: how about death?" (69) "*Help me, guys. Tell me how you've got on top of sex and death so they don't bother you*" (71; Updike's emphasis). He doesn't ask, because, like each of the four Rabbits, Harry does not want to discover his identity, but to have it discovered to him. "*Tsuris*," Bernie says, speaking for the three who have "sensed his silent cry for help, for consolation." "Sounds to me, my friend, like you got some *tsuris*. Not full-grown yet, not *gehoketh tsuris, but tsuris*" (72). And as they part, the trinity "in farewell cuff at him, even pinch the nape of his neck, as if to rouse him from a spiritual torpor" (73). "In Florida," Rabbit thinks in response to their caring gestures, "even friendship has a thin, provisional quality, since people might at any minute buy another condominium and move to it, or else up and die" (73).

This brief scene at the outset of the novel is extremely important, de-spite, or perhaps because of, the fact that the trinity of Jewish men never re-appears. The scene establishes the theme of the novel—that the existential search is a solitary journey that probably ends in death—as well as Rabbit's relaxed, almost flippant acceptance of this condition. And it is this attitude, this tone, that enlists the reader's sympathy and reduces that detachment that the reader, and Updike, have always maintained toward Rabbit.

Rabbit's journey leads him through various ordeals and trials: Nelson's bankrupting of the dealership by feeding his cocaine addiction; Judy's near-drowning; Thelma's death; sex with Pru; and above all, his heart attack. His response in each instance is predictable. He is angry and unforgiving with Nelson, whom he sees as weak and overprotected by Janice and Pru. He is proud of "rescuing" Judy (she was never in danger) because he sees this as atoning for his failure to rescue Rebecca, his daughter, whom Janice drowned accidentally in *Rabbit, Run*. Thelma's death touches him deeply, because he cared deeply about her loving him—a comic sidelight occurs at her funeral when we discover that Ronnie Harrison is Rabbit's doppelgänger, that part of himself that he dislikes ("Harrison" = "Harry's son," another example of Updike's delight in playing games with names [380]). Sex with Pru, mutually initiated, is something that "just happens" to Rabbit. There are few moral or ethical considerations. "All his life seems to have been a journey into the bodies of women" (468), he muses shortly before his final attack. A journey within a journey, traveled together: Pru sees to it that she comes twice on the trip.

This brief liaison leads to the climax of the novel: Pru's confession of the incident to Janice and to Nelson in order that Harry and Janice will not sell their house and move in with them. Rabbit is invited to a family discussion of the matter, and he does what he does, or desires to do, whenever he is faced with a crisis. He runs. Runs toward the novel's denouement.

The running at the end of this novel repeats the running at the beginning of *Rabbit, Run;* in fact, the whole denouement here repeats the initial action of the first novel, encircling and enclosing all four novels into a unified whole. Rabbit runs again to the South, and again he observes and comments upon the nation and its culture as it appears to him in talk and music on the radio and in the advertisements he passes on the highway.[5] And again he travels into the past, only now, at age fifty-six, it is a far richer, more complex past. And his ever-shifting attitudes toward sex and women, toward war and peace, toward politics, and so on, seem now to be summing-ups rather than, as so often in the earlier novel, petulant gripes. At any rate, he recalls his first flight and the gas station attendant who told him that "The only way to get somewhere, you know, is to figure out where you're going before you go there" (*Run* 28). Harry tries to find the station to tell the man that this time he does know, that his destination is his Florida condo, but the station has long since been replaced by a real estate office.

Rabbit must run toward his destination—toward his identity and toward his death ("buy another condominium . . . or else up and die")—without anyone's approval and despite anyone's disapproval. Such is the nature of the human condition, and Harry accepts it, moves in tune with it as always; and it is this acceptance that elicits our sympathy, our understanding. We are not sorry for Rabbit; we simply are closer to him, more in tune with him than we ever have been. Updike isolates him but does not detach him, the irony this time drawing us in rather than pushing us away.

In the crucial penultimate episode of this extended denouement, Harry's existential journey again circles back to the opening scenes of *Rabbit, Run*. In Deleon, after some chest pains, he goes back to the doctor, who advises him to lose weight and get some mild exercise, like walking, or else he may have another attack. He walks, and he comes across some young black kids playing Three, a version of Horse, on a playground basketball court. As he did in the first novel, Rabbit muscles in on their game. He doesn't do well. He is in a different culture at a different time; he is too old; the boys are black; he can't compete. He returns to the court the next day and talks his way into going one-on-one with a black eighteen-year-old. Summoning all his past skills, overextending himself in order to redefine himself, Rabbit beats the boy; then, as the ball falls through the hoop, he suffers a massive heart attack. "Pure horseshit," the boy says as the shot falls and Harry falls against him. Then the boy runs—he doesn't want to be blamed for this—leaving Rabbit alone on the court.

The novel could end there, dramatically and satisfactorily, with Rabbit having pushed the existentialist envelope through authenticity into the void. But Updike wants to tie up loose ends, and I think he wants to leave the question of Rabbit's death inconclusive. So he gives us a final scene, bringing everybody together in the ICU; and, at the very end, Nelson cries "Don't *die*, Dad, *don't*"; to which Rabbit responds, "Well, Nelson . . . all I can tell you is, it isn't so bad" (512). These are highly ambiguous last words, it seems to me—far more ambiguous than the collapse on the basketball court was.

Also, the title of the novel is ambiguous. Is "Rest" a part of "Rest in Peace," thus a euphemism for death? If Updike wanted us to be certain that Rabbit dies, why would he not have titled the novel more straightforwardly? He does so in two of the first three titles of the tetralogy, *Rabbit, Run* and *Rabbit Is Rich*. Indeed, the one indirect, intellectually playful title of the four, *Rabbit Redux*, is trashed in *Rabbit at Rest*. Running south, Harry sees a sign advertising Circus World, and Updike has him think, "not the one that's redux down in Sarasota. What a dumb word, dumb as faux, you see it everywhere suddenly, faux fun, faux jewelry" (462). Clearly, this is Updike's criticism of the "dumb word," not Rabbit's. Though he would be familiar with *faux,* he would not know the word *redux* if it bit him. It is Updike criticizing his own use of the word in the title, and, willy-nilly, calling our attention to the simple clarity of the other titles.

I think it's willy. I think, further, that given the publishing history of the four novels, we won't know for sure until the year 2000.

But the question of Rabbit's death is far less important than the cyclical nature of the ending, which ties the first and last volumes together and identifies Harry Angstrom once again and once and for all as Rabbit, dead or alive. And he can rest on that; that, after all, isn't so bad.

Notes

1. "It's the Going That's Important, Not the Getting There: Rabbit's Questing Non-Quest," *Modern Fiction Studies* 20 (Spring 1974): 13–27.

2. In the essay that follows, Ralph Wood discusses the dramatic tensions between Harry's pragmatic self and his transcendent idealism in terms of "a Cartesian vision of the soul."

3. All references to the Rabbit novels are to the Knopf editions.

4. Mark 8:22–26.

5. This running commentary (pun intentional) is a motif common to all the Rabbit novels. Indeed, it is so persistent and insistent as to be almost thematic. Updike uses Rabbit's point of view as a lens to comment upon American culture for most of the past forty years. It is not a point of view as intellectual or sophisticated or ironic as his own would be, but I believe that Updike sees it as therefore more distinctly American than his own. He makes this most clear in *Rabbit at Rest* when, after the incident with Pru but before Rabbit runs for what may be the last time, Updike appoints him as Uncle Sam in the Fourth of July parade in Brewer. He is a flawed Uncle Sam certainly, both morally and physically—he is fat, his beard doesn't stick, his hat doesn't fit; he has to pop nitro for his chest pains—but he is Uncle Sam nonetheless. And not in any ironic sense; by this time, Updike is too close to Rabbit to play that ironic game. Flaws and all, he is clearly more Uncle Sam than any unflawed Uncle Sam would or could be.

Ralph C. Wood
8 Rabbit Angstrom
John Updike's Ambiguous Pilgrim

The human condition in all of its irreducible ambiguity is the subject of John Updike's fiction. Not even in his tetralogy, with its quasi-epic dimensions, does Updike envision any grand scheme for our ultimate redemption. He offers something much more modest: the saga of a single, rather ordinary man as he has fared through four decades of American life toward his own death. Updike's Rabbit books serve not to account for the elite and privileged world of the Northeast (as in *Couples*) but rather to report on the popular culture of Middle America. As a man of the *gens* and not of the gentry, Harold C. (Harry, Rabbit) Angstrom is "one of us." He defines popular American life for the latter half of this century as his predecessors—Huck Finn, Nick Adams and Ike McCaslin—did for earlier times.

Updike confesses that *Rabbit, Run* was written not as the first volume in a tetralogy but rather as a counterpart to *The Centaur*. The two novels were originally intended to "illustrate the polarity between running and plodding, between the rabbit and the horse, between the life of instinctual gratification and that of dutiful self-sacrifice" (*Hugging the Shore* 849–50). Yet the full portrait of Rabbit Angstrom has required an entire tetralogy for Updike to vent this man's "urgent inner whispers," to celebrate his life-giving discontent, to sing his Whitmanesque song of egotheistic vagabondage. "The spirit needs folly," declares a character in *The Witches of Eastwick*, "as the body needs food" (96). From the very beginning of his career, Updike has professed this contrarian creed: "The heart *prefers* to move against the grain of circumstance; perversity is the soul's very life" (*Assorted Prose* 299).

Rabbit's enabling perversity makes him something of Updike's alter ego. Though he begins as a blue-collar laborer and remains uncultured in things literary and academic, Angstrom bears a rough resemblance to his creator: they are approximately the same age, they share an eastern Pennsylvania milieu, and they possess an uninhibited candor about matters personal and sexual. Rabbit lacks the sophistication to tell his own story, but Updike's narrator reveals his mind at work in ways both intimate and confessional. "Since his words enter into another's brain in silence and intimacy," Updike observes of the fiction writer, "he should be as honest and explicit as we are with ourselves" (*Hugging the Shore* 864). Present-tense narration—still a revolutionary technique in 1960 when Updike employed it in the first of the Rabbit books—serves as a brilliant device for revealing Rabbit's megalomaniac obsessions and adventures in all of their rushing inevitability.

Harry Angstrom is not only Updike's doppelgänger but also his hero. His heroism lies in his refusal to accept the plodding conformities of bourgeois life, even though he is hugely indebted to that life. While Updike refuses to censure Rabbit as a moral scoundrel, neither does he endorse him as an exemplar of the moral life. "Rabbit is the hero of this novel," Updike affirms, "but is he a good man? The question is meant to lead to another—What is goodness?" (*Hugging the Shore* 850). The answer remains profoundly ambiguous. On the one hand, Angstrom is an exemplar of the carefree liberty that has been the hallmark of American life almost from the beginning, doing his own heedless will with little regard for the consequences. On the other hand, Angstrom becomes an acerbic scold of our American naïveté about the limits of freedom, discovering the evil inherent in all attempts, especially his own, to throw off the shackles of obligation. He can hardly be called a pilgrim in the classic Christian sense, a man seeking clear passage from death and damnation to new and everlasting life. Yet as a soul with insatiable transcendent longings, Rabbit Angstrom is no mere worldling living complacently within the bounds of his own mortality. He is a man mired in insoluble ambiguity, a peculiarly American pilgrim.

Sinning That Grace May Abound: *Rabbit, Run*

When we first meet him, Harry Angstrom is—as his name suggests—a harried and anxious youth who is yearning, at age twenty-six, to be free from the binding commitments and responsibilities that life has thrust upon him all too soon. He is a former high school basketball hero whose dreams of glory are withering amidst the dull routines of adult life. Angstrom finds his job as a hawker of vegetable peelers to be morally degrading. He senses the nihilism inherent in modern advertising and marketing—its invention of conveniences and improvements that no one needs, its denial that only few things are truly worth having, its reduction of Greek wisdom and Christian revelation to Mickey Mouse salesmanship:

> Jimmie sets aside his smile and guitar and says straight out through the glass, "Know Thyself, a wise old Greek once said. Know Thyself. Now what

does this mean, boys and girls? It means, be what you are. Don't try to be Sally or Johnny or Fred next door; be yourself. God doesn't want a tree to be a waterfall, or a flower to be a stone. God gives to each one of us a special talent. . . . So: Know Thyself. Learn to understand your talents, and then work to develop them. That's the way to be happy." He pinches his mouth together and winks. (*Run* 9–10)[1]

Rabbit's one refuge from such cynicism lies in the ecstasies of sex. Yet these too have already begun to fail him. His wife, Janice, pregnant with their second child, is turning into a sloven with her endless drinking and television watching. Once their baby girl is born, she always seems to be crying. Even Rabbit's sexual life with his mistress, Ruth, has turned stale and predictable. Rabbit wants to get out of such a dead world, to let go, to run—to flee the life of grim effort and duty for the limitless realm of grace and freedom: "He used to love to climb the [telephone] poles. To shinny up from a friend's shoulders until the ladder of spikes came to your hands, to get up to where you could hear the wires sing. Their song was a terrifying motionless whisper. It always tempted you to fall, to let the hard spikes in your palms go and feel the space on your back, feel it take your feet and ride up your spine as you fell" (15).

As a thoroughgoing Freudian, Updike nearly always sees an inherent link between sex and death. Our medieval ancestors discerned that the most transcendent bodily exaltation is strangely akin to extinction; they called the weariness that follows orgasm "the little death." Updike also has in mind the escape from earthly limits that occurs in both death and sex. When Rabbit is sexually most liberated, he is most dangerous. His search for ecstasy often brings death into the world. It makes him less a heedless lecher than a diabolic mystic. Seeking spiritual no less than sexual deliverance, Rabbit turns his poor slattern Ruth into a goddess. Kneeling before his naked lover and kissing her empty ring finger, he calls their first encounter in bed "our wedding night." It is no mere spasm of pleasure that Rabbit seeks but rather a gnostic union of souls, not sweaty coition but unearthly bliss: "It is not her body he wants, not the machine, but her, her" (79). Though more amused than enchanted by such homage, Ruth understands that bodily concourse is a utopian plunge through pure air, a divine descent to nowhere. "It's like falling through," she says (86).

Though Updike makes kindly sport of Rabbit's desire to elevate carnality into spirituality, he does not mock his sacramental wonder before the world's beauty and mystery. After climbing Mt. Judge with Ruth, Angstrom ponders the glory implicit in such height: "It seems plain, standing here, that if there is this floor there is a ceiling, that the true space in which we live is upward space" (114). Though no longer a churchgoer himself, Rabbit refuses to regard the cosmos as godlessly suspended "in the middle of nowhere." Sunday worshipers streaming into the nearby church affirm the transcendence he now encounters only in sex and high places, "a visual proof of the unseen world" (91).

As one whose anguish-ridden condition is figured in his very name, Angstrom believes he would not be a creature both vexed and exalted with insatiable longings were there not a God seeking communion with him. "There's something that wants me to find it," he confesses (127). "His eyes turn toward the light," the narrator observes of Rabbit's botanical instinct for the sun, "however it glances into his retina" (237). Angstrom becomes a virtual evangelist for this unseen but all-invigorating presence. "I'm a mystic," he announces. "I give people faith" (144). Mrs. Smith, the elderly lady for whom Rabbit works as a gardener after he abandons Janice, confirms this self-estimate. "You kept me alive, Harry; it's the truth; you did. . . . That's what you have, Harry: life. It's a strange gift and I don't know how we're supposed to use it but I know it's the only gift we get and it's a good one" (224).

Rabbit's religious regard for his own élan vital seems to justify Cardinal Newman's observation that "mysticism begins in mist and ends in schism." Harry's egotheism is a guise for egomania, and it leads not merely to division but to death. With only his own inward deity to worship, Rabbit becomes merciless toward all his rivals, especially those who would make moral claims upon him. His faithless contempt for the pathetic Janice makes her embalm her dreams in alcohol. He also forces Ruth into ever more abject acts of sexual submission, finally demanding that she perform fellatio on him, as she has done for her other lovers. Yet Rabbit yields her little in return.

Rabbit's gnostic scorn for all outward obligations makes him a hot gospeler of subjectivity. "Goodness lies inside," he proclaims even to the end; "there is nothing outside" (308). As the prophet of inward self-indulgence, he would release others from their bondage to enervating self-sacrifice, teaching them that there is no penalty for self-abandonment. "If you have the guts to be yourself," Angstrom preaches, "other people'll pay your price" (149). Far from being a secular boast, Rabbit's egomania is deeply religious. Updike the existentialist believes that God has set humanity on the razor's edge between finitude and infinity. The burden laid upon every human being is to walk this narrow divide without plunging into bestial sensuality or orbiting into angelic abstraction. Rabbit regards the life of ethical duty as threatening him with an animalistic at-homeness in the world. Hence his desire to strike the shackles of moral constraint and to enjoy the frisson that comes from living at the juncture of time and eternity: "He obscurely feels lit by a great spark, the spark whereby the blind tumble of matter recognized itself, a spark struck in the collision of two opposed realms, an encounter a terrible God willed" (299).

Mainline American religion is helpless to quench or focus the fires ignited by such gnostic sparks. Jack Eccles, an Episcopal vicar whose name suggests that he is an ecclesiastic hack, has entered Christian ministry by way of family tradition rather than divine summons and theological conviction. He is a golfing priest who feels more at home on the greens than in the pulpit, a preacher scandalized by the scandalous faith he is commissioned to proclaim, a client-centered therapist who would rather lend an ear to the world's woes than declare its deliverance. Eccles can regard Rabbit's moral vagrancy only as a sign of ethical immaturity rather than spiritual evil. "With my Church," he declares to Angstrom, "I believe that we are all responsible beings, responsible for ourselves and for each other" (153). Eccles's humanist gospel leaves the running Rabbit theologically untouched, his miserable offenses neither checked nor redeemed. Even the unbelieving Ruth discerns that this ungodly man of God feeds Rabbit's spiritual fantasies: "The damnedest thing about that minister was that, before, Rabbit at least had the idea he was acting wrong but now he's got the idea he's Jesus Christ out to save the world just by doing whatever comes into his head. I'd like to get hold of the bishop or whoever and tell him that minister of his is a menace. Filling poor Rabbit with something nobody can get at" (149).

Updike sets the hard-boiled Lutheran minister Kruppenbach over against the soft-centered Eccles as his theological opposite and corrective. Kruppenbach is Updike's comical impersonation of a latter-day Luther. Unlike the suave Eccles, Kruppenbach is—as his name perhaps indicates—something of a horse's ass: a preacher who speaks at pulpit volume in casual conversation, a man of faith who looks ordained of God despite his crew-cut hair and sweaty undershirt, a Christian with a bullying creed. It is no surprise that Kruppenbach will have nothing of Eccles's sentimental idea of Rabbit as a pilgrim and mystic. He calls Rabbit a *Schussel:* a silly adolescent incapable of the seriousness demanded by the Gospel.

Yet it is not the sinning Rabbit whom Kruppenbach damns but rather the all-accommodating Eccles. Like Kierkegaard, Kruppenbach holds to the utter absurdity of the Gospel in the face of all reasonable panaceas for the human condition: "If Gott wants to end misery He'll declare the Kingdom now." As a Lutheran advocate of the doctrine that God's heavenly kingdom has little to do with the kingdoms of the earth, Kruppenbach insists that a minister must never confuse his holy calling with secular service. Christians come to church for a single reason, whatever their lesser motives: for the Good News, not for psychological therapies and political preachments. Kruppenbach thunders to Eccles that there is one true solace: "faith, not what little finagling a body can do here and there; stirring the bucket." Human existence is a great slop pan of suffering, he declares. The preacher's task is to command a raw youth like Rabbit Angstrom to carry his burden, to shoulder the load that Jesus Christ has borne for him: "You must *love* your pain, because it is *Christ's* pain. . . . There's nothing but Christ for us. All the rest, all this decency and busyness, is nothing. It is the Devil's work" (170–71).

Far from being a cool listener like Eccles, Kruppenbach believes that the minister should set his people afire with the scorching intensity of his own belief, scalding them with the lava of his conviction. Yet Rabbit's self-absorption is made of asbestos. Kruppenbach's faith is so vehement and otherworldly, so laden with anguish and torment, that Rabbit finds it no more suited to his condition than the cool suavity of Eccles's acculturated religion. Both ministers serve to confirm Updike's conviction that God is not dead or nonexistent so much as delinquent and hidden. There is much of Luther's dark conception of God as *deus absconditus* in the terrifying scene where the drunken Janice allows baby Rebecca to drown in her bath. Janice is responsible, of course, for having drunk herself into a stupor, and Rabbit is guilty for having betrayed her. Yet the fury of Updike's prose falls on neither the alcoholic wife nor the unfaithful husband, but upon the unintervening God who will not pull the stopper from the drowning baby's tub. In a passage of unparalleled metaphysical terror, Updike's narrator makes furious protest against the God who is present only in his absence:

> [Janice] lifts the living thing into air and hugs it against her sopping chest. Water pours off them onto the bathroom tiles. The little weightless body flops against her neck and a quick look of relief at the baby's face gives a fantastic clotted impression. A contorted memory of how they give artificial respiration pumps Janice's cold wet arms in frantic rhythmic hugs; under her clinched lids great scarlet prayers arise, wordless, monotonous, and she seems to be clasping the knees of a vast third person whose name, Father, Father, beats against her head like physical blows. Though her wild heart bathes the universe in red, no spark kindles in the space between her arms; for all of her pouring prayers she doesn't feel the faintest tremor of an answer in the darkness against her. Her sense of the third person with them widens enormously, and she knows, knows, while

knocks sound at the door, that the worst thing that has ever happened to any woman in the world has happened to her. (264–65)

Updike will have nothing of Leibniz's tame theodicy that rationalizes God's goodness with the world's evil by arguing that there is no divine disruption of secondary causes—for example, the buoyancy of water that makes it unbreathable. The Rabbit tetralogy asks how God can be forgiven his spirit-numbing withdrawal from the world, his heinous refusal to intervene at Rebecca's death no less than the Holocaust. God's truancy is also made evident in the extinguishing of the light that once shone in the church window across from Ruth's apartment. Absent all true transcendence, Rabbit lives by the only divine sign he knows—his egotheistic energy. By what other polestar can he steer, Updike asks, than his own inward flame? It drives Rabbit to make utterly contradictory claims about the eclipse of God. On the one hand, he declares *everyone* to be a victim, and yet on the other hand he confesses to the empty cosmos his own huge guilt: "*Forgive me, forgive me*" (248).

To Updike's own question of whether Rabbit is a good man, Angstrom's lover, Ruth, provides a clear answer. She calls him "Mr. Death himself. You're not just nothing," she adds, "you're worse than nothing" (304). She sees him as the Unmaker—the father of her own unwanted child, the cause of Rebecca's drowning and of the deep grief he has brought to everyone concerned. Rabbit is "worse than nothing" because he *thrives* amidst the metaphysical void. Having discerned the spiritual vacuum at the heart of a conventionally ethical life, Angstrom refuses to live it. Hence his final flight from the graveside service for baby Rebecca. Not only does he leave Janice to bear her now compounded grief, Rabbit also claims to act according to the promptings of the Gospel. Hearing Eccles pronounce the great scriptural promises of everlasting life, Harry lights out for the regions of unharnessed freedom. He runs in sheer antinomian justification of his own self-will.

This is the price we pay, Updike suggests, for human self-consciousness. Animals do not wreak such destruction; they kill only to satisfy their appetites. Rabbit Angstrom is the novel's hero, not because he is a good man but because, in a spiritually dead world, he strives mightily to keep his soul alive. He is no mere self-pleasuring hedonist but an exemplary and egregious sinner. His inward spirit is so transcendently important to him that he regards all communal bonds and moral duties as wearying by comparison.

The single hint at a more excellent way comes in a sermon preached, rather unaccountably, by the otherwise obtuse Eccles. His text is the account of Christ's conversation with Satan in the wilderness. Eccles interprets Jesus' encounter with the Tempter to mean that "suffering, deprivation, barrenness, hardship, lack are all an indispensable part of the education, the initiation, as it were, of any of those who would follow Jesus Christ" (237). Just as Kruppenbach insists that we see our suffering as Christ's own pain, so does Eccles declare true faith to be a *via crucis*—a pilgrimage through anguish, an endless wrestling with the self-contradiction of our spiritual animality. Such graciously embraced suffering has no appeal to Rabbit. He insists to the end that there are only two paths, "the right way and the good way"—the hard way of moral self-restraint and the soft way of sweet self-will. He refuses any third path beyond dull duty and delicious freedom: "Harry has no taste for the dark, tangled, visceral aspect of Christianity, the *going through* quality of it, the passage *into* death and suffering that redeems and inverts these things, like an umbrella blowing inside out. He lacks the mindful will to walk the straight line of a paradox" (237).

This is the most important moral and theological declaration in the entire novel. It reveals that Harry Angstrom's religious breakthrough is an ambiguous good. He has learned the truth that human beings cannot live without the adventure of the passions. Now he must learn the countertruth that the passionate life also has its limits, that pain and suffering are its necessary concomitants. Rabbit will be required to slow down, though he will never do so eagerly. He will cease scurrying like a self-preserving hare and begin plodding like a dutiful horse that pulls the world's load.

"Time Is Our Element": *Rabbit Redux*

Rabbit Redux (1971) carries Harry Angstrom beyond the comparative tranquillity of the Eisenhower years into the 1960s, the age Updike described as "the most dissentious American decade since the Civil War" (*Hugging the Shore* 858). As the title suggests, Rabbit has been "led back," restored to responsibility, cured of the uninhibited desire that afflicted his youthful years. Yet Rabbit's rehabilitation remains deeply ambiguous. He is still ensnared in the circumstances that proved so constricting in *Rabbit, Run*. Yet instead of fleeing the web of moral life, Rabbit here begins to affirm it. Against the grain of popular culture, with its mania for entertainment and material success, Angstrom learns that time is not our enemy but our element, that only the duties and fidelities of temporal existence enable us to become free.

As the self-avowed master of middleness, the serene singer of "things as they are," Updike was forced, rather unhappily, to face the apocalyptic ethos of the 1960s. Its strident demands for a radical reshaping of the social realm struck him as both foolish and pernicious. The extremists of the decade presumed that the old order could be overturned without destroying the good inherent in it. Their blindness to tragedy revealed, in his view, our American reluctance to admit the intractable ambiguities of the moral and spiritual life. Such a refusal is endemic to Rabbit's own naive notion that happiness can be had without suffering and sacrifice. The thirty-six-year-old Angstrom whom we here encounter is a man whose own moral contradictions are exacerbated by the chaos of the age. Though he finds dignity in his job as a Linotype operator, he is far from happy. On the contrary, his upwardly mobile life in Penn Villas leaves him trapped in middle-class mediocrity.

Janice has also imbibed the spirit of the times, having transformed herself from a homebound dullard into a liberated woman. Sexual experimentation is the mark of her new freedom, as she betrays Rabbit by having an affair with his friend Charlie Stavros. Now that Rabbit has become a responsible husband and citizen, Janice finds him much less erotically alluring. Rabbit reads his wife's infidelity as a sign of the rampant faithlessness inveigling the entire age. He is especially impatient with the antipatriotism of the black revolutionaries and the white protesters against the Vietnam War. Angstrom stands too greatly in debt to his country to let it be called racist and imperialist and power-mad. The American war effort was prompted not by self-interest, he insists, but by a sacrificial desire to make Vietnam another free and prosperous country like Japan. Hence his fury at the critics of President Johnson: "Poor old LBJ, Jesus with tears in his eyes on television, you must have heard him, he just about offered to make North Vietnam the fifty first fucking state of the Goddam Union if they'd just stop throwing bombs" (45).

Rabbit's moral spleen is prompted by his own moral failings. The more he splutters his rage against the decadence of the times, the more he reveals his own vacuity of soul. On the one hand, he righteously denounces the dread new "culture of narcissism," as Christopher Lasch would call it, with its endless gabble about looking honestly into ourselves, "searching for a valid identity," and thinking with "your whole person" (104, 110). On the other hand, this despiser of the counterculture not only takes up with a flower child named Jill but also gives bed and board to a black-power fanatic called Skeeter, even as Rabbit himself revels in the marijuana world, the sweet "lovingness of pot" (123). Even the hapless Jill can discern the contradiction in Rabbit. She tells him that, if he truly loved his country, he would want to make it better. "If it was better," Rabbit confesses in return, "*I'd* have to be better" (171).

The moral and spiritual poverty of the 1960s serve to make Rabbit as much victim as villain. It is an age dominated by television, especially the live coverage of the moon landings. These technological wonders provide no real sustenance for Angstrom's soul. Unlike the original New World landings, modern space exploration is empty with its own predictability: "Columbus flew blind and hit something, these guys see exactly where they're aiming and it's a big round nothing" (22). Such cultural vacuity leaves the empty Rabbit virtually vaporized by the decade, a time when—as Updike declares in another connection—"the Beatles spiritualized us all" (*Picked-Up Pieces* xv).

As a patriotic liberal turning reactionary, Rabbit is strangely drawn to two seraphic creatures of the age, a hippie and a black revolutionary. Skeeter Johnson is an avenging angel of wrath, a self-proclaimed messiah of chaos and destruction. He is an embittered veteran of the Vietnam War who hails it for shattering the American dream of uniqueness. We are a nation like all others, Skeeter says, a cockroach country that he calls the "Benighted States" of America. Ours is first among nations, he insists, only because we have turned the world's unacknowledged nihilism into a cultural and political principle. The hedonism of the ghetto, the self-indulgence of Detroit and Madison Avenue, the indiscriminate violence of Vietnam—all of these, says Skeeter, should be regarded with perverse pride rather than national shame. They make America the covert envy of the world:

> I'm not one of these white lib-er-als like that cracker Fulldull or Charlie McCarthy [who] a while back gave all the college queers a hard-on, think Vietnam some sort of mistake, we can fix it up once we get the cave men out of office, it is *no* mistake, right, any President comes along falls in love with it, it is lib-er-alism's very wang, dingdong pussy, and fruit. . . . What is lib-er-alism? Bringin' joy to the world, right? Puttin' sugar on dog-eat-dog so it tastes good all over, right? . . . We is *the* spot. Few old fools like the late Ho [Chi Minh] may not know it, we is what the world is begging *for*. Big beat, smack, black cock, big-assed cars and billboards, we is into *it*. Jesus come down, He come down here. These other countries, just bullshit places, right? We got the *ape* shit, right? Bring down Kingdom Come, we'll swamp the world in red-hot real American blue-green ape shit, right? (263–64).

The violence of Skeeter's rhetoric—blithely abjuring all subordination, willfully committing grammatical errors, imperiously demanding assent, brutally shoving sexual and scatological terms in his hearer's face—is in complete accord with his worship of the will to power. Updike seems thus to suggest that, when the American tradition of humane liberalism declines, a hard-edged nihilism rises up to replace it. As an ambiguous ex-liberal, Rabbit is helpless to resist Skeeter's dark love of brute force. "Wherever America is," Rabbit chauvinistically dreams, "there is freedom, and wherever America is not, madness rules with chains, darkness strangles millions. Beneath her patient bombers, paradise is possible" (47). Such obliviousness to the truth enables Rabbit not only to deny that he is giving shelter to this criminal pseudo-Christ but also to help him escape the police. Perhaps Angstrom salves his conscience by thinking that even a demon like Skeeter suffers, that he has been maddened by his experience in Vietnam, that the United States is no ideal republic, that black terrorism is sparked by white injustice.

Rabbit is saved from his enthrallment to Skeeter by a sudden turn that amounts to a virtual *deus ex machina*. The surprising event concerns Skeeter's disciple, a vaporous counterculture child named Jill. This rich girl who drives a Porsche and spouts Eastern mysticism is a nymphet who is spookily unpresent when Rabbit beds her: her angelic innocence makes her wholly impervious to sin and guilt. When angry neighbors burn Angstrom out for sheltering this hippie and her black revolutionary messiah, Jill dies in the fire. Once more Rabbit has become Mr. Thanatos. Yet his complicity in Jill's death, unlike his blithe disregard for Rebecca's drowning, awakens him to his own destructiveness.

The key to Rabbit's recovery lies in his response to his own dying mother's insistence that he leave the unfaithful Janice, flee the city, and thus seek his own rebirth rather than remaining passive like a lump of clay. Suddenly Rabbit discerns that this gospel of self-regard leads to a freedom that is laden with death. In a moment of acute moral discernment, the narrator records Rabbit's denial of his mother's call for him to run: "His cheeks flame; he bows his head. He feels she is asking him to kill Janice, to kill Nelson. Freedom means murder. Rebirth means death. . . . She is still trying to call him forth from her womb, can't she see he is an old man? An old lump whose only use is to stay in place to keep the lumps on top of him from tumbling?" (198). No longer the selfish *Schussel* whom Pastor Kruppenbach had so accurately labeled, Rabbit is learning to accept responsibility for the lives that are bound up with his. He is losing his gnostic urge to escape all earthly obligations. He is coming home to his true milieu: "Time is our element, not a mistaken invader. How stupid, it has taken him thirty-six years to begin to believe that" (374).

This chastened act of self-recognition enables Rabbit finally to be reconciled with Janice. They both admit that their lives are knotted inextricably together: "ties of blood, of time and guilt, family ties" (394). Confessing that they both have taken innocent life—she the baby, Rebecca, and he the girl,

Jill—they also admit their mutual betrayals and infidelities. "I feel so guilty," Rabbit declares. When Janice asks him to specify his guilt, he answers in typically Updikean fashion: "About everything." Hence his refusal to accept Janice's attempt to exonerate him of all blame. "I can't accept that," he replies (406).

Updike has declared in interviews that he rarely assigns his characters to so easy a fate as death, granting them instead the far more difficult destiny called life. Despite its apocalyptic atmosphere, therefore, *Rabbit Redux* has a comic conclusion that returns its characters to the quotidian world. Since the classic comic ending is marriage, this is the redemptive state to which Rabbit and Janice are led back. Their own home having been destroyed by fire, they are compelled to stay in a cheap motel called the Safe Haven. The moralistic manager suspects that they are a furtive couple in rendezvous. Rabbit and Janice are thus made to *pose* as the married couple they ineluctably *are*. Assuring the motel owner that they seek only a place to sleep, they keep their word, finding not sexual solace but the companionship of bodily rest. In the novel's final scene, Rabbit strokes Janice's naked flesh with an endearment that only matrimonial love can know: "He slides down an inch on the cool sheets and fits his microcosmic self limp into the curved crevice between the polleny offered nestling orbs of her ass; he would stiffen but his hand having let her breasts go comes upon the familiar dip of her waist, ribs to hip bone, where no bones are, soft as flight, fat's inward curve, slack, his babies from her belly. He finds this inward curve, and slips along it, sleeps. He. She. Sleeps. O.K.?" (406–7).

It is tempting to dismiss so jaunty an ending. Updike could have assuaged our incredulity had he situated Janice and Rabbit's reconciliation amidst the social and political Armageddon wherein they were first driven to distraction and alienation. Yet the ironic final question hints that not all is well that ends well. The Angstroms' renewed marriage will be haunted in the last two novels by their old troubles. Yet Janice and Rabbit are at least willing to risk connubial fidelity. They have learned that it is better to suffer while staying together than to thrive amidst alienated lives. That they live in an apocalyptically crazed age is not their chief problem; their real complaint lies with themselves and the ambiguous human condition they share.

Scattered Like Miraculous Bread: *Rabbit Is Rich*

Updike's third book in his tetralogy is a much more leisurely work than the first two. As an account of the late 1970s, the novel reflects the relative tranquillity of the time; the present-tense narration does not rush forward quite so rapidly as before. The apocalypse of the 1960s that spilled over into the early years of the new decade, with the fall of Saigon and the shame of Richard Nixon's resignation, seems an ancient memory. Economic inflation and the oil crisis are the only public cataclysms affecting Harry Angstrom's life. Yet it is a spiritually stagnant time, as Updike's coarsened diction and the blighted landscape reveal.

Angstrom's new problem is not marital or political, but financial. Janice has inherited her father's Toyota dealership, and Rabbit has become rich. Far from dwelling at ease in the Zion of financial prosperity, he is filled with dread about losing his new money. First he buys South African gold as a hedge against the falsely inflated value of Susan B. Anthony dollars. Then he swaps his Krugerrands for silver in fear that the price of gold will fall. In the novel's funniest scene, Janice and Rabbit lug huge satchels of silver from the exchange office to the bank, only to discover that their safety deposit box is too small for their large cache of coins. Their silver rolls wildly about the vault, until Rabbit finally gathers up three hundred of the metallic pieces and lugs them home. There he ponders the crazy ambiguity of his wealth: "His overcoat, so weighted, drags his shoulders down. He feels, as if the sidewalk now is a downslanted plane, the whole year dropping away under him, loss after loss. His silver is scattered, tinsel. His box will break, the janitor will sweep up the coins. It's all dirt anyway. . . . [T]hrough the murk he glimpses the truth that to be rich is to be robbed, to be rich is to be poor" (375).

There is more than a little self-pity here. The truly impoverished might rightly respond that it is they who have been robbed by such economic inequity. Yet Rabbit's confession points up Updike's fundamental contention that all people, even the rich, have their suffering. At age forty-six, Rabbit the once-lithe athlete is growing paunchy. It is not America alone that is running low on gas; so is Harry. He is more death-conscious than ever, thinking constantly of all the corpses that lie buried beneath the ground he treads. Reading of Skeeter's death in a shoot-out with police, remembering Jill's death by fire, and recalling baby Rebecca's drowning, Rabbit ponders the inescapable liability of his life: "There is no getting away: our sins, our seed, coil back" (33). Yet in our guilt lies our hope. "Without a sense of being in the wrong," Harry later observes, "we're no better than animals" (344).

Updike always links guilt with mortality, as if we were sinners not because we are fallen but because we are flesh. The scent of mortality-as-guilt thus pervades the entire novel. Like those who call life an incurable disease, Rabbit often envisions human existence as a progression toward oblivion. He fears no final judgment nor hopes for any resurrection from the dead. Even our personalities, he argues, are a series of perishing selves that we shed as snakes shed skin: "Our lives fade behind us before we die" (47). In a poignant bedroom scene, Rabbit grasps the fundamental human dilemma: "Life. Too much of it, and not enough. The fear that it will end some day, and the fear that tomorrow will be the same as yesterday" (354). Yet this same existential paradox keeps the sexual flame alight in Harry. He seeks to overcome the tedium of prosperity and the dread of death with the ardent eagerness of sexual expectation—"that cloudy inflation of self which makes us infants again and tips each moment with a plain excited purpose" (112).

Rabbit Is Rich is laden with a carnality that Updike's narrator describes with unprecedented rawness. It is at once a funnier and sadder kind of sex than we have previously seen. The anxiously rich Angstrom keeps thinking of *Consumer Reports* when he ought to be concentrating on more erotic matters. He pours Krugerrands over the naked Janice to arouse his desire for her. Already in 1981 Updike discerned that the American deification of sex would render it both dull and perverse. The wife-swapping scene at the end of the novel contains none of the usual Updikean ecstasy at the joy of illicit sex. Rabbit's anal intercourse with the menstruating, lupus-ridden Thelma proves to be an act more akin to death than life, an entry into "a void, a pure black box, a casket of perfect nothingness" (417).

Yet neither sex nor death can vex Rabbit as they once did. The real troubler of Rabbit's peace is his son. Though old enough to establish his independence, Nelson still lives at home, struggles to finish college, and impregnates his girlfriend before marrying her. The boy's irresponsibility is exceedingly irksome to the elder Angstrom, who conveniently forgets his own disastrous youth. Instead, the father waxes furious at a son made irresponsible by the cool and spectral medium of television: "Rabbit grunts. Spineless generation, no grit, nothing solid to tell a fact from a spook with. Satanism, pot, drugs, vegetarianism. Pathetic. Everything handed to them on a platter, think life's one big TV, full of ghosts" (161).

Angstrom is even angrier that his son repeats his own squalid history. Nelson is Rabbit but one generation removed, heedlessly committing his father's old mistakes. Just as Rabbit became a killer with his abandonment of Janice and Ruth, so does Nelson almost slay the child his wife is carrying. In a siege of anger at the drunken and pregnant Pru, Nelson half pushes, half watches her fall down a steep flight of stairs. Although both mother and baby are spared, Nelson soon flees as his father had done. Thus do the years circle upon one another, as history seems to accumulate like ever more burdensome baggage: "The more of it you have the more you have to live it," Harry thinks. "After a little while there gets to be too much of it to memorize and maybe that's when empires start to decline" (229).

There is no denying the pathos of Harry Angstrom's life. Thelma, his pathetic paramour, describes Rabbit's energetic embrace of life as both radiant and sad. The sadness is chiefly religious. God's putative agent proves to be a flaccid soul. Archie Campbell, the Episcopal minister who marries Nelson and Pru, has such a muddled faith that he has been nicknamed "Soupy." Harry's own waning faith makes God more memory than reality: "Now He had withdrawn, giving Harry the respect due from one well-off gentleman to another, but for a calling card left in the pit of the stomach, a bit of lead true as a plumb bob pulling Harry down toward all those leaden dead in the hollow earth below" (231).

Although *Rabbit Is Rich* exudes a melancholy found in neither of the first two novels, there are also signs of hope amidst the gathering gloom. When Nelson tries to "prove" himself as a salesman at the family Toyota agency by remarketing ancient gas-gulping convertibles, the results are at once funny and pitiable. In a fit of pique, Nelson smashes the old clunkers into a great heap of crumpled metal, prompting Rabbit to even crueler attacks on the boy's many failures. Yet finally it is not rage but pity that Angstrom pours out on poor Nelson. " 'I just don't like seeing you caught,' he blurts out to Nelson. 'You're too much me' " (208).

With middle-aged calming of his soul's troubled waters, Harry is learning that it is better to suffer the "daily seepage" (127) than to let life rush past in a single foolish spurt. Despite his murderous thoughts about Janice, he is bound to her by all the trouble they have endured together. The presence of Ma Springer, Angstrom's elderly mother-in-law, is also a reminder that their lives are not merely their own. Harry still chafes, of course, at the way the world is fencing him in ever more tightly. But his fury lacks its old bitterness and desperation.

Now that he no longer dwells on the raw edges of life, Rabbit has taken up golf again. He seeks neither to hit the perfect mystical drive down the center of the fairway nor to cultivate the leisured life he can now afford. He enjoys the game because it reflects the elusive magic of life itself: "Its performance cannot be forced and its underlying principle shies from being permanently named" (50). Yet Rabbit is not maturing into mildness and inanity so much as he is growing into suppleness and wisdom. The surprise graciously dawning on Rabbit is that his "inner dwindling" (97) contains a new liberty. This freedom is nicely figured in the novel's final scene. There Harry holds his new grandchild in his arms. Though complaining that she represents another nail driven into his coffin, Rabbit finds obvious delight in this newest Angstrom. The cowardly and cruel Harry has learned to forgive and receive, to let others feed off him as their very sustenance, and thus to experience the mystery of multiplied life: "In middle age you are carrying the world in a sense and yet it seems out of control more than ever, the self that you had as a boy all scattered and distributed like those pieces of bread in the miracle" (189).

Dying "Isn't So Bad": *Rabbit at Rest*

Since there is no English term for a fictional series longer than a tetralogy, Updike has declared *Rabbit at Rest* (1990) to be the last of his Angstrom books. The novel's only mystery is not whether but how and when Rabbit will go into the dark. Harry sees himself as but another moment in a great cosmic cycle whose biological pattern is circular and whose spiritual sum is zero: "The whole point of his earthly existence has been to produce little Nellie Angstrom, so he in turn could produce Judy and Roy, and so on until the sun burns out" (48). No wonder that the instant joy of drugs is so tempting for the young, as Rabbit's golfing buddy Bernie explains: "There are two routes to happiness. . . . Work for it, day after day, like you and I did, or take a chemical shortcut. With the world the way it is, these kids take the shortcut. The long way looks too long." Though an addict to sex rather than drugs, Rabbit agrees with the youth: "Yeah, well, it *is* long. And then when you've gone the distance, where's the happiness?" "Behind you," Bernie admits (58). Our most antinomian literary hero thus spends his last decade seizing the day, sinning his way to the grave.

The humbled calm that Rabbit seemed to have found at the end of *Rabbit Is Rich* is virtually absent in *Rabbit at Rest*. Now a fifty-six-year-old retired Toyota dealer afflicted with a failing heart, Angstrom remains a terrible hurricane of a man. He can still flatten other people's lives, even as he finally blows himself out. After almost drowning his granddaughter in a Florida boating mishap, Angstrom cuckolds his son and then leaves his wife. One final time, Rabbit runs, following the impulses of his own manic will. Yet nowhere in this final novel does Updike censure his self-seeking, other-forsaking hero. After all, Angstrom does no crime against life that life would not first do against him. "It's hell, to be a creature," he thinks, in an all-justifying complaint. "You are trapped in yourself, the genetic instructions, more strictly than in a cage" (105). With consummate artistry, Updike's narrator roams backward over the fields of Harry's youth, even as he drags us inexorably forward to his dying.

Still lurching ahead in the jumpy present-tense narration that Updike pioneered in 1960, Rabbit not only runs but also remembers and judges. He discerns in his own demise a sign that the entire American fabric is coming unraveled. "Everything falling apart," Rabbit laments, "airplanes, bridges, eight years under Reagan of nobody minding the store, making money out of nothing, running up debt, trusting in God" (9). Mr. Shimada, the Toyota executive who comes to investigate the problems at Rabbit's agency, complains in splendidly cracked English that America is no longer the wonder but the sinkhole of history:

> Nevertheless, these years of postwar, Japanese, man and woman, have great respect for United States. Rike big brother. But in recent times big brother act rike rittle brother, always cry and comprain. Want many favors in trade, saying Japanese unfair competition. Why unfair? Make something, cheaper even with duty and transportation costs, people rike, people buy. American way in old times. But in new times America make nothing, just do mergers, do acquisitions, rower taxes, raise national debt. Nothing comes out, all goes in—foreign goods, foreign capital. American take everything, give nothing. Rike big brack hole. (390)

Rabbit blames his family's calamities on the badness of the times. Surrounded by so great a cloud of troubles, who could have done much better? Yet Rabbit is no victimologist. Believing that things could have been much better than they are, he is enraged that Nelson has become a cocaine addict who has pilfered the profits from the family's once thriving Toyota dealership. Yet in his frenzy of accusation against Nelson, Rabbit remembers that his son is himself writ small—a youth saddled with his own vagrancy, irresponsibility, and egomania. Yet the parallels are not only negative. Just as Rabbit proved to be more than a *Schussel*, so is Nelson more than a fornicating dopehead. By the novel's end, he has been reconciled to his wife, even as he has found a cure for his drug addiction—if only by embracing the trite pieties of a twelve-step program. Nelson's grace before meals is vaporous with New Age spirituality: "Peace. Health. Sanity. Love" (402).

This descent to religious pragmatism, regarding whatever "works" as true and good, eviscerates Harry's life of true ultimacy. Sex and athletics were once his quick path to a glory that still glimmered with transcendence. As a youth waiting nervously to enter the game of life, Rabbit was obsessed with the God whose mystery seemed akin to his own mysterious future. Now the deity-hucksters of television are on such friendly terms with the Wholly Other that they enable Harry to forget God amidst the business of dying. His faith thus hangs by the unraveling thread of a double negation: "I don't *not* believe" (206).

> Funny, about Harry and religion. When God hadn't a friend in the world, back there in the Sixties, he couldn't let go of Him, and now when the preachers are all praying through bullhorns he can't get it up for Him. He is like a friend you've had so long you've forgotten what you liked about Him. You'd think after that heart scare, but in a way the closer you get the less you think about it, like you're in His hand already. Like you're out on the court instead of on the bench swallowing down butterflies and trying to remember the plays. (450)

Television and advertising are the purveyors of our everyday nihilism. They reduce everything to either amusement or consumption. Even the family, the primal institution of society, has become the subject of entertainment, though Rabbit can still tell the real from the feigned: "TV families and your own are hard to tell apart, except yours isn't interrupted every six minutes by commercials and theirs don't get bogged down into nothingness, a state where nothing happens, no skit, no zany visitors, no outburst on the laugh track, nothing at all but boredom and a lost feeling" (468). Despite this protest, Harry and his kin turn to television during times of crisis. After a near-fatal boat accident, when Rabbit and his granddaughter tack desperately back to shore they do not voice hymns of praise but empty jingles: " 'Coke is it,' Judy sings, 'the most refreshing taste around, Coke is it, the one that never lets you down, Coke is it, the biggest taste you ever found' " (140).

There being no God present to judge or forgive, no community to sustain or check, Rabbit faces death with all that is left: his inveterate eroticism. He fulfills, in a frightening way, the prophecy voiced by Freddy Thorne in *Couples.* Confessing a creed akin to Updike's own, Thorne declares that we dwell in "one of those dark ages that visits mankind between millennia, between the death and rebirth of gods, when there is nothing to steer by but sex and stoicism and the stars" (*Couples,* paperback edition, 389). After the eclipse of God, only sex remains divinely alive. In one of his last meditations, Angstrom offers this grimly hedonistic testimony: "One thing he knows is if he had to give parts of his life back the last thing he'd give back is the fucking. . . . A lot of this other stuff you're supposed to be grateful for isn't where it matters" (*Rest* 471).

Why not give thanks—with Garry Wills and Frederick Crews and a host of hostile critics—that such a shallow fellow has at last, like an old horse, been put down? The answer is not far to find. As Conrad said of Lord Jim, Rabbit Angstrom is one of us: the average sensual man, the American Adam in all of his dangerous innocence, the carnally-minded creature whom the moralistic religion and politics of our popular culture cannot encompass. When challenged by his cardiologist to define himself as anything more than a poorly functioning machine, Rabbit thinks in quintessential Updikean terms: "A God-made one-of-a-kind with an immortal soul breathed in. A vehicle of grace. A battlefield of good and evil. An apprentice angel" (237). This Cartesian vision of the soul as an addendum to the body, a ghost within the machine, denies the psychosomatic unity of human life. For Rabbit as also for his creator, we are not integrated body-souls so much as bifurcated spirit-animals. This means that we are the only creatures for whom sex can be more than a joyless act of instinct—it is also an erotic desire for spiritual exaltation. Yet such carnal urges require ethical control if they are not to become socially and personally destructive, even as these same passional drives prove exceedingly difficult to confine within a strictly ethical existence.

Such a sexually tragicomic condition lies at the center of *Rabbit at Rest*. The closer Harry approaches to death, the more he is obsessed with his own carnality. As he lies distraught in the Florida sand after being rescued from death's double assault—a heart attack during a boating accident—Rabbit does not turn his mind to Last Things. He stares up, instead, at the spandex crotch of his daughter-in-law's bathing suit. Alone in a North Carolina motel in a final flight from his Pennsylvania family, Angstrom masturbates "to show himself he's still alive" (448). Like the Reverend Thomas Marshfield in *A Month of Sundays*, Angstrom reveres the act of self-pleasuring as "the saving grace note on the baffled chord of self" (4). Rabbit also grants the dying Thelma Harrison, his lupus-ridden former mistress, one last peek at his penis. Such a deathbed sight is appropriate, he believes, for the one who taught him that sex is our true soul food.

Yet Rabbit dines largely alone at the banquet of carnality, even when he is having sex. The act of coition is not wondrously communal but strangely individual: it establishes his sense of self-worth, as he discovers his own value in being desired by another. Every available woman, even the Holocaust survivor he meets in the hallway of his Florida condominium, serves as a potential object of his sexual self-regard. To bed down his daughter-in-law is not, therefore, to cuckold his son and to commit virtual incest so much as to celebrate his own selfhood: "It had felt like he was seeing himself reflected, mirrored in a rangy young long-haired left-handed woman" (432).

Angstrom admits that males find their identity in their sexuality far more readily than do females. That women give themselves to men without self-interest is almost beyond his fathoming. In a telling confession, Thelma makes clear the reason: "You've never loved me, Harry. You just loved the fact that I loved you" (199). Sitting by his own wife at his lover's funeral, remembering Thelma in her wanton nakedness, Harry ponders the meaning of sex once more: "Women are actresses, tuning their part to each little audience. Her part with him was to adore him, to place her body at his service as if disposing of it" (374). Yet there are times when Angstrom praises "that strange way women have, of really caring about somebody beyond themselves" (305). He also confesses that the waters of thankfulness stream much more generously from women than from men: "in this [opposing] direction, men to women, the flow of gratitude is never great" (321).

Here lies the real ambiguity of Rabbit Angstrom's life. He has lived for five and a half decades by asking only a single question: "What's in it for me?" (227). Yet he knows that there is something drastically wrong with such a selfish life, and that the world has become an increasingly arid place as the pools of charity evaporate. He is haunted by the absence of nuns at the Catholic hospital where he undergoes angioplasty: "Vocations drying up, nobody wants to be selfless any more, everybody wants their fun. No more nuns, no more rabbis. No more good people, waiting to have their fun in the afterlife. The thing about the afterlife, it kept this life within bounds somehow, like the Russians. Now there's just Japan, and technology, and the profit motive, and getting all you can while you can" (272).

After a lifetime of "getting all you can while you can," Harry has learned a lasting negative lesson: his "failure or refusal to love any substance but his own" (328). Rabbit's life thus describes a wide arc that turns back upon itself in a literally fatal repetition. The fifty-six-year-old Rabbit suffers his deadly heart attack in the same place where we first met him in 1960: on the basketball court, trying one final time to win. Though his consuming egotism prevents his being a good man, he remains the hero of Updike's tetralogy: a man unwilling to quit, to surrender, to shrink into death like a defeated and pathetic victim.

Could Rabbit's life have been radically other than it turns out to be? Updike suggests that it could not. Progress and regress are, for him, opposite and ambiguous aspects of the single reality called life. We do not see further than our forebears because we are not mounted on their shoulders. All the forward motion is, in fact, a way of standing still. As our great elegist of life's heart breaking circularity, Updike reminds us that we are finished before we have barely begun, that our lives are but brief candles rocketed into the void. Thus did he choose to end his tetralogy in the early rather than the late autumn of 1989. In November of that year, a radically unrepetitive event occurred: the Berlin Wall was torn down, as one of the most hideous tyrannies of our century collapsed. What, one wonders, would Rabbit have made of this breaking of history's cycle, this strange new infusion of political and religious hope for so many millions?

Though ambiguity and repetition remain for Updike the final realities of human existence, they do not cancel its worth, as Rabbit learns in the end. He has fled to Florida, hoping there to escape the fury of his wife and son. Rabbit fears that there is no hope for mercy. Yet he finds it despite his utter unworthiness. The wife whom he has so often berated as a "dumb mutt" pronounces her last and unreluctant blessing upon her husband: "I forgive you" (511). Yet the prime reality remains Rabbit's own heroic confession that he is more sinning than sinned against, a creature whose sexual guilt and glory neither the angels nor the apes can know. Hence the dying Rabbit's refusal to give wise advice to his grieving son, even though the youth looks desperately to his father for a definitive last word: " 'Well, Nelson,' he says, 'all I can tell you is, it isn't so bad' " (512). Having no hope for the life to come, Harry cannot declare the end of his life to be unambiguously good. Yet neither will he call it an evil and unworthy thing. Together with those whom he has loved and harmed most deeply, Rabbit Angstrom faces his death with the self-consciousness that only human creatures can have. He is John Updike's pilgrim hero who has found both life and death to be wonderfully, terribly, ambiguously good.

Notes

1. All references to the Rabbit novels are to the Knopf editions.

Paula R. Buck

9 The Mother Load
A Look at Rabbit's Oedipus Complex

Is Rabbit a mama's boy? The same Harold Harry Hassy Angstrom—high school basketball star, "zilch" husband, lifelong womanizer who cuckolds his own son? It's so: the evidence is persuasive that John Updike's Rabbit novels present a case study of the oedipal conflict in the small-town American hero. Several critics have noted the connection between Updike's work and Freudian theory. Robert Detweiler, emphasizing art, offers a cautious point of view: Updike's characters "are first believable people with problems that may or may not have psychoanalytical labels" (*John Updike* 53).[1] Ralph C. Wood, however, makes a much stronger case: citing the autobiographical poem "Midpoint" as evidence of the author's egocentrism, he argues that Updike is, "indeed, more Freudian than Freud." In fact, Wood considers the struggle of "primary narcissism" against cultural strictures "Updike's call to arms" (202).[2]

Mary O'Connell and Judie Newman suggest meliorative irony in Updike's treatment of Freudian models. Working primarily from a feminist viewpoint, O'Connell stresses the "homicidal pattern" in the first three Rabbit novels, arguing that Updike "has been analyzing and challenging socially constructed masculinity," exposing its "limitations and proscriptions as the source of a great deal of unhappiness for both men and women" (3).[3] Newman offers a more directly Freudian analysis than O'Connell, yet she also believes that Updike's work, particularly his treatment of Rabbit as victim, "foregrounds the horrible price of social cohesion, its delusory basis, and the patriocentric nature of the Freudian idea." She suggests that Updike's commentary may be revisionist: "In the civilization of the Fifties the repressive father has been edged out, replaced by society itself which now acts directly upon the individual" (39).[4] One comment from Updike himself indicates support for this position. In a conversation with Frank Gado in 1973, Updike, discussing the undeniable yearnings of the id, says that "there is no way to reconcile these individual wants to the very real need of any society to set strict limits and confine its members" (109). His words suggest skepticism about the success of Freud's systematic attempts to explain, and perhaps resolve, this conflict.

Assigning a post-Freudian attitude to the Rabbit novels may well be valid, yet certain indicators suggest that Updike's depiction of life in Brewer, Mt. Judge, and Deleon is colored by biographical emotion, full of cultural lag, at least as much as by skeptical critical theory.[5] Updike, "the chronicler not simply of middle-class complacency, but of the ironic bind wherein we are all comi-tragically caught," offers Rabbit a full measure of sympathy for being caught in snares that seem to beg for Freudian analysis (Wood 205). Rabbit ducks into and out of uteral zones in misery until he finally understands that "the red cave he thought only had a front entrance and exit turns out to have a back door as well" (*Rest* 511).[6]

This alternate route leads to a spiritual resolution of Rabbit's struggles; in fact, Updike consistently asserts a sense of the divine in his main character. That he also uses Christian terms to frame Rabbit's eventual redemption indicates that Updike may be piecing together the two systems most significant in his own development.[7] What comes of the merging of Freudian and Christian clues is a poignant image of twentieth-century manhood in search of itself, substituting fragments of the World's Great Thoughts for personhood and community.

Updike brilliantly captures the sterile environment of postindustrial America in his description of Brewer, a latter-day Thebes. It is a relentlessly walled-in, dry place, suffering the slow death of all blue-collar towns in industrial Pennsylvania. Rabbit, one of its native sons, feels the crushing of the bankrupt economic and social systems: "If Kroll's could go, the courthouse could go, the banks could go. When the money stopped, they could close down God himself" (*Rest* 461). His dilemma, like that of Oedipus, derives from his lack of answers to riddles beyond his ken.[8] Inextricably bound to his hometown, Rabbit acts out the tragedy of making "natural" mistakes in an arguably unnatural world (105). Darting away on one seemingly futile flight after another, Rabbit returns to Brewer, always fighting for meaning, always looking to his family as the key. Persistence counts, as he tells his grandson, Roy: "If you don't stay to the end, the sadness sticks with you" (102).

One source of this sadness can be verified from the perspective of sociological determinism. Nancy Chodorow, noting Lévi-Strauss, recognizes the negative impact of the environment on marriage, an institution of central importance in the Rabbit tetralogy: "In our society marriage has assumed a larger and larger emotional weight supposedly off-setting the strains of increasingly alienated and bureaucratized work in the paid economy" (68). Updike shows what happens to such families: from cradle to cradle, generations of Angstroms create and battle monsters, themselves, and suffer under the load. Social determinism notwithstanding, a much more far-reaching analysis of Rabbit's angst can be derived from the ancient myth of Oedipus as reinterpreted by Sigmund Freud and refined further by Jacques Lacan.[9] Freud's contemporary audience resisted the thought that mother-son or father-daughter incest was a necessary, universal stage of psychological development.[10] Freud himself offers this riposte: "It cannot be said that the world has shown much gratitude to psychoanalytic research for its revelation of the Oedipus complex. . . . We must reconcile ourselves to the fact which was recognized by Greek legend itself as inevitable fate" (*Lectures* 207–8).[11]

Well aware that the open discussion of mother-son and father-daughter incest was taboo, Freud insists upon its value. He assesses the oedipal trilogy of the "devout" Sophocles as "fundamentally amoral": "It absolves men from moral responsibility, exhibits the gods as promoters of crime [breaking taboo] and shows the importance of the moral impulses of men which struggle against time" (*Lectures* 331).

Good news for Rabbit! Freud would have understood him: far from being a lone voice, Rabbit suffers consequences of needs unmet for him, his father, and generations of fathers before him. Expanding on the subject, Freud asserts that "mankind as a whole may have acquired its sense of guilt, the ultimate source of religion and morality at the beginning of its history, in connection with the Oedipal complex" (*Lectures* 332). He is deflated by the sense that his primary theory has been "rejected from real life" and "left to imaginative writing" (208).[12]

Updike's imaginative writing about the oedipal theory rings with respect for its verity. Consider his Freudian description of Brewer and its effect on Rabbit's immediate role model: Earl Angstrom, Rabbit's father, appears to his son as "one of the hundreds of skinny, whining codgers in and around this city, men who have sucked this same brick tit for sixty years and have dried up with it" (*Redux* 15). If Brewer is depicted as unnourishing mother, then Rabbit has no choice but to return to its "snug" streets so he can "[hurt] himself with the memory of his old self that clings to almost every corner of the Brewer area" (*Rest* 293, 181). In Freudian terms, Rabbit is showing neurotic symptoms of untreated infantile anxiety, a problem that can produce masochism: under the strain of missing a parent, "the child behaves as an adult; that is, he changes his libido into fear when he cannot bring it to gratification, and the grown-up who becomes neurotic on account of ungratified libido behaves like a child" (Freud, *Writings* 616).[13]

Marked by fierce, neurotic clinging, Rabbit hauls memories of Mom into every new situation; his lifelong quest for fulfillment arguably begins from a position of infantile deprivation, a condition that magnifies his arguably sexual desire for appropriate mothering. " 'Desire,' Freud explains, 'is a relation of being to lack. . . . Being comes into existence as an exact function of this lack' " (qtd. in Lacan, *Book II* 223). In the introduction to his *Three Essays on the Theory of Sexuality,* Freud directly addresses charges of overdoing the erotic element: critics, he claims, "should remember how closely the enlarged sexuality of psycho-analysis coincides with the Eros of the divine Plato" (xviii). The suggestion of divinity in Rabbit's character, often noted as a paradox, fits right in with Freudian thought.[14]

Jacques Lacan posits that "the Freudian world isn't a world of things, it isn't a world of being, it is a world of desire as such." Firmly endorsing the fundamental importance of Freud's work with the Oedipus complex, Lacan accepts no philosophical possibility of the divine: "All that life is concerned with is seeking repose as much as possible while awaiting death" (*Book II* 223).[15] He does, however, credit Freud with articulating a revolutionary concept of mankind: by assigning individuals the responsibility for recognizing and coming to grips with their unconscious motives, Freud sets them off on a "pursuit of the beyond," the possibility of coping with "lack": "In the pursuit of this beyond, which is nothing, it harks back to the feeling of a being with self-consciousness, which is nothing but its reflection in the world of things." Lacan defines Freud's accomplishment in terms that do seem to contradict his own nihilism: "This revolution brings man back into the world as creator" (224).

Updike puts Rabbit into a clearly needy position, leading him "unknowingly" through one bad relationship after another. Freud offers both a curse and a blessing: "Even if a man has repressed his evil impulses into the unconsciousness, . . . he is nevertheless bound to be aware of this responsibility" (*Lectures* 331). Like layers of gauze, Rabbit's experiences in "the world of things" blind him, in oedipal fashion, but only temporarily. Updike provides opportunities for Rabbit to see his own reflection and to articulate his own destiny. Lacan's "moment de virage" is most helpful here: he explains it as a "turning point in which the individual makes a triumphant exercise of his own image in the mirror, of himself. Through certain correlations in his behavior, we can understand that what occurs here for the first time is the anticipated seizure of mastery" (*Book I* 146). Rabbit has to wait for his really significant turning point; but when it comes, it comprises Greek myth, Freudian analysis, Lacanian linguistics, and Christianity. Rabbit—all but blindfolded in the layers of experience he has amassed—eventually does become a creator, the mystic that his friend Mrs. Smith has always known him to be: "That is what you have, Harry: life" (*Run* 207).

In the beginning, what Harry has, for better and worse, is his mother. Even a firm critic would have to see some common sense in one of the earliest applications of Freud's "pan-sexual" approach: "The person in charge of [an infant] who, after all, is as a rule, his mother . . . strokes him, kisses him, rocks him"; she is "only fulfilling her task in teaching the child to love" (*Three Essays* 89). If only she were fulfilling her task and doing it as naturally and successfully as this simple assertion would make it sound!

The system thickens immediately as Freud refines the mother's probably unconscious "intention": she "clearly treats [the infant] as a substitute for a complete sexual object" and "affords him an unending source of sexual excitation and satisfaction from his erotogenic zones" (Freud, *Three Essays* 89). Enter Mary Angstrom, the large-boned, raw-knuckled, cinnamon-scented amazon who almost palpably populates her son's every thought, waking and sleeping. She brings horror to the central character throughout the space of four novels, their number mirroring the squareness of Brewer and the tight world inscribed by the four corners of her worn, mighty, enamel kitchen table. She stands there often, "silent . . . with her wet cheek and red arms . . . a mad captive" (*Run* 155). Updike is careful to show this mother, like her son, as a victim.

Locked into a paternalistic society, as is her prototype Jocasta, Mary Angstrom is forced to work out in non-nurturing pall a life for herself and her family. Able to function only from her household, she is faced with a husband she considers weak and, worse, unsympathetic to her darling baby boy. Mary and her husband have spent many uncommunicative years; she ironically develops Parkinson's disease, which creates a physical halting in her already impaired ability to speak (*Redux* 15). Starved for affection, connection, Mary could count on one thing: her son always "gave her himself, his trophies, his headlines. Mom had seemed satisfied: lives more than things concerned her" (84). While she was trying to teach Rabbit to love, she was also teaching him to respect her power, a force "he used to fear more than anything, more than vampires, more than polio, more than thunder or God, or being late for school" (175). As his dreams later show, Rabbit has picked up both the thesis and the antithesis of maternal warmth from this woman: "Her tyrant love would freeze the world" (175).[16]

Calvin S. Hall explains in *A Primer of Freudian Psychoanalysis* that "actions involving the erotic zones bring the child into conflict with his parents, and the resulting anxieties stimulate the development of a large number of adaptations, displacements, defenses, transformations, compromises, and sublimations" (103). Indeed, the Rabbit series seems a dramatization of such developments. Let us first briefly consider the ramifications of Harry Angstrom's responses to oral stimulation at his mother's breast. In what Freud calls "the oral zone," each of five "modes" is a "prototype of a personality trait," establishing a model for "adjusting to a painful or disturbing state" (Hall 104).

The first mode, "taking in," can produce acquisitiveness (Hall 103). For Harry, not quite a model of the ambitious American consumer, acquisitiveness takes the shape of gathering gold and overeating.[17] In both cases, Updike blatantly sets forth the childish selfishness of his hero. Showing Janice his thirty pieces of gold, Rabbit feels "his prick firming up and stretching the fabric of his jockey shorts" (Rich 201). What makes this scene most interesting is that it takes place on the background of a "Pennsylvania Dutch quilt, small rectangular patches sewed together by patient biddies, graded from pale to dark to form a kind of dimensional effect, of four large boxes," echoing the four corners of Brewer's buildings and those of his mother's kitchen table (200–201). As he makes love to Janice, "Harry's skin is bitten as by ice when he lies on his back"; he soon switches position—suggesting that the homey, motherly quilt triggers discomfort and guilt (203). Always concerned for his own sensual well-being, an older Harry opts out of sharing a peanut bar with his grandchildren: "The first half is so good he eats the second and even dumps the sweet crumbs out of the wrapper and into his palm and licks them all up like an anteater" (Rest 7). This selfishness suggests Harry's hunger, which appears as a sublimation of his persistent neediness—now an oral fixation.[18]

The second mode, "holding on," may produce tenacity (Hall 104). In its most poignant form, this trait may best be illustrated by Rabbit's keeping clippings of his high school glory days long after anyone but him thought they were impressive: "resurrected from the attic where his dead parents had long kept them, even under glass the clippings keep yellowing" (Rich 2). Displayed in the Toyota showroom at the suggestion of Fred Springer, an unusually supportive father-in-law, the clippings have no value to a new breed of customer.[19] Even Rabbit eventually loses interest, leaving the impression that only mother had truly worshiped at this shrine and that retaining its unnatural echoes produces the compulsive mind-lock on youth that eventually chases Harry into his coronary (Rest 503–7).[20]

"Biting," the third oral response, can lead to destructiveness (Hall 105).

Dubbed "Mr. Death" by his lover Ruth, Rabbit eventually destroys several institutions—including his wife's loyalty, irrational as it is; and the one potentially adult love offered him by Thelma Harrison.[21] By now, the negative patterns in Rabbit's oral adaptations should be clear. Somehow he has not had enough to drink, so he does continue to search for mother's milk in the creamy (sometimes cocoa) skins of whores, waitresses, neighbors, friends, and relatives, all of whom frequently intermingle in dreams and fantasies and in reality to form variations on the images he has of his mother.[22]

"Spitting out," the response that leads to contemptuousness, takes at least two very interesting forms (Hall 105). Rabbit consistently disdains those for whom he feels responsibility, seeing them as burdens that he feels inadequate to carry. When his son, Nelson, confronts his seeming lack of affection for his family, Rabbit honestly responds, "I like everybody. I just don't like getting boxed in" (*Rich* 324). Consistently running from the limits of conventional adult behavior, Rabbit spits out epithets constantly: Janice is a mutt; Nelson is a bum; Roy, "from the numb look of his prick, will be a solid citizen" (*Rest* 120). Rabbit develops a fascinating identification with the United States government, which he sees as keeper of the world's inept masses; he feels himself "a float of a man, in a parade of dependents" (84); Updike masterfully brings this fantasy to life as he parades Rabbit down Brewer's Main Street dressed as Uncle Sam himself (371).

"Closing," the final primal oral response, is the one that Updike spares Rabbit. It leads to refusal and negativism (Hall 107). Rabbit's appetite for life persists through the last page of the last novel; only when he finally feels satisfaction of his rampant desires can Rabbit rest. His final action, the utterance of one last word, is the result of years of work. He earns his right to speak, to be, and to signify meaning beyond his individuality. As Lacan explains, "Desire emerges [and] just as it becomes embodied in speech, it merges with symbolism" (*Book II* 234). Until that moment, Updike puts Rabbit through extended neurotic paces.

As if dealing with the "pre-genital" complications of having Mary Angstrom of Brewer, Pennsylvania, as a mother were not enough, Updike manfully drags his main character through the tortures of the "sexual zone" (Freud, *Three Essays* 38). The presence of libido, "a quantitatively variable force which could serve as a measure of processes and transformations occurring in the field of sexual excitation" and "distinguishable from the energy which must be supposed to underlie mental processes in general," can be seen only when it attaches to an "object" (89). Unattached, this energy is "narcissistic ego-libido," a condition Freud considers "the original state of

things" (84). It is arguable that Harry Angstrom suffers both narcissism and
the inability to form a healthy attachment to an appropriate "object" other
than his mother.

Predictably, his first attempt to replace her is inappropriate: Rabbit's at-
tentions go to his sister, Mim. Freud asserts the presence of a new baby as a
standard challenge to any child: "When other children appear on the scene,
the Oedipus complex is enlarged into a family complex" (*Lectures* 333). In
Oedipus Myth and Complex, Patrick Mullahy explains that a boy child is
likely to replace the "faithless mother" by considering his baby sister as the
new love object (61). Updike uses this example of familial pathology as he
works Rabbit into a full-blown oedipal dilemma—while he is still in only the
earliest phase of sexual development (Freud, *Three Essays* 66). He has not
even begun to engage the woes of entanglement with his father, but his attitudes and behaviors already show much damage.[23]

That Mim is in fact a love object for Harry is most clear. Frequently recalling happy days of sledding with her, of sitting in the dark kitchen with
her, of needing to protect her, Rabbit eventually allows her to act as a whore
for him with Charlie Stavros to save his failing marriage with Janice. In fact,
he is so clear about his feelings that when Janice asks him to identify one
woman who would be "wonderful enough" for him, he replies, "Mim" (*Redux* 71). A clear assertion that Rabbit sees Mim and Mom as one (note the
similarity in names) comes in his remark to his hapless wife when he concludes, "I know Mom must have been sexy, because look at Mim" (*Rich*
136).[24]

Such a connection must have registered on Mary's radar, and clearly her
dubious love does Mim some sort of harm—at least from a conventional perspective: though Mim does escape Brewer, she does so by becoming a whore.
Such a development would be much more shocking without the benefit of
the Freudian perspective that "mothers resent their sons' choices, these new
versions of themselves"; Mary has presented Mim a clear challenge, one Mim
chooses to "resolve" in a reactionary way (Freud, *Three Essays* 94). Nevertheless basically sympathetic to her mother, she tells Harry, "Mom is a great lady
with nowhere to put it" (*Redux* 309).

Harry knows where Mom "put it": she is inside him, and so is his sister.
He sees Mim (possibly Mimic) as a tough Rabbit, somehow able to withstand
the maternal force he finds so overpowering: "She is himself, with the com-
bination jiggled" (*Redux* 316). Later in his life, Rabbit is able to recognize that
Mim is more than a sister: she is "himself transposed into quite another key.
. . . [A]s his own blood sister [she] had a certain unforced claim over him no

woman since has been able to establish" (*Rest* 76). She alone is the organic link between his mother's flesh and his own, and this connection creates a Freudian "ambivalence" that forms the basis for his identity crisis: Harry is part male and part female, living out the Freudian assertion that "every person is constitutionally bi-sexual" (Freud, *Three Essays* 66; Hall 110). His identity stretches beyond bounds of gender and of generation, paving the way for a plethora of real and imaginary transformations and transpositions: he begins to speak in the broken phrases his mother's Parkinson's has modeled for him; he sees Janice as Pru; he sees Nelson as a sissy; he envisions a black female Buddha as a sexual partner. Though Rabbit may appear "perverse" because he is out of touch with reality, a Freudian perspective allows for temporary "neurotic" distortions within the bounds of normal development (Freud, *Writings* 625):

> Over and above all of the other virtues of his [Freud's] theory stands this one—it tries to envisage full-bodied individuals living partly in a world of reality and partly in a world of make-believe, beset by conflicts and inner contradictions, yet capable of rational thought and action, moved by forces of which they have little knowledge and by aspirations that are beyond their reach, by turn confused and clear-headed, frustrated and satisfied, hopeful and despairing, selfish and altruistic; in short a complex human being. (Hall, Preface np)

When Harry enters his "phallic period," he is already fragmented and unsure of his personhood (*Run* 117; Freud, *Three Essays* 66). His father, the picture of personal impotence, is even more cowardly than his prototype Laius. Yet he is threatening—not so much because of his connection with Mary, but because of his resemblance to Mim. The clearest perspective on the issue comes from Jack Eccles, the minister. As he meets Mim for the first time, he can see it all: "Mrs. Angstrom's nose has delicacy on the girl's face, . . . but when her father stands beside her, Eccles sees that it is his height; their bodies, the beautiful girl's and the weary man's, are the same. They have the same narrowness: a durable edge that, Eccles knows after seeing the wounds open under Mrs. Angstrom's spectacles, can cut. . . . They'll get through. They know what they're doing" (*Run* 155). What they are doing is what Rabbit cannot manage: they are adapting to strengthen their own responses to the force of the mother load.[25]

Considering the role of the father in Harry's life is a relatively uncomplicated venture. Presented primarily as a hereditary deficit, Earl Angstrom offers little challenge to the developing force of his son. Already world-weary and defeated, he remains self-effacing, willing even to sacrifice his job if doing so will help Rabbit (*Redux* 211). Stymied by the negative turn Rabbit's life has taken, Earl bemoans his distress over his son's abandonment of Janice: "I just don't see how Harry could make such a mess. . . . He was a neat worker." In this same conversation, Earl does present the perfunctory oedipal clash by slapping his wife with his disgust for Harry and his sympathy for Janice: "He is my enemy. . . . That night I spent walking the streets looking for him he became my enemy. You can't talk. You didn't see the girl's face" (*Run* 151). The force of his remarks, however, is lost in his basically passive character; he seems to agree with his own father that life, death, all of "it is to be regretted but it can't be helped." Supported in his role as good guy by his coworker Buchanan, Earl—with his poor false teeth and painful vomiting—seems to die early, relinquishing his space to his son without much of a fuss at all (*Redux* 83, 96, 151).

Rabbit does seek surrogate fathers in the persons of Father Eccles, who spends a good deal of time concerned about his relationship with his own father; Stavros, hubris-filled lover of both Rabbit's wife and his sister; the unlikely Skeeter, in whose presence Rabbit feels safe going to sleep; and his Jewish golf buddies, who seem wise to him. The primary focus of his displaced love for his dad is his high school basketball coach Marty Tothero, a most predictable choice. Yet Harry finds enough similarity between his coach and his mother to make the paternal connection pale: "Next to [my] mother, Tothero had the most force" (*Run* 21). Updike makes the final judgment as he places father and son in a little dive near Verity Press: "Working ten years together they have grown into the love they would have had in Harry's childhood, had not his mother loomed so large between them" (*Redux* 14).

The truly frightening product that remains as a result of Rabbit's maladapted response to his dad is his sadistic treatment of central people in his life, primarily of his son, Nelson.[26] Earl's disappointment creates an indelible stain on his already twisted son; yet it will be this "reaction formation," the substitution of sadism as an active response to Earl's heinous masochism, that eventually saves Harry's integrity (Hunt 108). In one of the many unpleasant conversations among the Angstroms, Mim questions Rabbit's lack of assertiveness. The damning remark flies forth: "Never hurt a fly if he could help it, used to worry me. . . . As if we had a girl and didn't know it. Isn't that the truth, Mother?" (*Redux* 318). True blue, Mary stutters out her defense: "Never. All boy"; but the reader now knows what Rabbit has always known. He may be the mama's boy he fears his father may be. He may not know what a man should, could, must be—and until he finds the one human being who makes all such questions relative, he continues in his distress.[27]

Believing that his mother is "the only person who knows him," Rabbit launches a lifelong trek back to the uterus—even though he resists his mother's efforts to help him reenter the safety zone: at age thirty-one, Rabbit expresses his perception that "she is still trying to call him forth from her womb" and wonders if she can't see that "he is an old man" (*Redux* 175). Actually, he has a conflicting impression that she has already prematurely "shoved him out from shore" by sadistically informing him of the marriage of his first extrafamilial love, Mary Ann (*Run* 184). Rabbit does show some resentment toward his mother: "As a human being I'm about C minus. As a husband I'm about zilch. . . . Some life. Thanks, Mom" (*Redux* 91). Nevertheless, his attachment to her determines all of his responses to not only women, but most men; and it renders him forever horny in a most adolescent way (91).

As he attempts to form healthy attachments to other love objects, Rabbit encounters nothing but obstruction.[28] Both of his parents mark as the inception of his downfall his brief escape to Texas, where he encounters a whore (*Run* 152). The pivotal concept here is that she is "motherly" (28). A cursory list of succeeding surrogates becomes almost amusing. Janice, his bride, oedipally chained in her own right; Ruth, another whore, whom he abandons with child, though like a good Oedipus, he does so unknowingly; Lucy Eccles, the minister's wife; Mrs. Smith, whose own husband's name was Harry; Jill, who breaks the mother barrier into a mother-daughter dyad; Cindy, primarily a lust object who teaches him sailing, the one skill that can lead him toward a solution; poor Peggy Fosnacht, the walleyed mother of Nelson's only male friend; Thelma, the one person who sees in him the same kind of gift as did Mrs. Smith; and even the outlandish last-ditch effort Mrs. Zabritski, his aging neighbor in Florida—all keep Rabbit in a state of tumescent expectancy. He looks diligently until he finds the connection he most needs: general whoring around and the specific cuckolding of his father and his friends do not fill his need, but cuckolding his own son finally does the job. Without a Freudian perspective, we might see Rabbit as the "monster" even Tothero feared he may be; however, with one, something more insightful does develop (*Run* 46).

In the epigraph of *Rabbit, Run* Updike cites Pascal's *Pensées* 507: "The motions of Grace, the hardness of the heart; external circumstances." Freud credits the development of a healthy personality to "the ability to overcome frustrations, avoid pain, resolve conflicts, and reduce anxiety" (Hall

113). Updike expands upon each point of his epigraph, providing an instructive series of external circumstances that surely produce conflict and anxiety and, at long last, an odd measure of grace that softens Rabbit's defensive shell. He does develop a conscience, a superego, "the heir of the Oedipus complex because it takes the place of the Oedipus complex" (Hall 110).

"Hardness of heart" in Rabbit's case takes the form of sadistic behavior. Freud makes the explanation easy to comprehend: "It may be assumed that the impulse of cruelty arises from the instinct for mastery and appears at a period of sexual life at which the genitals have not yet taken over their later [progenitive] role" (*Three Essays* 59). Rabbit's genitals have surely been active and technically progenitive, yet he remains a psychological adolescent.

Meanwhile, his lack of mastery repeatedly evidences itself in acts of cruelty to those over whom he would be lord. Janice, Ruth, and in some small way all of the other women he would control feel the pain of his mental and physical blows. The most significant, though, is the "sadistic little squeeze" he gives the hand of his granddaughter, Judy; this hurtful act makes him pause: "He wonders why he did it, why he tends to do mean things like that, to women mostly, as if blaming them for the world as it is . . . without mercy" (*Rest* 98). The reason for this rare awareness of his own wrongness comes from his need to have a workable relationship with this little girl.

When he first sees her, he knows that she is part of the solution to his life's dilemma. She is one manifestation of Lacan's "mirror-stage," the process by which a person can see himself, even if reflected in someone else, "gaining an imaginary mastery over his body, one which is premature in relation to a real mastery" (*Book I* 79). Rabbit believes that Judy is "what he has been waiting for . . . fortune's hostage, heart's desire . . . another nail in his coffin" (*Rich* 437). Actually, his granddaughter helps to prepare him for an understanding of the complexities of the mature goal of reproduction and protection of his offspring, which has almost sadistically eluded him.

Though he is Nelson's biological father, Rabbit cannot reach a satisfactory level of paternity until he redeems the guilt he feels for his role in the death of his other child, Rebecca.[29] Drowned while Janice is in a drunken stupor as she tries to cope with yet another of Rabbit's babyish flights, the infant had produced a feminine version of goodness incarnate. Rabbit was sure of it: he knew she was "sure," too. Yet she dies and actualizes his horrifying premonition that he should look at her gently, "as if rough looking [would] smash the fine machinery of this sudden life" (*Run* 202). Just as he would have begun to develop a sense of healthy protectiveness—of "pity," the need to restrict cruelty—the object of his development is destroyed by a combination of factors including his irresistible urge to run (Freud, *Three Essays* 59). It was, as he says in his later years, as if "God had never wanted him to have a daughter" (*Rich* 421).[30] The loss of this daughter deprives Rabbit of his Antigone. It makes him feel one with death: it keys into his entire system, leaving him useless as a father to the son he does have. What it establishes is the certainty that he and Nelson share: "At bottom the world was brutal . . . no father protected you" (294).

Surely Rabbit becomes utterly incapable of protecting or pitying Nelson. In fact, he appears as a murderer of both Nelson's infant sister and his surrogate sister, Jill, and drives Nelson into a purely oedipal rage: "You fucking asshole, you've let her die. I'll kill you. I'll kill *you*" (*Redux* 279). Later, Nelson directs his rage at smashing cars, "fine machinery" of a type Rabbit can understand, and at beating his wife while he masochistically takes cocaine to escape his woes (*Rich* 124). Projecting his own insecurity about gender onto Nelson, Rabbit leaves his son without any form of paternal security.[31]

Rabbit's major acting out of this abdication of responsibility occurs at a logically Freudian point. Rendered impotent by a heart attack, he is deposited in a situation loaded with psychoanalytic overtones: Janice, now on her way to becoming a modern businesswoman, leaves her husband in the place that had for years evidenced Rabbit's ineffectiveness. It is Bessie Springer's, his mother-in-law's house; while there, he will sleep in Janice's "mother's old bed" (*Rest* 323). Though he characteristically has liked Bessie—even considered her "sexy"—he cannot convince her or her daughter/his wife that he can ever fill the shoes of the mighty Fred, mentor and magnate of Springer Motors (*Rich* 90). Cut out of his own home, his job at the lot, and any inheritance, Rabbit can only feel needy as he enters the charge of the current captive of the house—his daughter-in-law and his nemesis: Pru.

Drawn to her from the beginning, Rabbit knows that "having a wife and children palled for him, but he never fails to be excited by having, in the flesh, a daughter-in-law" (*Rest* 14). It doesn't take much of a leap to see what the attraction is: besides perpetrating the ultimate violence upon his son, Harry can finally make love to a big-boned woman with knuckles like those Mary used to rub raw in her awful kitchen: Rabbit resists telling Janice about the "instinctive bond he has with this girl. Pru is like his mother" (*Rich* 174). (Consider the irony of the name Prudence and the greater irony of her first name, Teresa, paired in every modern mind with the word *Mother*). Locked among layers and layers of limits, Rabbit can with this one woman effectively wipe out every taboo, every limit, every opponent. And how does he feel as he takes this forbidden fruit? As he places her hand on his penis, "his gesture has the pre-sexual quality of one child sharing with another an interesting discovery" (*Rich* 345). Having broken the incest taboo, Rabbit has made progress. At this new level, another manifestation of the mirror-stage, he "has the experience of seeing himself, of reflecting on himself and conceiving of himself as other than he is" (Lacan, *Book I*, 79).

Later, the treachery out in the open, a rehabilitated Nelson explains that Pru did what she did "to get in touch with her own father," and Rabbit responds that he had indeed sensed a "set-up" (*Rest* 480). Nonetheless, the unspeakable has occurred, and as Rabbit last communes with Pru, what he wins from her is her voice, "this woman-to-man voice. Who could ask for anything more?" (446). What Rabbit has done is to establish his *own* voice. Lacan would say that he has achieved a unique level of consciousness available to only a few: "not men as a herd," but to "men who speak," thereby introducing "something into the world which weighs as heavily as the whole of the real" (*Book II* 225). Rabbit wants to live without hurting anyone. Thanks to the Judy/Pru dyad, combined with a large dose of grace, he does manage to achieve his actual "moment de virage."

The most ironic form this grace assumes is that of a middle-aged woman named Thelma, who has inadvertently provided the emerging Rabbit an amazing shortcut—the alternative of anal intercourse, a truly dead end to his sexual compulsion (Hall 107–9, *Rich* 390–91). For him, penetrating this Freudian zone produces "no sensation: a pure black box, a casket of perfect nothingness." "Thank you," Rabbit says. "That I won't forget" (*Rich* 391). What Harry will remember is "that the red cave he thought had only a front entrance and exit turns out to have a back door as well" (*Rest* 511). Thelma unintentionally provides closure for Rabbit, eventually freeing him to perform a conscious act of altruism.

Freud provides plenty of space for "such accidental experiences" to intervene in psychological development; he notes that the degree of illness "apparently depends on intellectual development with the height of personal culture" (*Writings* 626, 628). Once elevated by his ability to voice personhood, Rabbit performs an act of threefold redemption. While sailing with his granddaughter, the "nail in his coffin," Rabbit experiences brine-filled baptism.

For once, he is able to synthesize body and spirit to create a worthy action; at last he is able to resolve his conflict between "the right way and the good way" (*Run* 254). Although Pru tries to blame the accident on her daughter (an oedipal given), Rabbit sees Judy's falling from the Sunfish into the sea exactly as we should think he would: he can now rescue his daughter,

Rebecca. More to the point, he can let go the phantom daughter and concentrate on a grace-filled amalgam of mind and matter: his living flesh finally reincarnated. What Rabbit lost when Rebecca died was himself: Janice had explained this connection to him as he first viewed his baby: "It was like having *you*" (189). Better yet, he can finally quiet his mother's voice. No more will she have the need to hiss, as she did at Rebecca's funeral, "Hassy, what have they done to you?" (268).

Risking his own body, he jumps into the element he most fears and extracts his granddaughter, his new reincarnation, from "this murky world halfway to death" (*Rest* 106). Thanks to her finally protective grandfather, Judy "gets out of Florida alive" (162). Hassy has also "delivered" himself into the present; and he has freed himself from one last overriding charge, the title of "Mr. Death" (*Run* 279). This Childe Harold is nearing the end of his pilgrimage.

Yanking himself into life itself, he too has "tangled with the curse" and finally sees it for what it is (*Rich* 28). Oddly, the controlling metaphor comes from Skeeter, the black revolutionary with whom Rabbit feels an affinity.[32] Explaining the big bang theory to Rabbit, this "hostile stranger descend[s] like an angel" and defines "strange holes in [universal] nothingness" through which "new somethingness comes pouring in." "It is where God is pushing through. He's coming, Chuck, and Babychuck, and Ladychuck. The sun is burning through. The moon is a baby's head bright red between his mommy's legs" (*Redux* 230).

To this vision, Nelson "screams" in response, "I don't want God to come, I want Him to stay where He is. I want to grow up like *him* [indicating Rabbit]—average and ordinary" (*Redux* 230). The question Updike poses here is whether Rabbit—with his references to moon shots and moonlike cuticles on God's fingers and his horror of the sky, especially manmade machines in the sky—is ordinary or not.[33] Does Everyman have a sense of the "ancient craziness of women," that this craziness is connected to the tides, that the tides are the truth, and that submersion in them is the only way to survive (248)?

Lacan, like Freud, believes that "Oedipus really does exist" in all of us, that he is Everyman, and that he "fully realized his destiny." Destruction of the old self is imperative, Lacan asserts: "the final point" is a "tearing apart, a laceration," when one "is no longer, no longer anything at all. And it is at that moment that he says the phrase . . . —Am I made man in this hour when I cease to be?" (*Book II* 229).

Harry understands that "Mother Nature [is] one tough turkey," capable of dealing death to her children, yet he clearly chooses to engage her life-producing properties (*Rich* 317).[34] He is at last able to address womanhood "being to being" and, having chosen life, readies himself for what may lie beyond (Lacan, *Book II* 223). In a discussion of "the beyond of Oedipus," Lacan denies a positive outcome, claiming that the legendary hero uses his voice to "call down extreme malefactions upon posterity and the city for which he was a burnt offering." Lacan claims that this speech warns the citizens of "Thebes," then and now, that they and we must face the agony of the speaker and own it: "If the speech which is his destiny begins to wander, it will take with it your destiny as well" (230). This point of view echoes atheistic/humanistic advice offered by big daddy Tothero: "Right and wrong were never dropped from the sky. We. We make them. Against misery" (*Run* 157).

Rabbit, however, chooses a more traditional, theistic framework in which to speak his final word—not at all a curse, but a benediction. He assigns the role of death-dealer to the heavens, relieved that his "skyey enemy" has found him at last (*Rest* 139). As he suffers his heart attack, he feels himself go "way up toward the clouds" (106). Moving skyward conjures standard images of God's locus, and Updike certainly addresses issues of the godhead. In fact, he allows Lucy Eccles to form connections among Tothero, Harry, Freud, and God himself: in a conversation about Rabbit's relationship with Nelson, Lucy asserts, "I think Freud is like God; you make it true" (*Run* 111).

Updike has already provided his main character with a positive Christian reaction to a purely negative Freudian stimulus: as his mother urges him to "pray for his own rebirth," Rabbit "feels she is asking him to kill Janice, to kill Nelson. Freedom means murder" (*Redux* 175). Instead, Harry opts to pray not for what his mother commands, but for mercy for all of his loved ones: "*Make the L-dopa work, give her [Mom] pleasanter dreams, keep Nelson more or less pure, don't let Stavros turn too hard on Nelson, help Jill find her way home. Keep Pop healthy. Me too. Amen*" (176; Updike's emphasis).

Updike's own choice of the Christian worldview shows in his hero who always seeks the light, but a milder light than that of the "violent," lonely sun; Harry Angstrom eventually becomes "the son of the morning" that Eccles saw him to be, that his parents had always intended when they sent him out to be able to "bask above that old, [dark] world into the sunlight, though they remained in the shadows" (*Rich* 117, *Run* 135, *Rich* 63, *Redux* 86). Resolution comes when Rabbit becomes Harry and finally participates in his own life through saving another. In one last, grand transformation, Harry accepts his maturity, the condition he had called "the same thing as being dead," as he willingly moves upward to become a "piece of the sky of adults" he had feared so long (*Run* 102, 11). The circular path—from the ground, through the water, to the heavens—brings him home.

Finally, the frenzied burrow seeker—bound to earth by biology, psychology, and a lack of vision—learns how to convert his naturalistic, mindless sexuality into mature human fatherhood. He shows mercy to his family in the end, assuring them, especially Nelson, that his new condition, even with its incipient threat of biological death, "isn't so bad." He can finally transcend. With conviction, he can say his final word: "Enough" (*Rest* 512).

Harry does become a star, whether or not he actually receives saving grace. No matter: rereading the words to the following hymn (familiar to Updike, Harold Angstrom, and other Episcopalians) with Freud in mind shows that compassion and mercy come in many forms and that "our father" is as likely to be heavenly as earthly.[35] Updike does present his main character and his readers with alternatives. For those "living" in Brewer or in Florida, alternatives are often . . . enough:

> Brightest and best of the sons of the morning,
> Dawn on our darkness and lend us Thine aid.
> Star of the East, the horizon adorning,
> Guide where our infant redeemer is laid.[36]

Notes

1. Though Detweiler entitles one section of his analysis "Oedipus in Pennsylvania," he maintains a cautious attitude about applying Freudian labels. For example, he offers only this sort of general assessment of the hero's dilemma: "A good part of Rabbit's frustration is that he seeks fulfillment of an ideal nearly as impossible to realize as his religious search: he wants to find in one woman the security of the mother and the excitement of the lover" (*John Updike* 55).

2. Robert Con Davis and Ronald Schleifer use nearly identical terms to define Freudian criticism: "ego psychology" holds that the individual must "negotiate between an id of insatiable appetites and a super-ego with standards of conduct impossible to meet" (281).

3. O'Connell offers an interesting historical "outline of gender theories" in her introduction, postulating that Updike remains "tantalized by the possibility of union" between antithetical elements of the "oppositional model and the superior/ inferior model" (3–12, 12).

4. Additional references to Newman's analysis of Rebecca's death appear in notes 29 and 30.

5. In his study *The Fiction of Philip Roth and John Updike* (1985), George Searles stresses that familial relationships are at "the center of [Updike's] vision." He

quotes an assertion Updike made in an interview with Charles Thomas Samuels in 1968: one of the major themes in all of the novels is "domestic fierceness within the middle class" (42). The emphasis on middle-class values supports the assertion that, irony notwithstanding, Updike seeks to dramatize the lives he sees, full of Freudian undertones though they may be.

6. I use the following editions: *Rabbit, Run* (New York: Fawcett Crest, 1960); *Rabbit Redux* (New York: Fawcett Crest, 1971); *Rabbit Is Rich* (New York: Fawcett Crest, 1981); *Rabbit at Rest* (New York: Knopf, 1990).

7. Updike's Christianity is well documented. Wood's *The Comedy of Redemption: Christian Faith and Comic Vision in Four American Novelists* (1988) characterizes "Updike as an Ironist of the Spiritual Life" (178–229). The other novelists—Walker Percy, Peter De Vries, and Flannery O'Connor—seem more truly ironic than Updike, even in Wood's thoughtful analysis.

8. Beleaguered by a "sphinx"—a winged lion with the chest and head of a woman, who kills those who cannot guess the answers to her riddles—the town of Thebes was facing disaster. Oedipus does find the answer he needs, thus saving the city and sealing his fate. Rabbit similarly finds an answer to the "riddle of life" articulated by his coach and surrogate father, Marty Tothero (*Run* 54).

9. A purely mythological interpretation of the Rabbit novels—despite many clear parallels—would preclude Harry's epiphany, which defies the fate of blindness and dependency.

10. See Lacan's "Desire, Life, and Death" for a comprehensive discussion of the concept of "resistance" (*Book II* 221–34).

11. Mary Daly's *Gyn/Ecology* examines Greek myths as "reversals" of earlier matriarchal mythologies, reflecting general rejection of myth-as-fate in later feminist criticism (8, 290–92).

12. Freud's attitude about literary depictions of the Oedipus complex is one of skepticism, asserting that his idea has been "placed freely, as it were, at [the] disposal" of art (*Lectures* 208). He implies his appreciation of Otto Rank's study of selected interpretations: *Das Incest-Motiv in Dichtung und Sage*, 1912 (*Lectures* 208).

13. For a full exposition of this syndrome see Freud's *Writings,* "Contribution II: Infantile Sexuality" (580–603).

14. Jeff Campbell notes the saint/sinner dichotomy in Rabbit's character and supports the "cad[dish]" reading, arguing that Rabbit "refuses to use his eyes to look beyond himself" (*Updike's Novels* 102, 103). Tony Tanner assumes a more positive point of view. He borrows an image from Updike's *The Centaur* and claims that "how an individual cell can rebel against the compromised environment is the subject of *Rabbit, Run*" (279). George Hunt takes the most "reverent" position, claiming that Rabbit "lacks the mindful will to walk the straight line of the paradox" between Christian views of goodness and evil but that "his eyes turn toward the light," a reading more in line with my thesis (197).

15. Lacan credits Jung with the "invention" of the term *complex* but agrees that "Freud gave us the first model of it, its standard, in the Oedipus complex" (*Book I* 65).

16. In *Rabbit, Run*, Harry's first dream is a vision of his entering an icy cave, where he encounters his mother, his sister, and his wife (84–85). Psychiatrist Mark Helm verifies an interpretation of frigidity. Later, Rabbit's mother dreams of a man inside a refrigerator, echoing Rabbit's image (*Redux* 172). Other obviously sexual dreams occur with frequency in the tetralogy; detailed treatment of them would be an interesting study.

17. Newman's analysis considers Rabbit's consumer mentality and his obsession with cars indications of his fixation in the anal phase, another reading that makes sense (65).

18. See Freud's definition of "inquisitiveness" as a "sublimated form of acquisition" (*Writings* 594).

19. Fred Springer's character is enigmatic because of his willingness to support his ne'er-do-well son-in-law. Suggestions that he is a two-timing husband and generally ineffective role model explain Rabbit's only use for him: he makes space for Rabbit to occupy (*Run* 186, *Rich* 2).

20. Rabbit's childhood reveries, which lace all four novels, would make an interesting study.

21. Ruth's damning epithet colors much of Rabbit's development (*Run* 279). What makes her presence bearable is her paradoxical belief in his essential goodness, a quality that actually annoys her. Thelma's role is interpreted later in this essay.

22. Rabbit's most psychoanalytically loaded fantasy occurs in the first novel as Rabbit considers the sexual attributes of Lucy Eccles against the background of a painting of canals. Here he actually addresses Freud, and maybe himself, as "you primitive father." An interesting touch is that Lucy's husband interrupts by announcing that their daughter is "getting into bed with [him]" (*Run* 279).

23. Both Freud and Lacan discuss the difficulty of "seeing oneself" in inappropriate "objects of attachment" (Freud, *Writings* 614–29; Lacan, *Lectures* 75–80).

24. On a birthday card for his mother, Rabbit finds a witty little juxtaposition of letters: "*It's Great to Get Up in the A.M. . . . to Wish You a Happy Birthday, MA.*" He notes that *ma* becomes *am* (*Redux* 85). (Along these lines, *Mom* can be read as *Mim* with an O for Oedipus, thereby completing her role as mimic of both mother and brother.) This card, I think, is a clue to Mim's role in Rabbit's big I AM at the end of *Rabbit at Rest* (512). At the point of death, Rabbit finally decides life and death, all of it, "isn't so bad."

25. Freud's analysis of the Electra complex has come under scrutiny, especially by feminist critics.

26. See Freud's *Writings*, "Contribution II: Developmental Phases of Sexual Organization," for a discussion of the origins of sadism (597–603).

27. During a hospital visit with a most discouraged Harry, Pru offers comforting, freeing balm: "What's a life supposed to be? They don't give you another for com-

parison" (*Rest* 174). Pru helps her father-in-law break the bonds of all conventional supposed-to-be's.

28. Freud's discussion of "object-finding" provides a clear explanation of this difficulty (*Writings* 614–29).

29. Newman offers an interesting analysis of Rabbit's sense of guilt, only heightened by his family. At Rebecca's funeral, though the responsibility for the infant's death "may be ascribed to Eccles, Lucy, parents, or society," the people closest to him blame Harry (38). Newman believes that by sparing Rabbit's father and sacrificing his daughter, Updike "suggests a deliberate undercutting of Freud's belief (in the primal crime, patricide) that society is based upon shared guilt" (39). No one who matters, Newman notes, is willing to comfort Rabbit by assuming responsibility for his or her fair share of the blame.

30. Again, Newman recognizes Rabbit's angst and assigns him a level of maturity that I would say does not develop until Harry is on his deathbed: she argues, "Only Harry sees through the welter of multiple causation to another responsible party—God" (38). At this early, tragic point in Rabbit's development, I think he, too, is simply seeking to assign blame.

31. O'Connell applies the ideas of psychologist Samuel Osherson to her oedipal analysis, concentrating upon Nelson's role as Oedipus, Rabbit's as Laius (186–208).

32. Harry's affinity with Skeeter has to do with personal politics. Though he is patriotic, Rabbit runs his own revolution against social tyranny, an idea underscored by the passages from a book ("by a woman historian yet") about the Dutch role in the American Revolution (*Rest* 86). Rabbit, of course, has grown up in Pennsylvania Dutch territory.

33. Harry sees airplanes as images of death, becoming obsessive about the Lockerbie incident. In one particularly oedipal encounter with Nelson, Rabbit snaps out a veiled death threat: "I'm not curious about your missing *your* plane" (*Rest* 176). The "death instinct" is a "neurotic" response related to masochism (Mullahy 57). Many of the characters—with the exception of Rabbit himself—show morbid and suicidal tendencies.

34. Father Robert E. Merritt, an Episcopal priest, perceives Rabbit's earthbound search as an Eden metaphor. Rabbit's persistent attention to trees, for example, bolsters his search for knowledge of both goodness and evil and his own version, "the good way and the right way" (*Run* 279).

35. In an interview with Jeff Campbell, Updike responds to the question "Do you see your sensibility as specifically Christian?" with the following clear answer: "I think so. I think Christianity is the only world frame that I've been exposed to that I can actually look through" (*Updike's Novels* 290).

36. One last note: in the 1982 revision of the Episcopal hymnal, the word *stars* replaces the word *sons*. I like that.

10 Jack B. Moore
Sports, Basketball, and Fortunate Failure in the Rabbit Tetralogy

> Growing up, when most young people struggle to define their tastes and develop their own sense of right and wrong, the star athlete lies protected in his momentary nest of fame. The community tells him that he is a basketball star. . . . They expect him to become an even greater athlete and to do those things which will bring about the fulfillment of what is wholly their fantasy. The adolescent who receives such attention rarely develops personal doubts. There is a smug cockiness about achievements, or a sincere determination to continue along a course that has brought success and praise. . . . His self-assurance is constantly reinforced by public approval. . . . Self-definition comes from external sources, not from within. . . . fame holds as much danger as it does benefit. . . . There is little chance . . . to fail without people knowing it, and no one grows without failing.
>
> *Bill Bradley,* Life on the Run *(120)*

For Rabbit Angstrom, basketball and his basketball life and high school stardom have become, together, grand tropes shadowing his life, a measure of his existence. The Rabbit tetralogy is about a person similar in many ways to the star athletes Bradley describes, young men who do not grow up or who, as they grow, do not develop in the fullness they might achieve, whose self-identity becomes shaky, who succeed in life only in their dreams of the past. Part of Reverend Eccles's explanation for Rabbit's first run from his wife and from responsibility is simply that "Harry has been in a sense spoiled by his athletic successes" (*Run* 142).[1] Rabbit, however, is anything but simple.

The inevitable question about Rabbit concerns whether or not he is a failure in life. That is the question I would like to answer through looking at the role played by basketball and, to a lesser degree, baseball in the tetralogy. Basketball hounds and bounds Harry's life in the series, and while his identity as a high school star does not totally define him as a person, it is a dominant subject in the four books, almost as much as his increasingly distant stardom as a high school player is a dominant fact of his life.

Rabbit's early athletic success comes after his inherent abilities and physical gifts are refined through discipline (his mother remembers "how hard he used to work practicing basketball" [*Redux* 57]), but he never seems able to relocate or reformulate this self-discipline in his life after basketball. Later, Harry often remembers the good times playing basketball or the good things he saw then. Ten years after his stardom, as he is making his first panicked run for freedom, he daydreams in his getaway car about Janice's depressing "unfrozen peas steaming away their vitamins" in "grease-tinted water" and "tries to think of something pleasant. He imagines himself about to shoot a long one-hander," but the dream collapses when "he feels he's on a cliff, there is an abyss he will fall into when the ball leaves his hands" (*Run* 24). This is an image of failure after sporting achievement. Still, the achievements were there. At the "Sunshine Athletic Association," Rabbit's high school coach recalls them "insanely" to a bunch of "old men mostly, but not very old, so that their impotence has a nasty vigor." Rabbit "twice set a county record, in 1950 and then he broke it in 1951, a wonderful accomplishment" (46). Two decades later, when son Nelson's wife, Pru, is in the hospital having her first baby and Harry in his mid-forties seeks greater living space than Janice's mother's house affords them, he remembers playing against Penn Park, where he's "always kind of dreamed . . . of living" (*Rich* 329).

Nearly always these details of Harry's past as a basketball star are dredged up to contrast with his present life. After his first heart attack, Harry has a sad, unconsummated meeting with Thelma Harrison, who is dying of lupus. Not long before, he had also experienced a frustrating go-round with Lyle, his wife's gay bookkeeper (who is dying of AIDS), while trying to look at the company's books so he can tell what is going on with Nelson, who is now heading the family auto business. In this context of despair, Harry remembers the marvelous Philadelphia Whiz Kids of 1950, like him boys of earlier summers: Richie Ashburn, Curt Simmons, Del Ennis, Dick Sisler, Stan Lopata. Harry never attained a professional level of play, but as a junior in his county B league the 1949–50 season he led all scorers with a record 817 points, a memory that helped "settle his agitated mood, stirred up by seeing Thelma and Lyle, a mood of stirred-up unsatisfied desire at whose fringes licks the depressing idea that nothing matters very much, we'll all soon be dead" (220). So high school stardom is still his relief, his stay against the thought of death's emptiness, but it does not offer lasting relief. Nor are his records permanent: they are eventually broken, for nothing lasts forever in sport or life. But clearly they are important to him as representatives of the long-passed zenith in his life.

Recovering from angioplasty in *Rabbit at Rest,* Harry lies in a hospital bed while his nurse, Annabelle, who is also possibly his and Ruth's daughter, takes his blood pressure and tells him to think of something soothing. He again remembers "playing basketball against Oriole High, that little country gym, the backboards flush against the walls, before all the high schools merged into big colorless regionals and shopping malls began eating up the farmland" (276). But as his archaic underhand foul shots suggest, in a few years his game became as outmoded as tiny high school gyms and towns without malls: basketball and America's basketball culture changed, and he was in some ways left behind, "The game different now, everything the jump shot, big looping hungry blacks lifting and floating there a second while a pink palm long as your forearm launched the ball" (*Redux* 25). By the time he's thirty-six, his style is both classic and obsolete. "Where'd you get that funky old style of shooting a basketball?" asks Skeeter, who now lives in his house with hippie chick Jill. "You were trying to be comical, right?" (239).

But Harry continues to play the sport. When he meets Jill's mother after Jill's horrifying incineration, his "guts felt suspended and transparent, as before a game. He was matched against this woman as he was never matched with Jill" (*Redux* 302). That was in his thirties. In his forties, in 1979, when *Rabbit Is Rich*, looking at "the yellowing basketball feats up on the wall" of the car agency he runs, Harry realizes that at the business he is "a center of sorts, where he had been a forward." It seems as a player he knew his proper position for greatest achievement. He was not really tall enough to play center, though at forward he was the star of "two all-county tens." At the agency he runs, his life is for a time "sweet" but also fat and unadmirable, stuffed with complacency (*Rich* 3–4).

Clearly, the best times Harry remembers are those early years when he played basketball, the time when at high school proms he danced with perfumed girls "in the violet light of the darkened gym, crepe-paper streamers drooping overhead and the basketball hoops wreathed with paper flowers." In his rich, late forties he remembers making love to Mary Ann, her body "nestling toward his hands, the space between her legs so different and mild and fragrant and safe, a world apart" (*Rich* 408). In his twenties he had remembered Mary Ann no less fondly, but already as belonging to a time of his irrecoverable past, recalling that after games when he was "tired and stiff and tough somehow . . . they would walk across mulching wet leaves through white November's fog to his father's car and drive to get the heater warmed and park and they would make love" (*Run* 165–66). The chain of events creating the context of this memory is rich in revelation, demonstrating his early fall from grace. Harry has a short time before coerced Ruth into taking him into her mouth because "tonight you turned against me. I need to see you on your knees" (157). Jack Eccles has called and awakened him as he lies in bed next to Ruth to tell him that his wife is entering labor. Rabbit tries to tell Ruth he must go to his wife, but Ruth, apparently asleep, is not responsive, and "lies there like some dead animal" (161). Harry rushes to the hospital and while in its waiting room listens for the cry of his child. Fearful and guilty, "he does not expect the fruit of Janice's pain to make a very human noise. His idea grows, that it will be a monster, a monster of his making. The thrust whereby it was conceived becomes confused in his mind with the perverted entry a few hours ago he made into Ruth. . . . His life seems a sequence of grotesque poses assumed to no purpose, a magic dance empty of belief. *There is no God; Janice can die*" (165; Updike's emphasis). This is precisely when he remembers having sex with Mary Ann in his father's car, Mary Ann "the best of them all because she was the one he brought most to" (166). If "most" means his stardom here, his concept of success is sad and very shallow. Unqualified, "all" seems to include Ruth and Janice and predicts all those we learn about later, certainly the whores when he is stationed in Texas, and Thelma Harrison, and, most disgracefully of all, his daughter-in-law.

"He came to [Mary Ann] as a winner and that was the feeling he missed since," that he would never quite recapture in the next three decades. In a beautifully narrated example of Pavlovian-Skinnerian learning through behavioral gratification, the process by which Rabbit's simple glory with Mary Ann is achieved is set forth: "the shouting glare of the gym," the "anticipation of the careful touchings that would come under the padded gray car roof, and finally "the bright triumph of the past game" that "flashed across her quiet skin streaked with the shadows of rain on the windshield, so that the two kinds of triumph were united in his mind" (*Run* 166). For a brief time Rabbit thought himself a winner, far from a failure.

An insistent motif in Rabbit's thoughts throughout the tetralogy is that he considers himself a failure. Others agree. "I *was* great," he tells Ruth early in their relationship, but "I'm not much good for anything now" (*Run* 64). As the series progresses to the point of Harry's near death, memory of his fame raises him up but also drags him down when he thinks of what he has lost. In *Rabbit Redux*, perhaps the most depressing of the four books, he often comments on his lowness. He says he wants Nelson to play ball so he can get "some bliss, to live on later for a while. If he goes empty now he won't last at all, because we get emptier." He apologizes "for his bulk, his bloated pallor, his dead fame" after he is half razzed, half praised as "the Big O [as in Oscar Robertson, not "the Big Zero"] of Brewer in his day" by a black coworker in the surrealistic scene at Jimbo's Friendly Lounge. To Jill's accusation that "you don't think much of yourself, do you?" he responds, "Once the basketball stopped, I suppose not." After this exchange, knowing Jill is wearing no underpants and that she has already made love with Skeeter previously that day, Harry and Jill have sex, and both cry. Jill asks Harry why he is crying and he says, "Because the world is so shitty and I'm part of it." When Jill is dead and Harry is about to get back together with Janice, he asks his mom, "Where do you think I went wrong? . . . my sister says I'm ridiculous" (31, 107, 178–79, 324). He does not appear to be fulfilling Coach Tothero's prophecy (or whiskey-inspired con) pronounced more than three decades earlier, that "a boy who has had his heart enlarged by an inspiring coach . . . can never become, in the deepest sense, a failure in the greater game of life" (*Run* 54–55).

In fact, Harry's doctor tells him in *Rabbit at Rest* that he has a heart enlarged from playing basketball, and it is killing him. "One doc told me," he says to Janice on her hospital visit, "I have an athlete's heart. Too big. . . . Too many pork chops on top of all that hustle on the court when I was a kid" (164–65), too many bags of corn chips like the one he buys—typically self-indulgent and self-destructive—a little later just after his angioplasty (327). Too much height, he complains to Thelma (204). His old basketball allies (heart and height) conspire with enemies he may have gathered to him with his early fame, to bring him low.

Even in *Rabbit at Rest,* the game Rabbit succeeded at when he was young, the local fame he achieved then, seems to cast a light that puts his present into a shadow. It is difficult to know whether to laugh or cry when Harry, an old, dying star, happily participates in his granddaughter's Fourth of July parade and is again, after his disastrous peccadilloes, welcomed back to the all-American fold: tall enough to march costumed and bearded as Uncle Sam, Harry is enthusiastically remembered by the celebration committee. "He was a Mt. Judge boy and something of a hero once. . . . The crowd as it thickens calls out more and more his name, 'Harry,' or 'Rabbit'—'Hey Rabbit! Hey hotshot!' They remember him." The crowd is "alive, affectionate. This crowd seems a strung-out recycled version of the crowd that used to jam the old auditorium-gym Tuesday and Friday nights, basketball nights, in the dead of the winter. . . . The whole town he knew has been swallowed up, by the decades, but another has taken its place, younger, more naked, less fearful, better. And it still loves him, as it did when he would score forty-two points for them in a single home game. He is a legend, a walking cloud" (362, 368, 370).

Updike's narration here is from Harry's point of view, like a film of Harry's life shot from his perspective. If only that film could stop now, how filled with glory would Harry's life appear. But Updike insinuates into his description another vision that runs alongside Harry's, so that the parade becomes grotesque in its display of Americana, with black faces in the crowd "as cheerful and upholding as the rest. And some Orientals [of course, Harry should be thinking "Asians"]—an adopted Vietnamese orphan, a chunky Filipino wife." Most ludicrous and horrible of all, close to the parade's front, "on a scratchy tape through crackling speakers, Kate Smith belts out, dead as she is, dragged into the grave by sheer gangrenous weight, 'God Bless America.' " Harry's "heart thump[s] worse and worse, [seeing] that all in all this is the happiest fucking country the world has ever seen."

But the book does not stop at this bizarre moment of epiphany. Harry's revelation is the "foolish" sort "he might have once shared with Thelma" (371), whose funeral he is attending in the following ritualistic scene during which he blurts to bereaved Ronnie Harrison that his wife "was a terrific lay" and Ronnie calls him a "cocksucker" (379). So much for marching to tunes of glory. The reality of his life is also that although he was "a wonderful athlete," that may have caused him to "psychologically dominat[e]" and thereby damage his son. And now partly because of his enlarged "athlete's heart" he has to "ride a golf cart and not do anything more violent than brisk walking" (*Rest* 189). As Harry lies probably dying in his hospital bed, Janice remembers "all the ways he was from the day she first saw him in the high-school corridors and at the basketball games, out there on the court so glorious and blond, like a boy made of marble," and then thinks of their empty condo, tidy except for the stacks of old newspapers Harry would never throw out, and the junk food crumbs in the wicker easy chair (500). Truly, as she thinks, "He had come to bloom early" (510).

Basketball is not the only sport that illuminates Harry's long trip to the hospital, where his family hovers about him in what they fear is their death watch, thirty years after the early bloom that preceded his long decline. Wayne Falke has written movingly and convincingly of the boring minor league game Rabbit takes Nelson to in *Rabbit Redux,* finding in the unpleasant scene Updike's "demythologizing of baseball" that "reflects" revisionist attacks on "self-serving delusions of the past" that "are not a sound basis from which to form one's own life or for a nation to build its own" (21). I would not wish to quarrel with Falke's analysis, though I would suggest qualifying it in three ways. First, Harry is watching the game, not participating in it, and generally he is critical about games at which he is a spectator. Watching organized games never gives Harry much pleasure. Second, while Harry's jaundiced observation of the depressing play transpiring before him doubtless reflects in many ways Updike's own vision—what he wants readers to see about the pathetic play the national pastime has become—the sequence must also be placed in the context of Harry's life at the time he is observing it, since what he sees, or rather, like a photographer, what he chooses to see and recapture in images, also reflects how he feels at the time, one of the many low points of his life. Janice, he has discovered, has been sleeping with Charlie Stavros, and she will shortly be leaving him. His own mother, nudged by Parkinson's disease, is sliding toward death. The country is sinking more deeply into the Vietnam quagmire, terrain that Harry wants his country to conquer and save. Teddy Kennedy has just the night before (July 18, 1969) slipped from his sunken car leaving Mary Jo Kopechne dead in the water off Chappaquiddick Island as Janice's father, old man Springer, a rabid Kennedy hater, gloatingly tells Harry. His work at the press is a task for an older world and is being phased out, outmoded at a time when in just one day (July 20) Neil Armstrong will walk on the moon. In space talk Armstrong's module is code-named *Tranquility,* a feeling Rabbit does not experience now. What's wrong? Rabbit sarcastically tells his opinionated father-in-law, "Things go bad. Food goes bad, people go bad, maybe the whole country goes bad." "Still," he says limply "about America" as he and the old geezer and poor, short, small-handed, uncompetitive young Nelson approach the baseball stadium, "it's . . . the only place" (*Redux* 76–81). Third, what he sees is a sparsely attended, bum minor league game, not the big-league sport whose hundredth anniversary great players like Bob Gibson, Steve Carlton, Johnny Bench, and Willie McCovey would celebrate in Washington, D.C., just a few days (July 23) later. The contest Rabbit and family see is hardly baseball at its best, for by 1969 minor league play was generally a pale replica of triple A and lower competitions that were so popular before television lured fans from green fields to tiny sets featuring the major league variety. But the game fits his mood and outlook at the time. The scene could have been far worse: Updike might have sent Harry to watch a Little League contest.

Teams and sports stars of the past are of little interest to Harry. He is not a particularly engaged fan or observer of athletic contests and their heroes throughout most of the Rabbit novels. But in *Rabbit at Rest* Harry shows more than fleeting interest in a triad of athletes, the baseball-football player Deion Sanders and baseball players Pete Rose and Mike Schmidt, all of whom serve as figures in counterpoint to his own athleticism and waning life.

"Neon" Deion Sanders is a new breed of athlete in the tradition of black and flamboyant Muhammad Ali, a brilliant, gifted hot dog, a fulfilled athlete whose life so far has not shown the downside of stardom as has Ali's. Also known as "Prime Time," he is at his peak and in and out of trouble that sometimes seems excused, as Bill Bradley would have expected, because of his athletic prowess. Early in *Rabbit at Rest*, Harry reads that the mayor of Fort Myers has stated that "football star Deion Sanders's recent arrest for assault and battery on a police officer could be partially blamed upon the unruly crowd that had gathered to watch the incident" (54). The mayor will later reverse this position when he "thinks his police acted properly in the arrest of Deion Sanders," a decision linked at least in the text with the immediately following news that "*Deadly pollution infects Lake Okeechobee.*" The juxtaposition seems either a parodic contrast comparing an ecological disaster to Sanders's minor misdemeanor that has been blown out of proportion to feed the corrupt taste of sports junkies, or a fusion of the moral and environmental rot blighting American life (92).

Harry's ambivalence toward Sanders and the charge against him is duplicated later when Nelson has a skimpy noontime breakfast with his mother in his parents' Florida condo. Nelson eats nothing and reads aloud as his father might have, "City reduces charge against football star. Lake Okeechobee's cure may be hard to swallow" (144), just prior to his mother's charge that he has a drug habit. The interest Harry and his son seem to share in Sanders's case intersects a short time later, when Nelson visits his hospitalized dad and the two briefly converse with some mutual feeling of regard and possibly love. Nelson tells his father that he has "noticed the Deion Sanders case is being pushed back into the sports pages and somewhere in Section B there's an article about fighting flab that'll give you a laugh" (177).

Out of the hospital, Harry reads once more about Sanders and a few other sports stars and the special perils and glories of stardom. A newspaper headline declares "Deion has right stuff" (linking him ironically to the astronauts of *Rabbit Redux*). Rabbit thinks Sanders should "enjoy it while he can. He calls himself Prime Time and is always on the TV news wearing sunglasses and gold chains." Harry has learned that neither gold chains nor, especially, golden lads can stay. Certainly athletic stardom does not last long: he "watches that big kid Becker beat Lendl in the U.S. Tennis Open final and gets depressed, Lendl seemed old and tired and stringy, though he's only twenty-eight" (*Rest* 470).

Rabbit's feelings about Pete Rose and Mike Schmidt are not similarly conflicted. Schmidt is for him a model, even noble, sports hero; Rose is not. In *Rabbit Is Rich,* Harry calls Rose a "showboat," and in *Rabbit at Rest* he faults him for succeeding more on hustle than talent. Since Rose has made more than the most of his relatively unexceptional abilities, Harry's judgment seems odd. Possibly Rabbit is showing his anger here at not having fulfilled himself at higher levels as an athlete, given his partly innate skills. For example, why did he *not* ever play ball in college at a time when many only slightly above average white players were given scholarships to good and not-so-good schools? Only toward the conclusion of *Rabbit at Rest,* in a rare moment of emotional intimacy with his son, does Harry relent, showing compassion for Rose. So for Rabbit, forgiveness is possible: forgiveness of Rose, perhaps forgiveness of Nelson, maybe forgiveness for himself. Forgiveness of failure shows growth, but forgiveness is not admiration. Harry tells Nelson, "Tell [Elvira] Schmidt is my idea of a classy ballplayer" (419).

If Rabbit's attitude toward Deion Sanders seems double, and if his attitude toward Pete Rose is clear while the reasons for it are murky, his high regard for Mike Schmidt and reasons for it are crystalline. Unchanging, always a Phillie, Schmidt was the consummate great player as great person, though some feel he was never fully appreciated by Philadelphia fans: a good-percentage hitter (.270 over sixteen years), a great-fielding third baseman (ten Golden Glove awards), a great power hitter (eight home run and three runs-batted-in titles), and an extraordinary team player (three National League and one World Series Most Valuable Player awards); no hot dog, a decent person.

In *Rabbit at Rest,* Harry is pursued—dogged, perhaps—by thoughts of Mike Schmidt, previously unmentioned in the tetralogy. Schmidt is for Rabbit close to what Joe DiMaggio was for Santiago in Hemingway's *The Old Man and the Sea,* an analogue for what he would like to be: courageous, skilled, stoical in the face of pain. Back in blossoming springtime Pennsylvania after his disastrous near drowning and subsequent collapse in Florida, Harry is pleased to note that at the start of the new baseball season, "Schmidt this year" (1989) had already hit "two home runs in the first two games," a great start for the veteran and doubtless reassuring to aging Harry, "squelching all talk that he [ostensibly Schmidt] was through" (181). Shortly after, on April 18, 1989, a doubtless pleased Harry hears Schmidt has hit his "five hundredth home run" and "is closing in on Richie Ashburn's total of 2,217 hits to become the hittingest Phillie ever" (220), an achievement that must be more significant or pleasing to Harry than Rose's never-mentioned record for the most hits or his major league record for at bats. A bit later Rabbit watches Schmidt hit his fourth home run "of the young season," and with the Phillies ahead by five runs he loses interest in the game. Since there are no basketball playoffs on television he "starts switching channels" (222) and then shuts off the set.

Schmidt is on a high, but Harry is not. While Harry reflects, "You can't live through these athletes, they don't know you exist" (233), he admires the way Schmidt faces decline. Harry, of course, like many other athletes, never prepared for his decline, and there is no evidence in the series that he even thought about its possibility until years after it had occurred. Unlike A. E. Housman's ironically lucky hero in "To an Athlete Dying Young," to whom Donald Greiner elsewhere in the present volume also alludes, Harry long outlives his days of sporting triumph and wild adulation, though he retains vestiges of his "renown." But here, finally, Schmidt is able to provide Harry with an alternate model of grace after pressure. This occurs at the time of probably the last unraveling of his life, after he has slept with his daughter-in-law but before she confesses their sexual act, after his angioplasty but before what seems his final collapse in Florida, after Nelson commits himself to rehabilitative therapy and while Harry is dragged into tedious family sessions, but before Mr. Shimada coolly cuts Springer Motors's distributorship ties to Toyota.

Rabbit finds comfort in Schmidt's stylish retirement—that he puts honor over money—repeating his pleasure that Schmidt "had the grace to pack it in when he could no longer produce" (487). His remark by itself could sustain many interpretations, could mean that Rabbit would like to display such grace by giving up life without fuss, or that once a person's vocational usefulness is over or once his performing skill is gone, he should leave the field of work or play quickly and quietly. When the systems begin to shut down (interest in baseball, interest in sex), a person should just help to turn out the lights. I am reminded here of a grim comment an aging colleague made about why he would never retire: "Retirement is death." But Rabbit adds to his remark about Schmidt's grace, "So there is life after death of a sort. Schmidt judges. Skeeter lives [Harry has at an earlier time received this incredible and doubtless literally false message]. And the weekend before last, a young black girl beat Chrissie Evert in the last U.S. Open match she'll ever play. She packed it in too. There comes a time" (487–88). There is degeneration and generation, and survival of sorts and decent retreat.

Immediately after this thought, Harry reads a headline about hurricane Hugo—"*Deadly Hugo roars into islands*"—and later that evening in a condo elevator he reassures a frightened woman with a "skeletal face" that "it'll never get here" (488). Like so much in the tetralogy, the passage is rich. Rabbit sees Schmidt as one who can continue his life past the period of his great ability and stardom—maybe Chrissie Evert too, who packed it in properly. This does not exactly ensure immortality, but it does suggest there is a good life possible after life at its peak has been passed. The activities a person can engage in at this time may be of reduced significance or pleasure, but they are activities, they are life. Of a sort. But really, you cannot stop a hurricane, only prepare for it. Ultimately some Hugo or other will reach you.

Death's inevitability has long intrigued Harry. He plays a game with death throughout his life so that his liveliness if not his goodness enables him to persist in, if not win, the contest. Mere activity is not quite enough for Harry, who compulsively plays basketball at what appears to be the end of his life. Earlier, in *Rabbit, Run*, he had been buoyed by the "touch" that "still lives in his hands" and "elates" and liberates him. But this momentary joy will not last. And while he never completely succumbs to the inevitable griefs that follow, neither will he ever again "reach the top" when "everybody cheers" (9). Still, in *Rabbit at Rest*, Harry, now fifty-six, plays the game of his life and probably his death. At first he merely watches the black kids who have replaced the white after-school players of *Rabbit, Run* as the objects of his attention or, thinking of their youth and not their sex, desire. Racially, culturally, and by age he is even more distant from the kids he had said kept "crowding up" thirty years before. What life of his own and his country's that has intervened between the two games is staggering. At first he merely watches the black boys, who "vary in heights and degrees of looseness, but all have that unhurried look he likes to see." Harry is alone in Florida where he has exiled himself, a state described in *Rabbit at Rest* as mainly loathsome and overbuilt. But the playground on which the boys cavort has developed its own character and "Rabbit is happy to think that the world isn't yet too crowded to have a few of these underused pockets left" with grass that has "crept onto the dirt court, in the middle, where the pounding, pivoting feet rarely come." Once again Harry is optimistic and (considering his routine racism) generous—"If he comes every day he'll blend in. Blacks don't have this racist thing whites do, about keeping their neighborhoods pure"—and wonderfully (or incredibly) naive about symbols of progress (486–87).

On his second visit to the playground, Harry plays Horse with two young black boys, at first tentatively, carefully easing himself in as an old, white alien to their game, and finally performing creditably as his innate and trained skills return, though he finally loses, thanking them for the game as they depart. He never deeply examines his motives for these late forays into black space and a sport he is too old to play, but his pleasure at performing well something he is good at is apparent. His "bit of basketball" leaves "him feeling cocky," but only briefly. Alone in his condo, he hears more news of a French airliner that has exploded over the Sahara. He concludes, "Every plane had a bomb ticking away in its belly. We can explode any second" (490–93). He does not articulate the thought, but it is clear that he knows his heart is his own bomb.

After he happily tells his granddaughter, Judy, over the telephone that he "played a little basketball with some kids not much older than you" (496), his third trip, as in a fairy tale, is most magical. The game he plays this eventful time is with a young black he thinks of as "Tiger," whom he sees as a boy who would probably resent being called a boy, "eighteen at least." Probably wondering if the white guy was again trying to take over his space, Tiger asks why Harry isn't playing around on his (white, wealthy) side of the island, and Harry answers that he's bored there. This seems not so much a comment on the depleted or empty nature of life in the white world as it is a comment on Harry's lack of function in it. Harry induces Tiger, who is in control of the turf, to play with him: Tiger against Rabbit in Twenty-one, the same game at which he beat his sister Mim probably forty years before. But Harry is old and out of shape: not the Western White World worn down, I think, but Harry paying the price for indulging himself in corn chips and Planter's Peanut Bars, sodium- and saturated-fat-rich snacks and unhealthy prepackaged, cholesterol-clogged dinners (502–4).

"Still, the sun feels good, springing sweat from his pores like calling so many seeds into life." Life and death jostle each other. He twists upward for one shot staring "straight into the sun" and can see nothing for a minute but the "red moon" of its "afterimage." The time is a complex one for Rabbit, showing him at his best and worst, living to the hilt almost heroically, and behaving foolishly. At least he gains Tiger's respect, as he had, grudgingly, gained Skeeter's sometimes. "Hey man, you all right?" his opponent and complicit partner in the game asks him. "How about coolin' it? No big deal." Harry thinks this is gracious of Tiger but also knows it shows weakness in himself, failure, the gap between what he once was and what he never moved beyond, never could become or attain in the same sharp way again, a sign of some eighth deadly sin of which he has been guilty. Harry thinks about himself derisively, "No big deal you aren't good even for a little one-on-one." He is "afraid he's going to lose the rhythm, the dance, the whatever it is, the momentum, the grace." In fact he has already lost these, if he is thinking of the perfection he could once reach and linger around during the short time of a game. What he does not realize is that life has larger rhythms and movements than a relatively simple game of sport and so will accommodate falterings that sport in its quick intensity will not. With the game's score eighteen all, with "neither player" calling "a foul," Tiger scores in close by whipping around Harry, Harry drops a long, heaved two-handed set shot that Tiger calls, admiringly, "pure horseshit," and then Tiger misses an imitatively long one-handed toss. Harry—or rather, as the text reads now, Rabbit—"grabs the rebound but then can't move with it, his body weighs a ton," yet manages with a last effort to leap up when Tiger "eases back a little" and then makes his shot as "his torso is ripped by a terrific pain" and "he bursts from within," then collapses on the court. Tiger, "shocked numb," says "pure horseshit" again, but, not desiring involvement, "walks deliberately away" and then "in the middle of the block, he begins to run" (504–6).

Harry next finds himself near death in the hospital, semiconscious and pierced by tubes. Even though he had been leading by twenty to nineteen and had not yet reached the required twenty-one (in this game, each basket is ordinarily worth one point and usually the victor must win by two baskets), he thinks of telling Janice "*I won*" but does not (511). Maybe Rabbit has won this small, Pyrrhic game, but more certainly he has suffered an infarction "right through the gosh-darn wall" and it appears to be ending his life (507).

So is Harry really a winner? Or is he a loser, a failure? Can anyone win in life? Harry fails Ruth in many ways but possibly succeeds in providing her with a daughter who seems a splendid person and who appears to be part of the process enabling Ruth to lead a more fulfilled life. He fails Thelma but succeeds in giving her someone to love completely. He is complicit in a dreadful act of adultery with Pru, but afterward she is able to shed the fear, torpor and self-loathing her relationship with Nelson has led her into.

Is Harry *presented* as a success or failure in life? Page after page reveals his flaws, his inadequacies small and large. A stimulating intellectual parlor game might be, what is the worst thing he does in the novel? Each book has its highlight low point, as when in *Rabbit, Run* he makes Ruth sink to her knees and perform fellatio as punishment and a sign of her love just before he deserts her, or when he pummels Janice in *Rabbit Redux* for sleeping with Charlie Stavros. To recall such episodes, just two among many, is to cringe at Rabbit's frequent terribleness.

Harry's life as an athlete illuminates these unquestioned flaws to reveal him in a different light. High school sport of course provides him with his greatest moments of success, but he cannot maintain this success that he, as a perfectionist, desires. In *Rabbit at Rest* he has these thoughts about a golf partner: "There's no satisfying him. Like Marty Tothero. . . . Get twenty-five points a game, Marty wanted thirty-five. . . . The soldier in Harry, the masochistic Christian, respects men like this" (64). His high school basketball stardom is good, giving him a rare, pure feeling of successful achievement, of near perfection, but it is also to him a sign of his later failure. Yet he grows falteringly and unevenly in ways he for the most part does not realize or give great, lasting significance to. At a very basic level, he proceeds from being a MagiPeeler demonstrator in *Rabbit, Run* to becoming a successful and rather knowledgeable car agency manager—not much intellectual or spiritual progress, perhaps, but a sign of his increased business acumen and responsibility. The Harry Angstrom who brags to Reverend Eccles in *Rabbit, Run* that he doesn't cry over being told he's "not mature" because "as far as I can make out it's the same thing as being dead" (90) grows in many ways. Also in *Rabbit, Run* he tells Ruth, "If you have the guts to be yourself . . . other people'll pay your price" (125), a condescending attitude he surely has lost by the time he takes responsibility for what he has done to Nelson, and worries as he lies dying, "*What else am I doing wrong?*" (*Rest* 511). By the time of *Rabbit at Rest* he is no longer the neanderthal of *Rabbit, Run, Rabbit Redux,* or *Rabbit Is Rich,* in which he claimed, "Women, once sex gets out in the open, they become monsters. You're a creep if you fuck them and a creep if you don't," and admitted, "intelligence in women has never much interested him" (*Rich* 38, 51). In *Rabbit at Rest* age and physical impairment have slackened his sex drive, though not enough to entirely quell his chauvinist fantasies or prevent his inexcusable tumble with actively willing Pru, which is occasioned, it seems, on both sides by a muddled excess of love as well as lust. But experience has modified him here too, for the better, as his playful tilting with the competent and acerbic Elvira demonstrates, and as his tender regard for and understanding of his granddaughter, Judy, shows. This latter relationship more convincingly proves his success as a grandfather, admittedly an easier task than fatherhood, but one at which Rabbit shows definite skill. He is much more tolerant with his grandchildren, recognizing he should not be so negative with them, that their needs must be considered over his, because, as he thinks when he realizes he is scaring Judy with his sarcasm, "When you get children growing under you, you try to rise to the occasion" (*Rest* 139).

He learns *somewhat* that he isn't *quite* the center of the universe. Ruth had said to him angrily that he wants her and his wife both because "You love being married to everybody" (*Run* 252). He thought about her, "She wants him to be content with just her heavy body, but he wants whole women, light as feathers" (64). The love *he* wants, the *entire* love, drives him even though that course is painful and dangerous to himself and others. When he is in the hospital in *Rabbit at Rest* and speaks with Ruth's daughter, the young woman mentions that her mother "knew quite a few guys before meeting up with my father"; Harry is "sad at the thought" and guesses that "she did." He thinks to himself, "Always he has wanted to be every woman's only man, as he was his mother's only son." But now, he does not even claim this "girl he thinks is his daughter" as his own, and even tells her he is "not sure" he has ever known her mother, which, except sexually, perhaps he has not (277–78).

Harry's presentation as a success or failure in life is uneven and not constant, certainly not clear. He never learns, for example, Mr. Shimada's message, the necessity of striking a proper balance "between needs of outer world and needs of inner being" (*Rest* 393), like the struggle between discipline and freedom, order and delight. But if Mr. Shimada has learned to practice this balance, it does not appear to have made him particularly human, or humane, for he seems, even if right in his decision to cut the Springer Motors from its Toyota dealership, cold and programmed, a bureaucratic hit man. Harry's style is not balanced but improvisational, which contributes both to his charm and to his harm to himself and others. "I don't really have a plan" he tells Eccles in *Rabbit, Run,* "I'm sort of playing it by ear" (88). But his often refreshingly enthusiastic or disturbingly risky running about never quite, to his credit, leads (at least for long) to personal chaos. As he tells Janice in the motel where they get back together at the end of *Rabbit Redux,* "Confusion is just a local view of things working out in general" (351). And some good things have been constant from the start: his actual openness as opposed to his theoretical closed-mindedness (he gets along well with blacks, comes to form a family with Skeeter and Jill, both of whom he really cares about, fantasizing in his grief over their deaths that he was a "father and lover to them" [331]); his ability to love (even perhaps Nelson); his willingness to be loved; a kind of (sometimes perverse) courage; his outrage at much shoddiness in American life; and, as he shows at the final basketball game he plays, the reason Ruth at the outset of the series says she "like[s]" him, " 'Cause you haven't given up. 'Cause in your stupid way you're still fighting" (*Run* 79).

If it is possible to split the protagonist of the series in two, something Updike does not do, and call the young version, the athlete, Rabbit, and the older man Harry, we might say that while it is good that Harry has Rabbit to remember, for he lived a time of peak and almost pure success, almost unalloyed joy, it is bad that he has so much trouble growing beyond Rabbit. What Rabbit does not know is how to suffer, a lesson he never learned as an athlete (in *Rabbit, Run* his old coach tells him "to avoid suffering" [233]), although he learned many other lessons good and bad as a sports star, such as the need to develop skill with practice, and that pleasure can proceed from self-centered enterprise. Harry's life is rich, complex, constantly changing, fascinating. It is a life of intense vitality and dreadful despair. He hurts people, betrays them, loves them, registers experience deeply. If he has been the cause of others' suffering, he has certainly endured suffering himself, usually of his own creation. But at the end Harry is more fully human than Rabbit had been, and that is the sign of his success. He has not made the best use of his life—who does?—but he has made rich use of it.

Considering the Rabbit tetralogy as a study in human success or failure, I would compare it to two of the many other extended sagas of male American life. The first is James T. Farrell's Studs Lonigan trilogy, in its totality a cautionary tale. Studs is a sad flop who dies in an early Depression world that seems to match his own spiritual emptiness. Religion, family, and government are crumbling institutions ("RIOT AS BANK FAILS," *Judgment Day* 315) from which he is unable to derive any sustaining values, partly because of his own lack of sensitivity to what is happening to him and partly because these enwrapping institutions have become corrupt. He and his world lack grace, and he possesses no resources that would enable him to rebel in any successful way. Instead he sneers and drinks and swaggers his life away, oblivious to the cries and signs of dissent that might supply some alternatives to his purposeless existence.

Out of work, his girlfriend pregnant, he is turned down rudely for a job and wanders, sneezing, in the rain to a "ten-cent burlesque show" with a "urinal smell" where he feels he might "become diseased or contaminated just by sitting in it." "Disgusted" by the "beefy women" grinding before him taking sex, by the sickly lustful men watching them, and by himself, he leaves the dispiriting entertainment and stumbles feverishly home, where he "feebly" throws himself into his parents' house and, like his world, collapses (*Judgment Day* 313–15). At his and the trilogy's end, he chokes and calls feebly to his mother that "it's getting dark," and then "there [is] a rattle in his throat." His eyes dilate, become blank, and finally there is "nothing in the mind of Studs Lonigan" but a "feeble streaking of light in an all-encompassing blackness, and then, nothing" (378).

What has ever demonstrated richness in Studs's aimless life? Surely not the brutal football game he and his buddies play in *The Young Manhood of Studs Lonigan*. His high point may have arrived in *Young Lonigan* when he walked in the park with Lucy Scanlan and kissed her as they sat in a tree and dangled their legs beneath them. Studs suffers throughout the trilogy, but in the sense that suffering happens to him. He makes no sense of it and does not change as a result of it except to deteriorate physically. In the truly depressing short story "Studs" ("the nucleus out of which the Studs Lonigan trilogy was conceived, imagined, and written" according to Farrell in an "author's note" appended to *The Short Stories of James T. Farrell* [347]), after Studs's funeral, rain falls on his grave, and in the story's last image "his old buddies are at work wishing that it was Saturday night, and they were just getting into bed with a naked, voluptuous blonde" (354). Studs's meaningfulness is his meaninglessness in a life that is similarly meaningless to him and in which he is quickly forgotten. His world is bad enough but no one should live like he does, or die like he does in it.

Studs Lonigan suffers greatly. Perhaps Studs's world is one—to paraphrase another Farrell work—he never made. Harry makes his own world, or some of it anyway, and also suffers in it. Natty Bumppo tries to create a good space for himself in a world he helps—against his desires, sometimes—to shape, but he does not suffer. Bad things happen to him; events like the wanton slaughter of pigeons in *The Pioneers,* for example, pain him. But he seems godlike and impervious to deep suffering—he never suffers to the core, to the bone, though he has much in his life to lament, such as the passing of ways of life that he loves. And I never sense that Natty, despite the tight adventures he so constantly finds himself enmeshed in, ever feels the anxiety for self or fear of success that self-doubting Rabbit does so frequently.

Beyond sharing some Adamic reverberations, as Donald Greiner notes in his essay in this volume, the Rabbit tetralogy might seem to relate to James Fenimore Cooper's Leatherstocking volumes only as a grim parody, though even here some parallels of diminishment are evocative (e.g., Natty's pride in his hunter's skill with his rifle compared to Rabbit's pleasure in his basketball talent: both are accurate shooters). The contrasts between the two characters are many and revealing about the worlds their authors had them inhabit (e.g., Natty's celibacy versus Rabbit's promiscuity).

But like Natty, Harry offers a constant critique upon the civilization that is growing up around him and replacing the old ways. Both Cooper and Updike use their protagonists to embody complex notions about the gains and losses heightened civilization brings. In Cooper's books, communities like Templeton in *The Pioneers* grow, giving promise of a new civilization, and that is good, but they are also powered by commercial greed, and that is not good. From *Rabbit, Run* to *Rabbit Redux* the movies have changed from *The Shaggy Dog* and *Gigi* to *I Am Curious Yellow, Midnight Cowboy,* and *Depraved,* problematic signs of progress, though men are walking on the moon. Natty's apostrophes to vanished forest silences are echoed in urbanized Rabbit's awareness that "The slope of cement is a buried assertion . . . of the land that had been here before the city" (*Run* 63). Rabbit is no solitary hunter like Natty, who ironically prepares the way for destroying the wilderness he loves, but he delights in discovering "where I guess a pioneer had a farm" on top of Mt. Judge. Ruth angrily asks him, "What do you think I care about your pioneer," and he says she should care, since she's "an American" (64). He is a bit of a latter-day pioneer observing, as he ages, the bad changes prosperity and communal growth have brought, thinking in *Rabbit Is Rich* that all of Brewer can now be seen only from the top of another hill where the "Pinnacle Hotel [is] now a site of vandalism and terror where once there had been dancing and necking" (31), and along Route 141 outside Brewer "shoppers pillag[e] the malls hacked from the former fields of corn, rye, tomatoes, cabbages, and strawberries" (4). Though he lives far earlier in green America than Harry, Natty could rue of his world, just as Harry does, that "we're using it all up" (*Rest* 326). Ecological devastation is constant in both series, from the deforestation of *The Pioneers* or just cutting down a lone tree that opens *The Prairie*, to the trees destroyed in *Rabbit at Rest* to make room for a Pizza Hut. And what would Natty, who so bitterly attacked destruction of natural resources to create "settlements," have thought of what has been done to Rabbit's Florida?

So despite vast differences in their situations and lives and in the literary modes of their representations, one in a historical romance and the other in a realistic novel, Natty and Rabbit—who on the surface may seem to have little in common save their desire to escape and their longing to return to a past world—would appear to share much that is meaningful. In a masterful scene concluding *The Prairie*, Cooper is able to summon up the sweep and range of Natty's rich life experiences at his death. The accomplishment of this scene is particularly amazing considering that Cooper still had two more novels to write in which to orchestrate events earlier in Natty's life, events that seem to resonate already in this deep scene of his dying. So when Natty sits alone under a tree, dying after a full life of turbulence and exploits, and the final word the often garrulous octogenarian adventurer speaks—almost the long novel's last word—is simply "Here," the effect is momentous (452). The word seems absolutely right and inevitable and sufficient, book-stopping. Whatever its many possible meanings, they all point to a rightness as summation of his flawed but well-lived life. Poor Studs Lonigan's final words were a "feeble" "Mother, it's getting dark" (*Judgment Day* 378). Natty is no Studs.

Nor is Rabbit, though he is also no Natty Bumppo. Rabbit's last word demands comparison with Natty's. He says "Enough," which indicates that he is in control of deciding what *is* enough as far as living is concerned, that he is in control of his part in the game sufficiently to determine that, to accept where he has arrived in life and to at least grudgingly accept his position. He calls his own game, as kids must when they play before referees blow whistles for them, and for Harry no referee beyond himself has yet arrived. Perhaps none ever will. Harry calls his game fairly. "Enough" suggests to me that he accepts responsibility for his flawed, rich life. Running away for the first time in *Rabbit, Run*—in *Rabbit at Rest* he will still think "nothing had a purity like running" (469)—young Rabbit meets a middle-aged man who apparently owns a backroads gas station, an old-timey sort of fellow who is also a farmer, who tells Rabbit where he is and where the different nearby roads will lead. He asks Harry where he wants to go and Harry replies he doesn't "know exactly." The man finally gives Harry some unforgettable if stock advice: "The only way to get somewhere, you know, is to figure out where you're going before you go there." Harry never does this. He says to the farmer, "I don't think so" (27). He improvises his life, often badly, but with many thrills and great activity. Natty always knew where he wanted to get to, but his problem was that when he got there, away from the world, the world always caught up with him, and he would have to move on, until there was really no place left to move to, which is where he was when he finally said "Here." Possibly Rabbit knew where he wanted to get when he practiced and starred at basketball, but not Harry, not afterwards, in life. "Enough" means OK, I'm satisfied to stop here, now that I am here, however I got here. This ending is to me neither banal nor disappointing.

Natty is better than the America he dies in, Studs Lonigan worse. Harry Angstrom seems about the same—no ideal, but far from the nightmare he can be and is at his worst. Though his early promise is never fulfilled the way his star potential held out the chance that it might be, in the performance of his life, through his intense and often loving engagement with life, through his suffering and some learning from it, he is, finally, no flop. He is successful whatever he thinks of himself, as a human being, no failure, no Hall of Fame candidate except in his depiction.

Note

1. I use the following editions: *Rabbit, Run* (New York: Fawcett Crest, 1960); *Rabbit Redux* (New York: Fawcett Crest, 1971); *Rabbit Is Rich* (New York: Fawcett Crest, 1981); *Rabbit at Rest* (New York: Knopf, 1990).

11 Judie Newman
Rabbit at Rest
The Return of the Work Ethic

Writing in 1988, I argued that the Rabbit trilogy cohered around one major organizing theme, that of the relation between individual and society, particularly expressed as the instinctual, sensual and libidinal dimensions of the human being in conflict with social constraints that are politically and economically determined. Updike quite clearly—though not naively—draws upon Freud's analysis of society as founded upon repression. To recap: for Freud, the methodical sacrifice of libido to work and reproduction *is* culture. Because the lasting interpersonal relations on which civilization depends presuppose that the sex instincts are inhibited, there is therefore a fundamental opposition between sex and social utility, and a huge price in individual happiness that must be paid for the benefits of civilized life. Most work requires that energy be directed away from direct sexual satisfaction, to produce the gains of technological civilization, a process arguably exacerbated in modern society in which desire is overcontrolled ("surplus repression") in order to maintain men as cogs in the industrial machine. In the Rabbit trilogy, Updike introduced this central conflict in explicitly Freudian terms in *Rabbit Run*, proceeding to examine in *Rabbit Redux* the potential MacLuhanite sensual liberation of the individual, freed from toil by the new technology, and in *Rabbit Is Rich* the ways in which society may deform and exploit the instincts by the creation of mass fantasy in order to repress once more.

The reader who turns to *Rabbit at Rest* will find few immediate surprises. Work, technology, and instinctual indulgence remain the central organizing concerns of what is now a tetralogy. Once again Updike stages the Freudian psychomachia of society as opposed to instinct, dramatizing both the gratifications and the failings of the American Dream. But with one major difference. In *Rabbit at Rest*, in contrast to the libidinal economy of scarcity in the preceding volume, desire is overindulged, actively encouraged by a society intent on keeping its members unquestioningly inside the American myth. In the America of *Rabbit at Rest*, notions of play, games, leisure, and holiday occupy center stage, together with their commodification in the leisure industries, whether official or unofficial. The novel opens in the emblematic locale of Florida, as Nelson arrives for a short vacation with his father, now in enforced retirement and entirely at leisure. The legitimate attractions of Deleon—golf, theme parks, cinemas, and bingo—are shadowed by commodities equally productive of engineered happiness. While Harry has been overindulging in food and play, Nelson has been acting on the same imperatives. Ironically, in the subsequent action, it is Nelson's permanent holiday of crack cocaine addiction that triggers Harry's return to work to safeguard the family business (an image that unites the forces of work and reproduction) and the forcible reassertion of the work ethic in the shape of Mr. Shimada, who terminates the Springer Motors Toyota franchise on the grounds that they all "play" too much. Despite the pleasurable emphasis of their advertising slogans ("I Love What You Do for Me, Toyota" [375]),[1] Toyota technology demands the sacrifice of individual happiness to the corporate culture.

In its broad strokes, the plot clearly indicates Updike's continued interrogation of the Freudian repressive hypothesis. The ambivalent role of technology in liberating/enslaving the protagonists is emphasized in the chemical technology of crack cocaine, which almost ruins the family as both an emotional and financial entity. In a parallel plot, medical technology offers Harry physical salvation (a choice between angioplasty and a coronary bypass) but reduces him to a soft machine, a spectator on the activity of his own heart, displayed on a television screen, "a typical American heart," "tired and stiff and full of crud" (164). Both male protagonists appear to end the novel in a state of newfound happiness, but an apparently commodified one. Nelson, born-again in a narcotics clinic, substitutes faith for his addiction, but in a form that has such a mechanistic emphasis that it appears as merely a means of reducing the individual to conformity. Harry is last seen floating in a morphine haze after a massive heart attack. The two have apparently swapped places, with Nelson, sober and abstemious, at the bedside of his father, who is described as floating "in a bed of happy unfeeling" (504). In the outcome, the indulgences of each of the two men represent less the lineaments of gratified desire than a surrender to the death instincts, a return to a pain-free state of nonbeing.

As a result, the novel interestingly reverses the structure of its predecessors. In *Rabbit, Run,* Harry's indulgent holiday from virtue with Ruth is ended by the death of his daughter and a return to family and repression. In *Rabbit Redux* the excursion with Jill and Skeeter again closes with death and a return to the family, as well as a job in the family business. In *Rabbit Is Rich* an actual excursion (to a Caribbean playground) brings Harry into metaphoric contact with death and nothingness (the sexual encounter with Thelma, terminally ill of lupus) and returns him, chastened, to the fold. (He is last seen holding his new granddaughter in his arms.) *Rabbit at Rest,* however, begins in leisure, then makes a brief return to the world of work, only for Harry to restage his original "run" once more, this time definitively, returning to die on the basketball court in Florida as the circle of the tetralogy closes upon him.

In this connection, the political dimension of the novel is worth foregrounding. In Updike's work, economic forms and fictional form continually interact. The structural reverse reflects America's own self-identified reverses, its position of global domination under threat from the new "Asian tiger" economies. When Nelson plans to replace the Toyota franchise with a shop selling jet skis, expensive toys for a leisured society, Harry argues caution in the face of imminent Depression: "We don't have any discipline! We're drowning in debt! We don't even own our own country any more!" (411). Nelson's view is that nobody works for necessities anymore, that the profit is in toys and fads, in other words that work has become play—and conversely, play is work. In Mr. Shimada's analysis, the United States has opted for a society based upon instinctual gratification and has lost its technological lead as a result. After a preliminary polite conversational skirmish with a saleswoman on the subject of playing tennis (in his heavily accented English he appears to be asking her if she *prays* [381]), he delivers an authoritative verdict: "Toyota does not enjoy bad games prayed with its autos" (387). Extolling the virtues of discipline, Shimada notes the American lack of happiness in indulgence and places the blame firmly on too much freedom, too little order, and on both Nelson's and Harry's games: "Not just son. Who is father and mother of such son? Where are they? In Frorida enjoying sunshine and tennis" (387). Mr. Shimada's speech is entirely consonant with Updike's description to Iwao Iwamoto of the change in values in America, as opposed to the image of Japan that reflects the Freudian hypothesis: "We picture Japan as a very efficient and orderly place, with everything in its place and very industrious. And any industrious people have repressed a great deal in terms of pleasure-seeking, or feeling, even. One of the phenomena that I've noticed in my lifetime has been a loss of the sense of the urgency to work" (Iwamoto 122). Expanding to his theme, Updike noted that for his own father work had a sacred importance (he had to work or his family would starve), whereas Updike's own sons did not take work so seriously: "I think this creates a kind of vacuum which has to be filled with other things—with romance, or sex, or even games" (122).

In the novel, Updike inscribes this particular opposition of indulgence/ achievement in global political terms, as the cold war (the ultimate image of repression, at home and abroad) comes to an end, and America finds itself liberated into insignificance, consigned to the sidelines "like a big Canada" (352). In its political dynamics, baldly stated, the novel appears to argue straightforwardly in favor of repression in the service of an older American code of family values, the work ethic, technological progress, and the right of America to global domination. But Updike is never quite as simple as this. The plot of *Rabbit at Rest* is very carefully engineered in order to strike a series of variations on the central theme; the reader's experience is thus of a finely nuanced succession of debating points scored with or against the Freudian hypothesis, together with its political agenda.

Rabbit at Rest divides into three long sections, FL (Florida), PA (Pennsylvania), and MI (Myocardial Infarction): the latter's substitution of a coronary for a place-name converts the whole of America into the site of one giant heart attack. In the opening sequence Harry is poised between two alternatives—play as death or pain as life. Florida, where life is a "perpetual vacation" (41), has necrotic rather than erotic overtones, the airport terminal (aptly named) offering large windows onto the runways, "so if there's a crash everybody can feast upon it with their own eyes" (7). Chewing peanut brittle, Harry, unwittingly feasting on his own death, meditates obsessively on other deaths (Max Robinson, Lockerbie, Roy Orbison) and on a culture that is, in his view, in terminal tailspin: "Everything falling apart, airplanes, bridges, eight years under Reagan of nobody minding the store, making money out of nothing, running up debt" (9). When Harry scares his family by getting lost in the terminal, Nelson's comment foreshadows the end of the novel: " 'Suddenly we looked around and you weren't there.' Like Pan-Am 103 on the radar screen" (25). In conversation with his father, Nelson had derided the values of the work ethic, the Toyota emphasis on rules and discipline and the absence of creativity. His grandfather's era had allowed for more freedom: "Grandpa was a dealer. . . . He loved to make deals. . . . It was fun. There was some play in the situation" (8). The conversation is set in Deleon named for Ponce de León, the "discoverer" of Florida, but pronounced by the local people "Deal ya in"—conjoining the imagery of finance and play, commodification and game. Just like his father, Nelson promptly gets "lost," in quest of a different kind of dealer, to supply his habit. The losses attendant on indulgence are foregrounded in the Florida sequence, which moves from minor "missing persons" incidents to a near-fatal accident to Judy, the potential heir to the curse of Rebecca and Jill, and to Harry's heart attack.

The theme is firmly established in an extended sequence that concerns Harry playing golf, a game in which his losses are dual—the game itself, and twenty dollars to his opponents. The dialogue of the scene continually contrasts play (the game, the foursome's comments) with death and pain. Conversation ranges over politics, drug addiction, disease. The central theme is stated by Bernie Drechsel: "There are two routes to happiness. Work for it, day after day, like you and I did, or take a chemical shortcut." In his view it is unsurprising, given the state of the world, that kids take the shortcut cocaine, described as "instant happiness" (57). Immediate gratification, rather than the long haul, is Nelson's choice, and by implication, America's. Nelson describes the experience of cocaine as "feeling no pain" (147), and in this he is not distinct from the political choice of his father's generation. "Rabbit liked Reagan. . . . Under Reagan . . . it was like anesthesia" (61). Bernie (his memories of heart surgery still fresh) cautions: "When you come out of anesthesia, it hurts like hell" (61). Bernie and his Jewish friends, fellow adherents of the work ethic, represent a set of values in which repression in the service of work and family is primary. "The soldier in Harry, the masochistic Christian, respects men like this. It's total love, like women provide, that makes you soft and does you in" (63). The Jewish/Christian opposition dramatizes, however, an alternative way of reading the work/play dynamic, reminiscent of that developed in *Rabbit, Run* between good works and grace, Eccles and Kruppenbach. For Bernie golf is "just a game" (5), not, as Harry intermittently sees it, "infinity, an opportunity for infinite improvement" (65). Ironically, Harry loses the game because he is hampered by repressed emotion, following a family row: "I couldn't get my ass into it, I couldn't release. I couldn't let go," he explains (68). In *Rabbit, Run*, Updike had suggested the possibility of reading Harry's playfulness less as social irresponsibility than as presocial innocence, instinctual openness, even spiritual grace—values lost to social man. Though the connection between play and grace is only vestigially developed in this initial game, it recurs in the game with which the novel closes.

In general terms, however, in the Florida sequence, play features repeatedly as pain or loss. Harry remembers holidays as "Torture" (48), though he himself promotes an "educational ordeal" (50), a visit to the Edison house, in preference to an excursion to the attractions of Disney. The house displays grounds full of exotic trees, apparently a triumph for nature and indulgence. (The eye lingers on the sloth tree and the apparently immortal banyan.) Nature, however, is firmly subordinate to culture here. All the trees had been imported in the search for a substitute for rubber. The Edison house proclaims technological triumphalism, a monument to the invention of the storage battery, phonograph, toaster, waffle iron, and other examples of the type of technology that has liberated the Angstroms into leisure. They remain bored, irritated, or impatient and retire speedily to McDonald's, where bingo is available in one corner. While Janice (about to become a career woman when the business collapses) watches *Working Girl,* Harry and Roy play a video game: *Annihilation.* Roy's attention span is too short to enjoy a long movie. He had already left *Dumbo* halfway through, before events turned upbeat. Presciently Harry points out that "it all works out. Roy, you should have stayed to the end. If you don't stay to the end the sadness sticks with you" (100). Both grandchildren, however, appear constitutionally incapable of the long haul. In front of the television, Judy continually channel-surfs, possessed by "a gluttony for images" (78) almost as devouring as her grandfather's appetite for snacks. Judy's television-watching offers an apt image of the fashion in which the Angstroms are being formed and molded by the mass fantasies disseminated by the media. Family dinner in the "mortuary calm" (31) of Valhalla Village is dominated by technological play, bingo numbers blaring from a loudspeaker. Harry can see Judy speak, and Pru's mouth move in response, but the sound track is that of the bingo caller. When Judy watches television, her attention is held, if not for long, by a film, *The Return of Martin Guerre,* the tale of a man who usurps another man's wife and family. Harry rather enjoys the idea: "There ought to be a law that we change identities and families every ten years or so" (84). As well as an in-joke for the knowing reader (the tetralogy appears at ten-year intervals), the comment is proleptic. In the event, Harry will take over Nelson's job and, for one night, his wife. Judy's channel-surfing vividly reveals the instability of the family in an America dominated by exchange values. In *Rabbit Is Rich* the wife-swapping episode introduced the notion of individuals as mere counters in emotional barter. Now whole families are interchangeable: "Faces, black in *The Jeffersons,* white in *Family Ties,* imploringly pop into visibility and then vanish" (77).

In the pursuit of easy happiness, the Angstroms risk dehumanization. Harry's bedtime reading, identified by Stacey Olster ("Rabbit Is Redundant") as Barbara Tuchman's *The First Salute,* restates the problems of the novel in broader historical terms: "Fantasies about America produced two strongly contradictory conclusions that in the end came to the same point of injecting some caution into the golden dreams. . . . Climate in the New World . . . made men listless and indolent, they might become happy but never stalwart. America . . . 'was formed for happiness, but not for empire' " (*Rest* 85).

Harry's reaction to this admonitory comment is telling. Hilariously, as he drifts off to sleep, he surfs the page much as Judy surfs the channels, transforming Tuchman's solid history into sexual double entendre: "Expectation of lucrative commerce . . . tangled issue . . . increased tension . . . neutral bottoms . . . French vigorously" (86).

If channel-surfing features initially as an image of technological short-circuiting of emotional affect in a society that sacrifices the long perspective to immediate gratifications, it takes on a different guise in the incident, Sunfish sailing in the Gulf, in which Judy and Harry almost die. Libidinal pleasures, with the implicit threat to family cohesion, culminate in a real threat, in the surf of the ocean itself. Harry has been offered a cheap deal on the hire of a Sunfish by the son of one of his golf partners, Gregg Silvers, a "holiday facilitator" (116) who makes his living out of the leisure industry. Harry notes that beneath his perpetual tan he is older than he at first appears: "He shouldn't still be horsing around on the beach" (118). In the locker room, immediately prior to embarking, Harry had been meditating on the opposition of natural pleasure to social repressions. Roy is circumcised. Harry is not. He wonders whether, had he been less sexually responsive, he might have been a more dependable person. "From the numb look of his prick Roy will be a solid citizen" (118). On the beach the immensity of the ocean, its "raw glory," entrances him, especially in contrast to the "hemmed in" nature of his own native state. Pennsylvania is remembered as a land "dingy with use," a *worked* nature, where even the wild patches "had been processed by men" (119). Out in the Gulf, however, one puff of wind is enough to capsize the boat. Play almost does result in death, as commodified pleasure is transformed into an encounter with nature red in tooth and claw. Struggling heroically to save his granddaughter's life, Harry suffers a heart attack that is presented as life-giving pain: "Joy that Judy lives crowds his heart, a gladness that tightens and rhythmatically hurts, like a hand squeezing a ball for exercise" (132). Although in agony, Harry "feels good, down deep" (138), rescued from anesthesia into life. Singing to keep Harry from lapsing into unconsciousness, Judy can at first only remember snatches of television commercials. "It is like switching channels back and forth" (139), though her attention seems to linger, appropriately, on "Coke is it!" But slowly her voice strengthens, and the songs increase in length, as she returns to those of the past, children's classics from the movies of the Depression years. As play becomes a desperate struggle to survive, a long haul back to the safety of the shore, it is only Judy's existence that prevents Harry from giving in to death.

In the aftermath, Pru attempts to retranslate the event back into a lighter vein, suggesting that instead of being trapped, Judy was merely hiding from Harry "as a sort of game" (159). The suggestion registers a truth of a kind. A game that had got out of hand almost did kill Judy, and *will* kill Harry. American free play, unrestrained indulgence, poses a threat to Judy's survival, whether directly (the crack dealers who threaten to kidnap Nelson's family) or, more generally, in the attenuated human relationships and lack of responsibility of a generation that no longer puts its children's welfare first. Nelson's squandering habits have already consigned Judy to outgrown clothes and a shabby home; more legitimate entertainments have produced a child whose gluttony for a rapid succession of images forms a parallel to her grandfather's snack-damaged heart. Harry's heart may be physically endangered. The hearts of his family risk underdevelopment, their emotions attenuated by media substitutes.

In the hospital Harry has two television screens to watch: his own heart on a monitor, and a football game. Nature has again thrown a spanner in the cultural works; the game is almost invisible as the result of a sudden fog. Television coverage has been reduced to the sideline cameras, and spectators at the game can see even less than Harry, drugged to the eyeballs in a hospital bed. The game cannot be abandoned—it is costing the sponsors a million dollars a minute. As an image of America it could hardly be more telling.[2] Nobody knows what is really going on; there is an unbridgeable gap between real action and media image. The crowd "rumbles and groans in poor sync with the television action, trying to read the game off the electronic scoreboard" (161). They are actually present, but their understanding and reaction is attuned only to the media. In contrast to the spectators, Harry, his vision less clouded as a result of his brush with death, goes beyond the commodification of America into a deeper sense of ludic existence. "The game flickering in the fog, the padded men hulking out of nothingness and then fading back again, has a peculiar beauty bearing upon Rabbit's new position at the still centre of a new world" (162).

Harry's is a lone intuition, however, amidst a plethora of images of bodily commodification. Around him the image of his heart—damaged, struggling, real—is juxtaposed with television commercials, notably one for Gallo wine (gallows humor here), which sells the product on the basis of an erotic plot line, as customer and liquor saleswoman date. " 'It was perfect,' the girl in the commercial sighingly says. . . . [Y]ou can see that they will fuck, if not this date the next . . . all by the grace of Gallo" (165). Janice ("a channel that can't be switched" [168]) hangs equally starry-eyed on the jargon of the heart specialist, intent on restoring the physical process to smooth function without any awareness of the emotionally calcified hearts around him. Judy, channel-surfing again, pauses only on images of physical violence. Bruce Lee's kung fu kicks alternate with the surgeon's plans to violate Harry's body, fading into nude bodies, and a film in which a man changes into a werewolf. On screen, bodies metamorphose painlessly, instantly interchangeable, in the fiction of play that is American culture. The implication is that the next generation will have precious few desires to repress—they are easily, if unsatisfactorily, gratified by a form of media play that sidelines reality in a fog of mystification and commodification. Bodies and hearts have become only constructed products. America is no longer simply surrendering to pleasurable emotion as opposed to sacrificing all to the work ethic. It is confusing the two, turning all forms of emotion into marketable product, all play into work. In a real economic sense, America *capitalizes* on family affections, while simultaneously deforming them to commercial ends. Even more disturbingly, Roy has learned from his experiences (as he demonstrates by painfully yanking out his grandfather's nose tube) "the idea of inflicting pain to show emotion" (313). In this he is distinctly representative of the underside of the American Dream, his actions generalized in Charlie Stavros's comments on punk fashion: "Pain is where it's at for punks. Mutilation, self-hatred, slam dancing. For these kids today, ugly is beautiful. That's their way of saying what a lousy world we're giving them" (237). Harry's implicit choice of pain as opposed to political and emotional anesthesia has both its representative and its darker side.

Back in Pennsylvania, Harry embarks on a period of convalescence and treatment that restores his heart in both physical and emotional senses—angioplasty repairs the muscle, and the near-death experience sharpens his emotional take on the world. The extent to which he has come to his senses (sensually and sensibly) is underlined in the description of Pennsylvania. The return to his native state carries suggestions of a return to an older, less befogged condition in which Harry is able to disentangle libidinal pleasure from the mystifications of America, to see its attractions and its dangers. The question posed for the reader is whether this is an advance on the earlier state of anesthesia. Emotion is restored—but potentially redemonized. No longer tired of life, Harry appears to yield to sensual gratification, committing, in the act of adultery with his daughter-in-law on which the sequence closes, the one act of sensual indulgence that is, even in the permissive 1990s, utterly taboo. Harry returns to Pennsylvania in the spring as blossom erupts about him, "a sudden declaration of the secret sap that runs through everybody's lives" (179). Cruising through town, his eyes rest on women in running tights

("Young animals need to display" [182]), on a young Hispanic girl in a lilac party dress, decorated with a cloth rose ("She is a flower" amid "a swarm of boys" [183]), and a half-naked boy kissing his girl, all of them representing "lives that are young and rising like sap" (184). The emphasis on the irrepressibility of nature is continued in Harry's memories of Mary Ann ("his to harvest" [185], her underpants described as "stuffed with her moss" [184]) and in his awe-stricken reaction to a street of pear trees in bloom, their heart-shaped leaves bending into one another to form an enclosure almost as enchanting as Mary Ann's, over his head.

This America—an America of happy indulgence—contrasts with Harry's later experience, particularly in his relationship with Thelma. Thelma (relocated in a new housing development that is skimpy on trees, and decidedly not representative of natural overabundance) has loved Harry only within the masochistic framework of Freudian repression, sin, and guilt. (She understands their relationship as having "enriched her transactions with God" [193] by giving her something to be guilty about.) A conventionally good housewife and mother, Thelma's secret affair with Harry embodies the Freudian economy, in which family and work take precedence over sensual gratification. The latter has not been lacking (Harry remembers Thelma's plush sofa with needlepointed scatter cushions and lace antimacassars as conveniently positioned for oral sex). By bringing Harry news of Nelson's cocaine habit, however, Thelma transforms a potentially erotic tryst into characteristic sadness: "Why don't you like me to make you happy? Why have you always fought it?" As Harry admits, "We've never been exactly set up for a lot of happiness" (200). A second factor also comes between Harry and consummation—his own fear of AIDS, a new and powerfully repressive element in the dynamic relation of eros to culture. As the plot develops it transpires that Nelson's associates in the scam that ruins the Angstroms are two gay men, both of whom are to die of AIDS. If the national, political reference to the Japanese has disquieting elements, the sexual politics of the plot are even less reassuring. Because of unrestrained indulgence in "unnatural," nonreproductive desires, the family business totters. Racial and gender betrayal are both potentially present in the plot. Everything appears to support the Freudian case for repression as necessary for social health. Indeed, when Nelson attacks Pru, Harry features entirely as the voice of order. Nelson's attack is described as a typical product of a society that is glutted by images and which expresses its emotions by violence. Nelson felt "like a monster or something had taken over my body and I was standing outside watching and felt no connection with myself. Like it was all on television" (258). When Nelson takes refuge in psychobabble and therapy-speak, Harry asserts an older set of values: "We can't expect society to run our lives for us. . . . There comes a point when you got to take responsibility" (265).

Harry's angioplasty also appears to register Freudian imperatives, if in quasi-religious guise, as the opposition of grace/good works shadows that of pleasure/toil. He reflects that the hospital is no longer run by nuns. Vocations have dried up, and the days of deferred gratification are over: "No more good people, waiting to have their run in the afterlife. The thing about the afterlife, it kept this life within bounds, somehow, like the Russians. Now there's just Japan, and technology, and the profit motive, and getting all you can while you can" (269). In a wonderfully apt phrase, Harry telescopes God, the cold war, and sexual repression in one image. Now the Iron Curtain is coming down on all counts. Angioplasty enacts Harry's worst nightmares, of invasion and violation. In the process he becomes, successively, a soft machine, a media product, a woman, and a gay man. Harry has persistently resisted surgery on the grounds that it constitutes an unnatural violation. "You, the natural you, are technically dead. A machine is living for you" (266). When Charlie Stavros objects that "You're just a soft machine" (234), Harry silently resists, envisaging himself as "a vehicle of grace" (235). Opting for angioplasty rather than open-heart surgery, he is horrified to discover that the process is carried out under local anesthetic, and that he can watch it all on television. As "The Rabbit Angstrom Show" unfolds (on several television screens in the operating theater and the monitoring room), Harry observes the catheter snaking into his heart and wonders "if this is what having a baby is like, having Dr. Raymond inside you? How do women stand it, for nine months? Not to mention being screwed in the first place. Can they really like it? Or queers being buggered?" In his view, "godless technology is fucking the pulsing wet tubes we inherited from the squid, the boneless sea-cunts" (270). Indeed, his voice is now high, "as if out of a woman's throat" (271). Even worse, imagistically, the act is not located in the vaginal so much as the alimentary realm. Harry repeatedly describes the plaque in his heart muscle as if it were food debris—"Rice Krispies" (270), for example. The operation involves a catheter expanding (a balloon inflates) in order to clear the artery of its blockages and open up a larger internal space. The description is clearly tumescent. Harry sees "a segment of worm thicken and swell, pressing the pallid Rice Krispies together" (270). Because of the injected dyes, his only other sensation is that of "knifelike sweet pressure in his bladder" (271). To add to his complete humiliation, the two doctors agree that the procedure has been entirely successful, in tones reminiscent of a beer commercial, "like those voices on television that argue about the virtues of Miller Lite" (271). Even worse, it transpires that, without even recognizing it, Harry has had a heart attack anyway, or as the surgeons put it, "some new Q waves and . . . an elevation of the creatinine kinase myocardial enzyme, with positive MB bands" (281). The language of the heart offers its own mystifications, its own forms of exploitation.

It is his perception of the violation of his masculinity, his individuality, and his heart that motivates Harry's adultery with Pru. In committing this particular act, Harry marks a decisive division between his own desires and state-sponsored indulgence. Incest with one's in-laws is not generally a feature of the plot line of soap opera: this is an event that cannot be reassimilated into the comfortable schmaltz of American "family values." It is, as far as Harry is concerned, a purely libidinal event, in opposition to both Freudian repression and the commodified gratifications previously on offer to him. The encounter takes place while Janice is out taking an exam as part of her return to the world of work. Janice has already sacked Nelson from the car lot; temporarily he has been sacrificed to the business and removed from the family group. Both Janice and Thelma are no longer objects of libidinal fantasy. Janice, converted to power dressing and hulking shoulders, is now "electric, businesslike" (292), resembling a television newscaster. Bearing news of Nelson's embezzlement, she appears to be wearing contact lenses, tears "prepared for him during the station break" (292). Her language lends her a preprogrammed quality, with her need to "process" after all the "trauma" (298). Thelma, meanwhile, has herself become a soft machine, dependent on the process of dialysis for life, with a permanent shunt attached to her arm.

In contrast, the sexual encounter, in the spare room that is permeated with the green, wet fragrance of leafy trees, overtly draws upon suggestions of natural spontaneity and innocent emotion. In the past, before Nelson (safeguarding the domestic structure) cut down the great copper beech tree that shaded the room, Harry experienced the sound of rain in its leaves as the most religious experience of his life. He still associates nature with grace and innocence, in the realm of the presocial. In bed, Harry places Pru's hand on his erection with a gesture that "has the presexual quality of one child sharing with another an interesting discovery" (341). To the accompaniment of the affective fallacy—crashing rain, thunder and lightning—Pru disrobes "as if in overflow of this natural heedlessness . . . lovely much as those pear trees in blossom . . . were lovely . . . a piece of Paradise" (341).

The irony here is that, although Harry is spontaneous, Pru is not. Indeed, she has chosen quite consciously to sleep with Harry in order to safeguard

her own family unit. Before their encounter, Harry and Pru spend the evening on the sofa watching television, particularly *The Cosby Show,* in which
Harry admires Phylicia Rashad's wide smile, "implying that indecency is all
right in its place, its wise time, as in one of those mutually ogling Huxtable
snuggles that end many a Cosby show" (332). Judy however, interrupts,
switching to the image of a huge turtle "determined to defend its breeding
grounds" (332). Unknown to Harry, Janice is planning to sell their house, in
order to pay the debt to Toyota, and move back in with Nelson and Pru.
Watching *Unsolved Mysteries,* Harry had been struck by the fluency of the
witnesses; America has become "a nation of performers" (334). It does not
strike him that Pru is one of them, even when she joins him, scantily clad
(but equipped with condoms), laments her enforced sexual abstinence, and
huddles close to him while carefully checking his capacities ("Does Janice say
you can't fuck? What did your doctor say?" [340]). Describing the ruin of her
life, Pru wails, "I had my little hand of cards and played them and now I'm
folded" (339). But in fact she is playing with considerable skill: both in the
sexual game (Harry feels "expertly used" to provide two orgasms), in the
finely calibrated performance that he never suspects of being a role, and in
the long-term strategy of which it is a part. In America play has a use value,
as Pru demonstrates, defending her breeding grounds.

Harry's ignorance also carries a political point. Shortly before leaving
the hospital Harry had met Annabelle, the woman who may be his daughter
by Ruth. Annabelle had left Brewer for an independent life but has now returned to live with her mother. She contrasts with Harry's sister, Mim, remembered as "a leggy colt of a girl dying to break out of Brewer, to kick or
fuck her way through the fence" (283). Once out, Mim never came back to
the fold. Harry then has a peculiar dream in which Ruth appears to be living
with him and Janice, and his embrace of her is "semi-permitted, like an embrace of a legal relation" (288). The house in which they are living is the
Springer house, the polka dots on Ruth's dress are the pear blossom. Harry
reflects that "two men for a woman and vice versa is just about right, just as
we need two kinds of days, workdays and holidays" (302), underscoring the
connection between the adulterous triangles of the tetralogy and the work/
holiday opposition. As the dream suggests, on some unconscious level, Harry
is aware of Janice's plans—though he converts them into erotic fantasy. Again
he is politically typical. His ignorance is that of a nation fed on dreams,
which now wakes up to economic and affectional scarcity. Remembering
Reagan, he comments, quite unselfconsciously, that Reagan "had that dream
distance; the powerful thing about him as President was that you never knew

how much he knew, nothing or everything" (291). Harry's own situation reveals, however, that ignorance is not bliss. The dream of happiness for all, guilt-free and permitted, has terminated. Harry may happily envisage sharing himself with two mistresses; he does not envisage being forced by economics to include a son, daughter-in-law, and two kids as well.

Where the Florida section of the novel ended with an encounter with nature which was a corrective to mass fantasy, the Pennsylvania sequence closes with an encounter that is much less "natural" than Harry thinks. Pru is almost as much an actress as Phylicia Rashad. As the final section of the novel reveals, Harry gets his manhood back only in illusion—and in the service of Pru's economic ends. In addition, at the car lot he discovers that technology has "screwed" him economically as well as physically: Nelson has exploited the computerization of the bank to extract five car loans in the name of a dead gay friend. When Harry marches in a Fourth of July parade as Uncle Sam, a role for which he is apparently fitted by his service during Korea and his past as a sports hero, his masculine strutting is rather belied by his appearance. The wig makes him look like "a very big red-faced woman" (357). Citizens keep asking him for directions, "because he is dressed as Uncle Sam and should know," but he has to admit that "he doesn't know anything" (359). This is a "holiday and liberty" occasion—in American terms *the* holiday celebrating liberty—and the crowd that turns out to celebrate the American Dream appears to Harry "younger, more naked, less fearful, better" (365), the roads lined by "a cheerful froth of flesh" (364) creating in him the impression that "this is the happiest fucking country the world has ever seen" (366). (The erotic emphasis is relentless.) Harry's own happiness, however, is drug-assisted. It is the Nitrostat tablet that has opened up his veins "like flower petals uncurling in the sun" (365). The parade is immediately followed by an account of Thelma's death, raving, angry and hallucinating, an American nightmare. A less celebratory communal ritual is staged in her funeral, at which Harry and Thelma's husband, Ron, former basketball teammates, almost come to blows. At the end of the funeral the two, "with a precision as if practiced, execute a criss-cross" (374), games players to the last.

The most skillful player, however, is ultimately revealed to be Pru. When Janice finally tells Harry of her plans, she assures him that there is no way Pru can resist. Janice holds the economic power: she still owns the Springer house. But in revealing her adultery with Harry, Pru plays her trump card, as Janice recognizes: "She didn't seem repentant, just tough, and obviously not wanting me to come live in the house. That's why she told" (427). Pru has defended her breeding grounds in adept fashion, a performer who is both inside and outside the game, able to manipulate the others to her own ends. Nelson is also able to exploit the American commodification of affection. When Nelson learns that his father has made love to his wife, his reaction is telling. He doesn't hit him, or her, or howl, or scream. He sets to work, without delay, to set up a family therapy session: "He says this will need a lot of processing" (427).

Faced with this distinctly unenticing proposition, Harry flees. As Jeff Campbell comments in his essay in this volume, Nelson's therapy is an extension of the machine world, a creed that is entirely organized around the idea of refining the human product. Nelson does not seem to think or feel, he processes. Fatter, he resembles in equal parts Harry's mother-in-law (395) and a television evangelist (396). As the heir to the Reverend Eccles, his faith is "faith that the process will work" (398), faith in "God as we understand him" (397). Ironically, his recovery is total. He has transformed his initial libidinal excess into work (a career opportunity as a social worker) and rewritten it in "family" terms, as a mere symptom of his problems with Harry. For Nelson, the addiction is now less important than "getting the relational poison out of your system" (416).

Harry's flight, a completion of the interrupted escape attempt of *Rabbit, Run*, is not, however, a straightforward escape. On the debit side he has escaped responsibility, indulged his libido handsomely, and fled the world of work to that of permanent holiday. On the other hand, the Florida to which he returns is not the same world as that of the opening sequence. On his daily walks he moves away from the mass vacation locale to an older working community that supplies the labor for the hotels and condos. It is important to note here that Updike displays the economic underpinnings, other people's sacrifices, that make the permanent holiday possible and that they are black sacrifices. The black area of town, with its old-fashioned houses, chicken coops, and general stores is reminiscent of Harry's childhood, familiar and vital. Harry's identification with the black community may be naive, but it marks, at least, a clear advance on his earlier racism.

What is it exactly that kills Rabbit? Or who? Play (as the immediate cause)? Overindulgence (hence a heart attack)? Adultery? Flight from the consequences of adultery (and an angry Janice)? Or is her "hardheartedness" more responsible than his? Should responsibility be laid at the door of Pru, fighting for her family? Or Nelson, indulging his desires? Or is Harry's death in part a return to individual responsibility in opposition to the therapeutic, the commodified, the fantasy? Three points are important here. In the first place, if Updike doesn't *quite* kill Harry at the end, it is perhaps for good reason. In a sense this is not the novel in which Harry dies, but the novel in which he comes back from the dead (a form of living death), albeit briefly, to choose a better death. Second, it is important to emphasize that this death is a choice, and third, that it is a choice which aligns him with a different political and economic position.

Updike multiplies a plethora of suggestions that Harry is ready for death. Watching the basketball game, Harry thinks of Mike Schmidt, "who had the grace to pack it in when he could no longer produce," and Chrissie Evert, who "packed it in too. There comes a time" (481). He makes a last call north, to speak to his grandchildren, but is unable to hang up: "He had to make the child do it first. Chicken in a suicide pact" (490). Thereafter, in the Mead Hall of Valhalla Village, the former cold warrior sets to work to eat-to-die, retiring to dream of a curious reunion with all his dead, including, in some future incarnation, Roy, now fully grown. In choosing to play his final game, Harry also opts out of a commodified and materialist world. In his youth Harry had been an ardent believer in capitalism, as represented by Kroll's department store, despite his awareness of "the panicky gamble of all this merchandising" (454). When Kroll's closes, he realizes that "the world was not solid and benign, it was a shabby set of temporary arrangements rigged up for the time being, all for the sake of money." He comes to the conclusion that the gamble of capitalism, its deals and speculations, is no longer based on "good faith" and that nothing is sacred: "If Kroll's could go, the courthouse could go, the banks could go. When the money stopped, they could close down God himself" (455). In the event, this turns out not to be so easy. On the drive south, *play* actually does turn into *pray,* if in somewhat farcical terms. A Supreme Court ruling against organized prayer before football matches has infuriated the South. The mayor of Montgomery leads prayers at the fifty-yard line, in Alabama local ministers in the bleachers join spectators in the Lord's Prayer, and in Pensacola prayers are declaimed through bullhorns to the audience. As a result of his heart attack, Harry comes to feel that he is "in His hand already. Like you're out on the court instead of on the bench swallowing down butterflies and trying to remember the plays" (443). For Harry, the rehearsals are over. "Play" in its indulgent, "bread and circuses" sense no longer stands between him and a firm grasp of political and social reality. His bedtime reading suddenly reveals to him the costs of the American Revolution, in Tuchman's account of atrocities. Up to this point, "He has always thought of the Revolution as a kind of playful toy war, without any of that grim stuff" (492). Harry has always been torn between rebellion and conformity. Now he decides that "he loves freedom but a grassy field is his idea of enough" (479).

The endgame (on a grassy court) is clearly emblematic. In the alternative Florida that Harry has discovered, work and play seem to be held in creative balance. The game is played in an "unhurried" and cooperative fashion, "all together making a weave, nobody trying too hard" (480). Harry also advances beyond his earlier, defensive homophobia, unworried by the boys' suspicion of him (they take him for a "cheesecake" who is after "a black boy's dick" [483]). In the final game, Harry plays alone against an opponent who, in symbolic terms, embodies all his former nightmares. The boy is black, with "Indian" (495) high cheekbones, and is wearing a tank top decorated with a snarling tiger. He unites in one person the threats of black America, the Asian tiger economies, and ancestral guilts. Harry notes that he is an extremely skillful and deliberate performer "making good serious economical moves" (495). He is also a dealer. He offers Harry some "Scotty"—a euphemism for crack, as his gesture of cracking a whip implies. (The reference is once more to television: *Star Trek* and its catchphrase, "Beam Me Up Scotty.") Yet although Tiger clearly has the whip hand in the game, he is also described as "gracious" (498) and his play is based on an honor system, calling his own fouls on himself. Harry has plenty of warning of impending death, but courts it as if it were paradise. He feels "as if his tree of veins and arteries is covered with big pink blossoms," while the pain in his back is "spreading, like clumsy wings" (498). As he leaps, to die in play, he goes "way up toward the torn clouds," beaming up in a fashion that is about as transcendent as Harry's own limited consciousness will allow: "He feels something immense persistently fumble at him" (499). As "the social net twitches" and a neighbor calls the emergency services, Tiger, the heir to the younger Rabbit, feels "the impulse to run" (499) and takes off, one step ahead of the paramedics, whose emergency sirens suggest to the bystanders the beginnings of hurricane Hugo, the natural cataclysm that coincides with Harry's death.

The tetralogy ends on an ambivalent note. On the plus side, Harry has (at least in his own experience) swapped commodified gratification for real sex, and anesthetized deathliness for a real death. Janice also experiences a reawakening of naked emotion. When she sees Harry, she is hit by a wave of enormous feeling and realizes that her hardhearted silence had been "a kind of addiction" (503). Janice is nonetheless still ready to maintain her toughness with Nelson ("after a while the mother in you dies just like heart muscle" [501]), who appears to be quite unregenerate. At the close, as Nelson whines by his deathbed, Harry wants to put him out of his misery: "*Nelson,* he wants to say, *you have a sister*" (504). But the message is garbled. The existence of Annabelle remains "an old story, going on and on, like a radio nobody's listening to" (275). Here there is no soap opera deathbed confession and re-union. The story—in its secrecy, its repression—is from another era in content and medium. It is not just a question here of lost content, but of a form of story that can no longer be told to the television-attuned Angstroms. As a result, Nelson's little sister is lost to silence—as Harry falls into the embrace of her proverbial namesake—Little Sister Death.

Notes

1. *Rabbit at Rest* (London: André Deutsch, 1990). All subsequent references are from this edition.

2. A very similar image of a fogbound game as national symbol (baseball in this case) occurs in Anne Tyler, *Ladder of Years* (London: Chatto and Windus, 1995), 131ff.

James Plath
Verbal Vermeer
Updike's Middle-Class Portraiture

> Praise *Disney,* for dissolving *Goofy's* stride
> Into successive stills our eyes elide;
> And *Jan Vermeer,* for salting humble bread
> With Dabs of light, as well as bricks and thread.
>
> *Updike,* Midpoint *(38)*

André Malraux once wrote, "Whenever we have records enabling us to trace the origins of a painter's, a sculptor's, any artist's vocation, we trace it . . . to the vision, the passionate emotion, or the serenity, of another artist" (281). This is certainly true of Updike, who, in addition to praising the art of animation, has said of his own work, "One can give no more than what one has received, and we try to create for others, in our writings, aesthetic sensations we have experienced. In my case . . . the graphic precision of a Durer or a Vermeer" (*Picked-Up Pieces* 36).

Of all the artists Updike mentions in his writing, none is cited more often than seventeenth-century Dutch painter Jan Vermeer, whose near photographic depictions of household scenes from everyday bourgeois life are recalled in Updike's own fictional portraits of upper-middle-class domesticity—particularly those set in his native Pennsylvania, where the Dutch historically settled. Vermeer, unlike most of his genre-painting contemporaries, deemphasized humorous and narrative elements and instead concentrated on the arrangement of objects and the play of light within an interiorized space, what Malraux called "a simplified color harmony shot through with light" (339). Because he treated objects and humans equally, the former acquired a sense of importance, and the latter a kind of memorialized stasis—each "favored" by the artist's even, modulated light. It was not until the 1860s—when French impressionism was emerging and the public's attention was drawn to surfaces, shadow, and light—that Vermeer's work first began to be appreciated and his artistic vision accepted. Now, of course, his view of the world is considered modern: the fracturing of spaces, the equal treatment of objects and humans as forms, the notion of form as content, and, most importantly,

A Maid Asleep by Johannes Vermeer. Oil on canvas. The Metropolitan Museum of Art, Bequest of Benjamin Altman, 1913 (14.40.611).

a harmony based on color and tonal juxtapositions, brought about by Vermeer's innovative use of daylight.

Vermeer's was a world of the commonplace, of private moments far less moralistic or anecdotal than are found in the paintings of his contemporaries. Action, when it does occur, is restricted to a single common activity or gesture, while the cool atmosphere of Vermeer's surfaces creates a state of suspended animation: a woman pours milk into a pitcher that never becomes full; a "procuress" collects for a night of passion, though her customer's hand never leaves her breast; and a lace-maker's fingers effortlessly hold onto taut threads as if they were life itself. In Vermeer's interiors, folds of tapestry, maps, letters, loaves of bread, household vessels, chairs, and musical instruments become as much of interest as the equally static human elements, and modulated broad sunlight seems to select areas randomly to highlight or "glorify."

In this respect, Vermeer was some two hundred years ahead of his time. As Peter Caldwell wryly observes in *The Centaur,* "That Vermeer himself had been obscure and poor I know. But I reasoned that he had lived in backward times" (78). In a later echo, Updike told a Boston television audience that the painter he admires most is Vermeer, adding, "I, myself, in my attempt to be an artist in words, have looked to museums—especially modern museums—as some sort of example of what art might do now. The little *frisson* or big *frisson* I get in the museum is something I hope to translate into my own writing" (Lydon 218–19).

Ironically, Updike's apparent attempts to apply painterly techniques to fiction—"to transcribe middleness with all its grits, bumps, and anonymities" into something more magical (*Assorted Prose* 186), or to appreciate the life-giving effects of light on commonplace subjects and objects—has elicited nearly the same critical lack of understanding that greeted Vermeer during the painter's lifetime. As Donald J. Greiner so succinctly observed, Updike's critics are disturbed by "the lavish care expended to tell the tales not of heroic men but of little people living little lives" (*Updike's Novels* 1). Arthur Mizener noted in his review of *Pigeon Feathers* that Updike has a "highly negotiable talent for adorning his stories with a cosmatesque surface of very great and radically irrelevant decorative charm" (45), while Robert S. Gingher concluded that Updike has an "exquisite, photographic ability to capture and preserve the small details, the quotidian minutiae which fill the spaces of his characters' lives," but questioned the author's suburban subject matter and "message" (98).

If one considers Updike's fiction as deliberate attempts at visual-to-verbal transformations in the manner of Vermeer, such criticisms border on praise. Consider Paul Theroux's review of *Too Far to Go,* for example: "It seems odd . . . that the grace-note of Updike's fiction should be optimism—a radiant box of corn flakes in the kitchen mess, a cascade of Calgonite offering an epiphany in the dishwasher, and so forth—because his people are not so much learning marriage as pondering a way out of it" (7).

With Updike, however, it *is* enough to find radiance in the commonplace, because his characters find in such moments a means of elevating the quality of their otherwise ordinary lives, and in the process they experience a reaffirmation of life itself by noticing, as did Vermeer, how light brings substance to life. Light is definition, light is order, light is life. In Genesis, according to Christian mythos, God's command that "there be light" was the second act of creation, and the first to impose distinction or order on an otherwise dead and formless world. When the day or, in the case of the Rabbit tetralogy, a life ebbs, resulting, as the Wallace Stevens epigraph to *Rabbit Is Rich* explains, in "The difficulty to think at the end of the day, / When the shapeless shadow covers the sun / And nothing is left except light on your fur," for Harry Angstrom and other Updike characters it is important, at least, to notice and appreciate that light.[1] From the very first Rabbit novel, Harry Angstrom has seen the world from eyes that are more painterly than working class. Before he bolts, he

> walks back as far as the lit kitchen window . . . and on tiptoe looks in one bright corner. He sees himself sitting in a high chair, and a quick, odd jealousy comes and passes. It is his son. The boy's neck gleams like one more clean object in the kitchen among the cups and plates and chromium knobs and aluminum cake-making receptacles on shelves scalloped with glossy oilcloth. His mother's glasses glitter as she leans in from her place at the table. . . . Nelson's big whorly head dips on its bright neck and his foreshortened hand, dots of pink dabbles toward the spoon, wants to take it from her." (*Run* 20–21)

The surface play of light may seem extraneous or frivolous to critics, but it is extremely important to Updike, for light alone favors one object over another, and it alone has the power to transform the ordinary into the extraordinary. And no Updike character is more "photosensitive" than Harry Angstrom—the ex-jock and frustrated MagiPeeler salesman who uses language more suited to a painter. Just as Vermeer sometimes drew attention to tables and fabrics in the foreground by blurring them slightly and foreshortening them to bring about a confrontational angularity, Updike/Rabbit refers to Marty Tothero, Rabbit's former coach, as "foreshortened" (*Run* 41), which brings disturbingly closer an image that, for Rabbit, is different from the one he remembered as a youth.

Rabbit is also the Updike character most likely to objectify women in moments of reflection. As more than a few Updike scholars have noted, Rabbit is a creature who finds comfort in solid objects, who sees magic in moments of everyday life, especially when, as Fitzgerald did with his "dream girls," Harry thinks about females. Typically, when Harry contemplates the opposite sex, it occurs within a pocket of reflective space where, like Vermeer, Rabbit/Updike is able not only to notice the effects of light upon certain aspects of a subject, but to imagine or contemplate the symbolic associations. When, in *Rabbit Is Rich*, a pregnant Pru is overwhelmed by her wedding reception and Harry notices her feeling isolated in a roomful of people, he also notices a green glossy egg: "Held against her belly the bauble throws from its central teardrop a pale knife of light" (255). Although the palette is different, the technique is unmistakable. In Vermeer's *Woman in Blue Reading a Letter*, a pregnant woman, her back in shadow and her front bathed by light as she faces the window, holds a single letter suggesting correspondence from her husband. The only other "props" in the painting are two empty dining-room chairs framing the solitary figure and a map of the world hanging on the wall, which suggests a greater world beyond the implied two-person drama suspended in time.

Updike has described himself as a "highly pictorial writer" (*Picked-Up Pieces* 509), believing that "Narratives should not be *primarily* packages for psychological insights, though they can contain them, like raisins in buns. But the substance is the dough. . . . The author's deepest pride . . . [is] in his ability to keep an organized mass of images moving forward" (453). Later, Updike wrote that he "could see that [James] Thurber had a lot of trouble fitting his furniture around his people" (*Hugging the Shore* 840). For Updike, the arrangement of images—people included—is every bit as important as chronological narration.[2]

Like Vermeer, Updike is acutely aware of the relationship between his characters and the objects that surround them. As in Vermeer's *Woman in Blue Reading a Letter*, rather than "fitting his furniture" around people, Updike describes his people and objects with the same loving care, each having the same formal value. In a Vermeer painting, action is implied "offstage" through such doors and windows left deliberately open, affording the human "objects" of the painting quiet spaces in which to contemplate. Such Vermeer-like rooms occur throughout Updike's fiction, especially in the Rabbit tetralogy. Though such compositional moments occur with more frequency in the earlier novels, an older Rabbit is still able to see scenes with a painterly eye. In *Rabbit at Rest*, when Harry explores the room that used to be Nelson's, "now little Roy's," the door is ajar, and as he enters he notices that "light enters it not as sharp slices from the proximate streetlights above Joseph Street but more mistily, from the lights of the town diffused and scattered, a yellow star-swallowing glow arising foglike from the silhouettes of maples and gables and telephone poles. By this dim light he sees Pru's long body pathetically asleep across Roy's little bed." The soft and revealing light by which he views Pru is contrasted immediately by Janice and Nelson looking for him in the "bright hall" (265).

Likewise, when Harry falls asleep "drinking a Schlitz while channel-surfing with Judy," he wakes with the painter's eye for detail, noticing that "the luminous bar beneath the door is gone but a kind of generalized lavender light . . . picks out the planes and big objects of the bedroom. A square bureau holds the glassy rectangle of Nelson's high-school graduation photo; a fat pale chair holds on one arm Harry's discarded linen trousers, the folds of cloth suggesting a hollow-eyed skull stretched like chewing gum" (116). Though Updike only at times composes scenes this thoroughly in the manner of a Vermeer, the painter's compositional strategies—windows, penetrating and defining single light sources, dark figures against a light ground, attention to shadows and light, and a selective number of objects—occur in Updike's fictional descriptions with regularity.

The tendency toward offstage implied action is evident as early as *Rabbit, Run,* where Updike gives his characters a wide variety of textual space to inhabit. Some subjects exist in the foreground (Rabbit), some in the middle distance (Janice/Ruth/Tothero), and others in the background (Eccles/Kruppenbach/relatives). It is likewise interesting to note that the theological debate that dominated *The Poorhouse Fair* is drawn into the background of Updike's second novel, because of the positioning of the two ministers. As George Hunt observes, one half of the theological argument (Kruppenbach) is presented totally "offstage," while the other half (Eccles) is always projected in shadows (41), or, as Joyce Markle notes, drawn primarily in green (9)—a color that tends to recede into the background. As a result, the religious debate is never projected toward the reader as it is in *The Poorhouse Fair,* when one-third of the novel is devoted to the subject. Likewise, the Vietnam debate that loomed so large in the foreground of *Rabbit Redux*—with Skeeter and Rabbit spouting antiwar and patriotic jargon—is relegated to the background in a later novel, *The Witches of Eastwick,* where the subject is only briefly and unemotionally mentioned. Suggesting a feature that gives Vermeer's work a power lacking in most of the Dutch genre paintings of the same period, Updike's characters are always sensitive to what lies outside the "pictures" they inhabit. But also like Vermeer's subjects, they are so enchanted by the world of solid objects within their reach that they seldom care to look beyond these fictional rooms or beyond the world of their own senses.

What makes Vermeer a genius among his contemporaries, as well as among modern artists, is his unique ability to select and arrange common objects in configurations that are as formally correct as they are informally apparent. Harmony begins with the selection of images, something of which Updike seems fully aware. As he told one interviewer, "Rather than energy and violence at all costs, I prefer things to be neat and precise: 'domestic' writing. I prefer Vermeer to Delacroix" (Salgas 178). This appreciation for selecting the right objects is evident in *The Centaur*, where the narrator, Peter Caldwell, laments the "dull innocence" of his 4-H Club members in their unfortunate choice of objects to favor with light: "We met in the church basement, and after an hour of slides illuminating cattle diseases and corn pests, I would sweat with claustrophobia, and swim into the cold air and plunge at home into my book of Vermeer reproductions like a close-to-drowned man clinging to the beach" (74).

Vermeer's—and Updike's—appreciation of painting's power to redeem everyday life from mediocrity is best explained by Jill in *Rabbit Redux*. When she tells Harry and Nelson to "think of a painter" whose momentary feelings are permanently recorded on canvas, Nelson responds, "What's the point?" "The point is ecstasy," she says. "Energy. Anything that is good is in ecstasy" (158–59).

Love of detail and compositional harmony are what Updike and his fictional characters strive for and most admire. An appreciation of the sensual becomes near-sexual. In *Marry Me*, for example, when Jerry Conant takes his mistress to the National Gallery of Art in Washington, D.C., he seeks out the wall bearing three Vermeers: *A Lady Weighing Gold (Pearls)*, *Girl with a Red Hat* and *Young Girl with a Flute*. "Oh, God," he moaned, "the drawing; people never realize how much *drawing* there is in a Vermeer. The wetness of this woman's lips. These marvelous hats. And this one, the light on her hands and the gold and the pearls. That *touch*, you know; it's a double touch—the exact color, in the exact place" (37).

Conant, after seeing the exactness of the three Vermeers, is reminded that both he and his mistress are married to others—a reality that intrudes upon his dream-date/dream-state. He tells Sally, "Now you and me . . . are the exact color, but we seem to be in the wrong place" (37). Of this scene—in a moment of appreciation for Updike's painterly approach that is rare among critics—Elizabeth Tallent writes, "It is as if, for a moment, they have actually entered a Vermeer, a sort of fragile stasis, a beautifully becalmed realm in which the light streams reassuringly from a single direction. . . . The moment is almost inevitably precarious" (43).

Hunt, meanwhile, noticed in *The Centaur* that Peter's "childhood passion for Vermeer reasserts itself in his narrative . . . through his attempt to render with delicacy and simplicity the ordinary domestic scenes of his boy-hood" (56). But it can also be argued that Updike too "reasserts" his child-hood passion for Vermeer through narratives that strive for the same magical elevation of the commonplace—not only in these two fictional instances where Vermeer is mentioned so prominently, but in the whole of Updike's suburban corpus. While the Vermeer scene from *Marry Me* is actually not, as Tallent suggests, drawn in the same manner—the singular light, for instance, is not present—she nevertheless touches upon several key points that deserve further study.

That his own domestic scenes are drawn in the manner of Vermeer is suggested by other passages where allusions to the Dutch painter occur in conjunction with a comparable description. In *Couples,* Piet in his bedroom, moving in a Rabbit-like way, "hopped across the hearth-bricks worn like a passage-way in Delft and sharply kicked shut Angela's closet door, nearly striking her. She was naked. . . . Angela had flinched and now froze. . . . A lu-minous polleny pallor, the shadow of last summer's bathing suit, set off her surprisingly luxuriant pudenda . . . her tipped arms seemed, simple and sym-metrical, a maiden's . . . sighing, immersed in a clamor of light and paint, the Hanemas dressed and crept to bed" (9). The briefly open door, the yellow tints, the shadows, the reference to the village of Vermeer's birth (the subject of his only painted exteriors), the notion of a moment suspended in time, and, most especially, the luminosity of light are all components typically found in Vermeer's work. So, too, the narrative element is minimized, and, as in Vermeer's work, there is an implied rather than developed moral dilemma, suggested not so much by content as by competing tonalities and juxtaposi-tions. Plotting and action are never dominant.

There is first and foremost what Updike has called "the window of fic-tion" (*Hugging the Shore* 196), where light streams in from a single source. Like Vermeer, Updike seems fascinated by the effects of modulated light upon an object. Most of Vermeer's paintings and many of Updike's interiors have windows that, by virtue of their placement, are important composition-ally. Even in such later novels as *The Witches of Eastwick,* such settings are common, by night as well as by day: "[Sukie] turned off the bathroom light and went into the bedroom, where the only illumination arose from the street lamp up at the corner" (137). Vermeer paints not impressionistically but sym-bolically, using areas of sunlight to draw attention to the surfaces he has se-lected, more creator than reporter. Light and shadow always determine the *values* of objects, using the term in the painterly sense of tonal variations, as well as in the moral-philosophical sense (mores) and the evaluative (worth) sense.

Updike often finds disfavor with feminists because of his treatment of women. While a painterly reading of Updike's work may not necessarily exonerate the author from such charges, it should at least be pointed out that Updike treats his women more like art objects than sex objects, having deliberately chosen to highlight the female form in his work. It is a curious cultural phenomenon that while the restriction of subject matter to the female form is acceptable in painting, a similar artistic celebration in fiction is thought of as preoccupied or sexist. Yet, it is apparent from Updike's work that he is indeed engaged in the glorification of the female body that visual artists attempt. In describing "One's Neighbor's Wife," Updike writes, "Her hands, oval and firm, bear no trace . . . of awareness that they are sacred instruments—much like those Renaissance paintings wherein the halo of the Christ Child, having dwindled from the Byzantine corolla of beaten gold to a translucent disc delicately painted in the perspective of a 3-dimensional caplike appurtenance, disappears entirely, leaving us with an unexpectedly Italian-looking urchin" (*Hugging the Shore* 5). Following this elaborate art-historical introduction, Updike launches into a long, painterly description of her "pussy" as he imagines it would look in sunlight. Critics react to the latter with some measure of shock, surprise, or amusement, without considering that Updike could, in fact, be serious about the subject matter he has chosen to "paint," fictionally, in rarefied light.

Joyce Carol Oates is among those who take exception to Updike's objectification of the female: "His energies are American in this prolific and reverential housing of a multitude of objects, as 'Nature' is scaled down, compressed, at times hardly more than a series of forms of The Female" (58). It should be remembered, however, that Vermeer treats his characters and objects alike, painting what amounts to still lifes. Characters do not occupy the center stage as they do in genre painting, conventional portraits, or historical narratives. People are as likely or unlikely to be favored by the grace of Vermeer's light as the other objects in the paintings. In Vermeer's work, light and shadow establish order: the relationship of things to each other. And yet, most of Vermeer's canvases portray middle-class women "glorified" by light or made beautiful by the envelope of solitude and quietness that surrounds them and allows the viewer to appreciate "woman" as a formal concern, as an object in relation to other objects in the painting.

Like Vermeer, Updike modulates his light to consider his women in quiet, intimate moments. But modulation is the key, as Rabbit discovers when he first enters Ruth's apartment vestibule and finds that "abruptly, in the cold light of the streetlamp which comes through the four flawed panes of the window by his side, blue panes so thin-seeming the touch of one finger might crack them, he begins to tremble" (74). "Harsh direct light falls on her face," making "the creases on her neck show black" (79). When Rabbit goes to the window to draw the shade in order to control the flow of light, "Ruth's eyes watch him out of shadows that also seem gaps in a surface," and the "curve of her hip supports a crescent of silver" (79–80). But light both reveals and glorifies. Rabbit "drinks in the pure sight of her," noticing how "she keeps her arm tight against the one breast and brings up her hand to cover the other; a ring glints. . . . Light lies along her right side where it can catch her body as it turns in stillness; this pose, embarrassed and graceful. . . . So that when her voice springs from her form he is amazed to hear a perfect statue, unadorned woman, beauty's home image, speak" (81). That Updike's method is deliberately painterly is clear from a revised paperback version (Fawcett Crest, 1983) of the same scene, where "[Ruth] sits upright with her fat legs jack-knifed sideways and her back symmetrical as a great vase. . . . As one arm tosses her brassiere over the edge of the bed the other, on his side, presses against her breast so he won't see. But he does see; a quick glimmer of tipped weight" (79 paper).

Here, Updike's attempt to create the kind of dynamic stasis Vermeer's women inhabit is most clear, as is the attempt to paint, fictionally, a light that both hides and discloses. The passage also illustrates the way Rabbit gravitates toward fleshy women because they remind him of substance, of solidity, of the kind of Rubenesque women memorialized in classical art. Later, when Harry and Ruth are in the public pool, he notices how "standing in the water she looked great, cut off at the thighs like a statue" (133 paper)—another addition that does not appear in the original hardcover version.

Poolside in *Rabbit Is Rich*, Harry is similarly struck by the way light strikes a chunky Cindy Murkett as she stands on flagstones and "dry sun catches in every drop beaded on her brown shoulders, so tan the skin bears a flicker of iridescence" (172). More than male fantasy, the description hinges on contrast—dry sun metaphorically "beaded" like pool water on brown skin—verbally employing the beads of light and iridescence so typical of Vermeer's canvases. Light helps to define Cindy's appeal for him, which becomes clear later when, sleeping alongside a repugnant Janice, he thinks, "How quickly Cindy's [plump] footprints dried on the flagstones behind her today! The strange thing is he can never exactly picture fucking her, it is like looking into the sun" (188–89). His thoughts eventually turn to the comforting solidity of memory, of interiors, of Ruth and "the privacy of this room. This island, their four walls, her room. Her fat white body out of her clothes . . . one long underbelly erect in light" (190).

Vermeer's women are always objectlike, frozen in a single, simple action, fleshly solid, and, from their posture and facial expressions, emotionally sound, though thoughtful. Women in Vermeer represent constancy, and while in Updike's fiction the male is typically the activist, it is always the female who is the source of strength, who, as Tallent notes, is often compared to the solid earth: Woman = Terrain (25).

Just as Vermeer painted still lifes with humans, rather than portraits, Updike also seems to have a sense of his characters as objects with formal value, interested in how they fit in the world, rather than the activities in which they indulge. Harry Angstrom is an "order-loving man" (*Run* 13) who, despite age and the way in "his inner life too Rabbit dodges among more blanks than there used to be, patches of burnt-out-gray cells where there used to be lust and keen dreaming" (*Rich* 13), is still able to have his senses awakened by the call of light. *Rabbit Is Rich* begins, in fact, when Ruth's daughter drives into the Toyota dealership, "milky-pale and bare-legged and blinking in the sunshine" (13), and Rabbit, still able to be surprised by the "long day's lingering brightness" (46), finds new life apart from his mechanical routine.

Rabbit sees forms, colors, and tonal masses the way an artist might, and yet for him true "life" is the result of his ability to paint reality more brilliant than it is in actuality, a talent that is largely peculiar to him in the novel, but which other Updike heroes share. When he and Ruth go hiking up a mountain at the park, Ruth complaining as they walk, he suggests that she take off her shoes. Here Rabbit's artistic eye sees beauty again in the strangest of objects and the most ordinary of actions: "Bare of stockings, her white feet lift lightly under his eyes; the yellow skin of her heel flickers. Under the swell of calf her ankles are thin. In a gesture of gratitude he takes off his shoes, to share whatever pain there is." He then tries to kiss her, but Ruth thinks it "a silly time; her one-eyed woman's mind is intent on getting up the hill" (*Run* 111). Again, while Rabbit's remarks appear sexist under a feminist reading, in the context of Vermeer and the painter's eye, sex is not the issue. If one eye is closed, the world becomes flattened and two-dimensional in appearance, something that Rabbit—and apparently Updike—dreads. Twenty years later, at a party, Rabbit perceives "the entire deep space of the room . . . with appointments chosen all to harmonize. Its tawny wallpaper has vertical threads of texture in it like the vertical folds of the slightly darker pull drapes . . . lit by spots on track lighting overhead . . . and the same lighting reveals little sparkles, like mica on a beach, in the overlapping arcs of the rough-plastered ceiling" (*Rich* 290). In this setting, which in Harry's eyes has depth, texture, and the selective play of light, other couples carry on ordinary conversations and fail to notice details. Among such people, "Rabbit worries that the party is in danger of flattening out" (292). Likewise, with Ruth at the top of Mt. Judge, Rabbit *sees,* while Ruth's vision is restricted to ordinary perspective: "In the lower part of his vision the stone-walled cliff rises to his feet foreshortened to the narrowness of a knife; in the upper part the hillside slopes down, faint paths revealed and random clearings. . . . Ruth's gaze, her lids half-closed as if she were reading a book, rests on the city" (*Run* 112).

In a similar scene with Ruth in her apartment, Rabbit asks if he should pull down the shades before they make love. She responds, "Please, it's a dismal view." Rabbit, however, deliberately looks to see what could possibly be so dreary, as if it were another challenge to his own powers of artistic imagination. What he sees is a sight so lovely that "he feels gratitude to the builders of this ornament, and lowers the shade on it guiltily" (*Run* 79–80). His powers of perception awakened, Rabbit sees Ruth as "great and glistening sugar in her sifty-grained slip" (79). Being able to *see* enables Rabbit to create life and perfection where none, to the rest of the world, exists, and men as well as women comprise the "non-seers."

By contrast, dumbness and dimness seem to be interrelated for Updike. At the funeral of Rabbit and Janice's baby, "Mourners move into the sunshine. . . . at last beyond the dark recession of crowding rocks he has seen a patch of light; he turns, and Janice's face, dumb with grief, blocks the light. . . . He hates her dumb face. She doesn't *see.* She had a chance to join him in . . . the simple factual truth, and turned away in horror" (*Run* 293). In *Rabbit Redux,* likewise, Harry notices when "a shape, a shade, comes forward in the kitchen. He expects it to be his father, but it is his mother shuffling in a bathrobe, yet erect and moving" (92). Updike embraces the traditional-archetypal associations of light equaling truth, salvation, information, and transformation, with darkness and shadow embodying the opposite.

For a time Rabbit's wife does, in fact, experience the creational feeling that accompanies a new way of seeing. In *Rabbit Redux,* having begun an affair with Charlie Stavros, she thinks, "One of the nice things about having a lover, it makes you think about everything anew. The rest of your life becomes a kind of movie, flat and even rather funny" (53). Rabbit, although somewhat driven by sex, is nonetheless driven more by the artistic impulse;

perspective permits him to love life itself, though everyone around him might seem jaded.

Ruth, self-conscious about her size, is hesitant to let Rabbit see her. But Rabbit, before making love to his heavy ex-prostitute, "sits on the corner of the bed and drinks in the pure sight of her. . . . Her belly is a pond of shadow deepening to a black eclipsed by the inner swell of her thighs. Light seizes her right side as her body turns in its stillness; rigidity is her one defense against his eyes. She holds the pose until his eyes smart with echoes of white. When her voice breaks from her frozen form, he is startled" (*Run* 80–81). As long as she is cooperatively motionless, Rabbit is able to paint a still life of her, to notice the way light makes even this large and coarse woman more beautiful— the way Vermeer's plain-looking models acquired a quiet beauty in the stasis he crafted with his modulated rooms full of light. In *Couples,* likewise, Piet is able to see Foxy's face in bed next to him "like a candleflame motionless . . . like the roads of his native state, or the canals of Holland" as long as her face is "perfectly steady" (201).

While making love to Ruth, Rabbit creates "a lazy space. He wants the time to stretch long, to great length and thinness," and feels the painted quality of the scene as "at the parched root of his tongue each register their colors" (83). In his re-visioning of Ruth he remakes her so that her most noticeable physical defect is nearly negated. In dim light, Ruth "stands by the edge of the bed, baggy in nakedness" (86), but an intensified, remodulated light recharges Rabbit's ability to see the world through the wonder-filled eyes of a child, and, as in Vermeer, a secular scene becomes almost holy, so baptized by light:

> From deep in the pillow he stares at the horizontal strip of stained-glass church window that shows under the window shade. Its childish brightness seems the one kind of comfort left to him. Light from behind the closed bathroom door tints the air in the bedroom. The splashing sounds are like the sounds his parents would make when as a child Rabbit would waken to realize they had come upstairs, that the whole house would soon be dark, and the sight of morning would be his next sensation. He is asleep when like a faun in moonlight Ruth, washed, creeps back to his side, holding a glass of water. (86)

The baptismal effects of light are here accented by water imagery, the traditional medium and symbol of baptism. Ruth, who is "baggy" in her flesh, leaves to get Rabbit a glass of water, while the light triggers Rabbit's creative impulse. When she returns, Rabbit is asleep, but, if the point of view is consistent, dreaming. In moonlight, washed, Ruth becomes something more delicate and youthful, more dear/deer: a faun.

Given Updike's painterly disposition, if Rabbit does indeed seek to recapture lost youth, it is not youth itself that he seeks. Rather, it is the rediscovery of the wonder-filled way children see the world, as if for the first time. José Ortega y Gasset writes that "the child sees in palpable presence what our imagination is too weak to visualize" (60). A passage from *Rabbit Redux* illustrates how in Updike's mind childlike wonder gradually diminishes with age:

> Mom's room has lace curtains aged yellowish and pinned back with tin daisies that to an infant's eyes seemed magical, rose-and-thorns wallpaper curling loose from the wall . . . a kind of plush armchair that soaks up dust. When he was a child this chair was downstairs and he would sock it to release torrents of swirling motes into the shaft of afternoon sun; these whirling motes seemed to him worlds, each an earth, with him on one of them. . . . Some light used to get into the house in late afternoon, between the maples. Now the same maples have thronged that light solid, made the room cellar-dim. (95)

Updike says that his own "sense of childhood doesn't come from being a father, it comes from being a child" (*Picked-Up Pieces* 519). To the infant-Rabbit the room has the greatest magical potency, the most brilliancy. Even to the child-Rabbit the room has the power to become other "worlds," as long as some light is still able to get in through the thickening maples. To the adult-Updike, however, brilliant and magical vision is furthest removed, the room made "cellar-dim" by the growth and age of the narrator and the stand of maples that choke off the creative force of sunlight. Piet, in *Couples,* states the relationship between light and growth more bluntly: "Vague light becomes form becomes thought becomes soul and dies" (213). This progression is evident throughout Updike's fiction, with characters representing each stage. Only brilliant light redeems, prolongs, or creates life—and brilliant light is what Rabbit and other Updike characters gravitate toward, as if it were a fountain of youth.

Vermeer's subjects are never old, and they never age. Whether in moments of listening, talking, reading, or pouring milk, they always seem to have the same sense of rapture and contemplation of the ordinary. Where Vermeer and Updike like to dwell is at the first and most sensual level of creation, that moment closest to the birth of an object through the midwifery of light: the present. Thought muddles the vision and the ecstasy of seeing/ being; likewise, the soul worries too much about future salvation and past sins to be much alive in the present.

Rabbit "hates all the people on the street in dirty everyday clothes, advertising their belief that the world arches over a pit, that death is final" (*Run* 234). Typical of Updike's narrative personas, Rabbit associates life with light, and darkness/drabness with death. When he sees his baby at the hospital, "the smile of the nurse, foreshortened and flickering cutely between his eyes and the baby's nose, reassures him that he is the father" (218).

Rabbit, through his painterly vision and his desire to render ordinary objects more brilliant, is the great creator, the great artist who is called "the old Master" (*Run* 176), with a capital M, as if in allusion to the Dutch Masters. "I made you," he tells Ruth (109)—just as a former basketball teammate reminds Rabbit that their coach—"The man who made us immortal" (176)—created *them*.

Updike has meant for his novels to raise the questions "What is a good man?" and "What is goodness?" (*Picked-Up Pieces* 496), and he seems to be quite aware of the precarious position in which artists and creators find themselves. There is a thin line between creation and illusion, and the artist is always faced with the positive and negative aspects of dreaming. "Hold tight dream girl," Harry says in *Rabbit Is Rich* when he has intercourse with a snoring, sleeping Janice (55). In many respects, Rabbit is an illusionist, a magician who pulls himself out of the dull darkness of a hat from day to day, largely because of his childlike vision. This is evident in a moment of crisis, when Rabbit's artistic vision momentarily fails him again: "The details of the street—the ragged margin where the pavement and grass struggle, the tarry scarred trunks of the telephone poles—no longer speak to him. He is no one" (*Run* 283). Nothingness for Rabbit—and Updike—is not just Barthian nothingness, and dread is never only Kierkegaardian. It is also represented, and in fact *created*, by a loss of the creative imagination, a temporary suspension of the ability to see sparkle and wonder in the commonplace. Banal existence and routines are as much a nothingness as the natural Christian fear of death's finality, for as Updike writes, his characters "go back to work; that's the real way that people die" (*Picked-Up Pieces* 509).

In *Rabbit, Run,* when the hospital atmosphere makes Harry momentarily remorseful over his irresponsible behavior, and he and Eccles sit together in the maternity waiting room, he sees himself briefly as others have; he sees that he embodies not only the positive, childlike side of youth, but the negative, childish side as well. Weighed down by the atmosphere and by the "blackness" of the minister he is nonetheless drawn to, his life seems to him "a magic dance empty of belief" (198), a charge Ruth takes up later in the novel after the baby dies. "Why don't you look outside your own pretty skin once in a while?" she says (301–2).

In a way, Rabbit and other Updike heroes hide in surfaces as much as they revel in them, so engaged in re-creating reality and re-painting what they perceive as dull routines or unsavory circumstances that the world they ultimately inhabit becomes a private one, one is in constant danger of becoming all-exclusive of the outside world, and of so-called reality as it exists for others. They create and are reluctant to leave their magical Vermeer-like rooms, the surfaces that contain them becoming like membranes, or neo-wombs. Thus, Updike's heroes are caught in a curious paradox, similar to one that Emerson describes: "We are not very much to blame for our bad marriages. We live amid hallucinations, and this especial trap is laid to trip up our feet with, and all are tripped up first or last" ("Illusions" 275).

Rabbit must become a child in order to see the world anew each time he looks at the repetitions that accompany familiarity and the simple process of aging. As Eccles tells Rabbit, "Children are very sacred in psychology" (*Run* 126). Yet, with the positive aspect of becoming a child—childlike wonder and vision—comes the negative aspect: self-centered childishness. Children largely occupy the present, appreciating moments with a fullness adults can never achieve because their own minds are always preoccupied, always occupying more than one plane of time. Rabbit lives totally in the present, with no thoughts for his future, and really no great preoccupation with the past. Though numerous critics have suggested that Rabbit seeks a return to glory, he spends little time thinking about the past. No descriptions exist, for example, of his high school team in action, or locker room memories. His is a world of moments, of the fullest possible appreciation for the present—which is why Thelma, the grade-school teacher who "chooses" the childlike Rabbit during a triangular night of mate-swapping in *Rabbit Is Rich*, likes him. "You're so glad to be alive," she says (418).

Rabbit, like other Updike heroes, notices Vermeer-like rooms in real life, or creates them if none seem to exist. He notices people as they sit alongside windows, and charm in such places as the Eccleses' spare bedroom, where the human element is present only in a photograph: "Sunshine, the old clown, rims the room. Two pink chairs flank a gauze-filled window buttered with light that smears a writing desk furry with envelope-ends. Above the desk is a picture of a lady in pink stepping toward you" (*Run* 206).

Just as Vermeer reused rooms for his paintings of domesticity, so, apparently, has Updike. In *Rabbit Redux,* the bedroom where Harry awakens next to the runaway Jill is similarly described: "Sunshine, the old clown, rims the room. The maple has so many leaves fallen morning light slants in baldly" (301). Rabbit knows what Malraux has said, that "for a certain moment of history a picture or a statue speaks a language it will never speak again: the language of its birth" (317), and artistic creation—living fully in the present—becomes a way of "freezing" time, of preserving moments, and consequently, of preserving or providing for the salvation of self. Space is threatening for Rabbit, who finds comfort in interiorized, self-contained moments of idealization and creation. Having left Janice again at the end of *Rabbit, Run,* Harry is balanced on a "small fulcrum" weighing opposites. One alternative is "the right way and the good way, the way to the delicatessen—gaudy with stacked fruit lit by a naked bulb—and the other way . . . to where the city ends. He tries to picture how it will end . . . and he doesn't know. He pictures a huge vacant field of cinders and his heart goes hollow" (306). "There is light, though, in the streetlights," and it lights the way for Rabbit's curtain call (306). As soon as he perceives the luminosity, the scene is once again transformed: "to his left, directly under one [streetlight], the rough asphalt looks like dimpled snow. He decides to walk" (306), and eventually run, toward the light.

Once again, the ability to perceive motion in stillness—buildings in darkness under the spell of light—literally lights the other-world of dark, empty space that Rabbit finds so threatening, yet which seems his only escape. Feeling trapped by a marriage to a woman he no longer loves, having impregnated both of the women in his life, and having indirectly caused the death of his daughter, the irresponsible, childish side of Rabbit prompts him to run. What gives him the impetus, what "trips" or triggers his final flight, is the childlike ability to perceive newness in old forms, the play of light that bleaches the dark asphalt white and gives motion to thresholds—steps and windowsills—making the darkness seem somehow less threatening.

Updike, in his essay on "Emersonianism," cites an essay on "illusions" that contains a passage most applicable to the ending of *Rabbit, Run* and to the critical writings of those who have not fully appreciated the way Updike continues to experiment with visual-to-verbal art transformations: "Even the prose of the streets is full of refractions. In the life of the dreariest alderman, fancy enters into all details and colors them with rosy hue. . . . Great is paint; nay, God is the painter; and we rightly accuse the critic who destroys too many illusions" (Emerson, "Illusions" 273). In running—in seeking to avoid the trap of dull reality—Rabbit chooses the world of illusion. A non-artist, he nonetheless glories in his ability to paint his world more beautiful than it is. His flight is symbolic of imaginative flight, that leap from the "real" world needed in order to create an ideal world. Although Rabbit is, as critics have noticed, childish in his response to the world, he is also childlike in his desire to see in it something better.

A Vermeer-like reading of Updike's work certainly helps to explain why, curiously, Harry Angstrom is more intellectually contemplative than most men of his class, education, occupation, and regional roots—or why Rabbit seems to notice light the way only a painter or art student can. To notice such light is to notice detail; to imagine or create such light, as Harry often does, is to rival a painter or the Creator himself. Light, for Rabbit, is the mantle of a creator. When, for example, Harry engages Charlie Stavros in small talk and sympathizes with his problems in *Rabbit Is Rich,* he is absolved by Charlie's simple pronouncement, "What can *you* do?"; even metaphorical light is rejuvenating: "This is what he wants to hear; relief bathes him like a kind of light. When you feel better, you see better; he sees all the papers, wrappers and take-out cup lids that have blown across the highway from the Chuck Wagon, lying in the bushes just outside the window, getting soaked" (270).

Updike, by his own admission and by critical consensus, is a poet of middleness and commonness, the very realm from which Vermeer chose his raw materials. In Updike's words, "It is a function of art to show us the paradise that, disguised as the ordinary, surrounds us as we live" (*Hugging the Shore* 630). Answering charges that his characters are too ordinary, Updike responds, "Either everyone is a hero, or no one is. I vote for no one" (*Picked-Up Pieces* 518). Typically his characters are upper middle class—never lower and seldom higher in station. His "heroes" are Linotypers, carpenters, bricklayers, salesmen, teachers, writers, artists, ministers, or middle-management executives. To make such ordinary lives seem extraordinary through careful abstraction has been one of Updike's main aesthetic principles, something that is evident in all that he has written. "There is a way of working with rotten wood," Harry observes, "and making it as solid as marble, and like marble swirled and many-shaded" (*Rich* 282). Throughout the Rabbit tetralogy, Harry depends upon such observations—the effects of light upon objects—to get him through tough moments. When, for example, in *Rabbit Is Rich* he has erection difficulties responding to Janice, he turns to light for help: "He resolves to suck Janice's tits, to give himself a chance to pull himself together, this is embarrassing. A pause at the top, you need a pause at the top to generate momentum. His spit glimmers within her dark shape above him; the headboard of their bed is placed between two windows shaded from the light of sun and moon alike by a great copper beech whose leaves yet allow a little streetlight through" (52–53). As in Vermeer's interiors, light beads and glistens, not on a woman's pearls, but on Harry's spittle, and the stream of streetlight angling in between two windows is all it takes for him to notice the composition of the room and feel better. Harry's painterly imagination and thoughts of shadow and light provide a similar comfort when a conversation with Nelson turns tense and he thinks of the rain outside and the garden, where "the smallest scabs of earth, beneath the lettuce and lopsided bean leaves perforated by Japanese beetles, are darkening, soaking, the leaves above them glistening." Such thoughts divert Harry from "studying Nelson's stubborn clouded face" (*Rich* 118).

Form, not narrative action or thematic content, is at the core of the "magic moments" that are essential to Updike's fiction and to his characters, for in order to respond to the challenge of making ordinary lives seem extraordinary, his characters must never travel great distances or have a great deal of exceptional things happen to them in their lives. What happens to them is what happens to all men and women: they inhabit Middle America, they eat, they work at middle-class jobs, they have sex, and, in facing death, they wrestle with their middle-of-the-road religious beliefs.

In Vermeer, "The visible definition of female shape had been his continual purpose: progressively he had discovered in it the character of a monument" (Koningsberger 59). By contrast, the absence of light can produce a similarly striking effect. In *Rabbit, Run,* when Harry, a former teammate, and two women double-date at a restaurant, light has a direct influence on the way things are perceived. When one of the "girls," Margaret, speaks, "a serious shadow crosses her face that seems to remove her and Harry, who sees it, from the others, and takes them into that strange area of a million years ago from which they have wandered; a strange guilt pierces Harry at being here instead of there, where he never was. Ruth and Harrison across from them, touched by staccato red light, seem to smile from the heart of damnation" (178). Here quite clearly the light—and absence of light—is symbolic as well as selective, and those who, like Harry, are able to perceive the effects of light will have their vision appreciably altered. Light, as in Vermeer's paintings, has the ability to re-create or appreciably change reality. Light is associated with disclosure and demystification; shadow, with mystery. In Vermeer, areas of highly concentrated information (light) are alternately juxtaposed against areas of noninformation (shadow). Articulated areas of a painting always need to be supported by nonarticulated areas, and vice versa. Updike, of course, is also aware of this principle, for such nonarticulated areas support his Sunday skaters who, in "the pattern of their pirouettes," are "silently upheld" (*Assorted Prose* 186).

When Updike uses light to describe his scenes, a contrast is somehow involved, whether pictorial, symbolic, or thematic. Often pictorial light will be paralleled by suggestions of the symbolic or thematic. In the same double date mentioned above, Harry is feeling the first traces of remorse over his affair with Ruth when he notices "a colored girl in an orange uniform that he guesses from the frills is supposed to look South American . . . and he sees her back is open halfway down her spine, so a bit of black bra shows through. Compared with this her skin isn't black at all. Soft purple shadows swing on the flats of her back where the light hits. . . . She doesn't care about him; he likes that, that she doesn't care. The thing about Ruth is lately she's been trying to make him feel guilty about something" (174). Rabbit notices how the light hits "the flats of her back," but what is also illuminated for him in seeing her turned away from him—as figures are often positioned in Vermeer's canvases—is an intimate moment colored by indifference, rather than vulnerability. Seeing the light and making the association immediately prompts Rabbit to think of an obvious contrast in Ruth's behavior.

If the notion of form-as-content is kept in mind, this layering of black-and-white/shadow-and-light can account for certain puzzling aspects of Updike's fictions that at first seem thematic in nature. Critics have, for example, been somewhat perplexed by the fact that Peter Caldwell, in *The Centaur,* narrates the story of his father while lying next to his black mistress. But Updike, with his painterly eye, knows that light without shadow is dull and weak, incomplete. Formally, they depend upon each other. This is no more apparent than in *Rabbit, Run,* when Harry sees his infant daughter in her bassinet "somehow dimly, as if the baby has not gathered to herself the force that makes a silhouette" (232). Although the scene foreshadows the baby's death by drowning, it is important to note how interdependent light and darkness are for Updike. Without a shadow, there is no life: yin and yang separated. Just as Harry in *Rabbit, Run* feels a force pulling him toward the minister, Eccles, a "tug drawing him toward this man in black" (105), often the things that appear most dynamic in Updike's world are those objects and scenes that display the tense balance that results from the clean juxtaposition of colors. Fuzzy areas of tonal overlapping are rare in Updike's suburban fictions, and when blending does occur, it is decidedly negative.

In the pool scene from *Rabbit, Run,* for example, Harry sees "a clear image" of Ruth in the water, her bottom "a round black island glistening" and bubbles breaking as she swims (142). "The air sparkles with the scent of chlorine," and Harry rejoices at how clean she feels to him: "Clean, clean. What is it? Nothing touching you that is not yourself. Her in water, him in grass and air" (143). In the lengthy, glorious description of Ruth-as-monument that follows, Harry once more revels in the light that surrounds them. But then after she emerges from the water and joins him on the lawn, he notices "chalk highlights" on her tanned skin, his idealized image of her starting to blur, to fade. In defining "clean," Harry thinks like an artist. Chalkiness in art indicates an inability to control the intonation of those areas that pretend to be illuminated. After seeing such an area on Ruth—perhaps an indication of a lapse in his own ability to paint life more brilliantly—Harry looks over Ruth's slightly tanned "dead body" with its "chalk highlights" to a pair of girls who embody light and darkness in more striking contrast: "the lighter figures of two sixteen-year-olds standing sipping orange crush from cardboard cones. The one in a white strapless pecks up at him from sucking her straw with a brown glance, her skinny legs dark as a Negro's" (144).

Critics have been puzzled by the fact that Updike's men are fascinated by black women or often take black mistresses, but to a painterly eye such striking contrasts create a formal tension and harmony of balance. At the all-black bar where Harry first sees the white teenage runaway Jill, "the blacks fit around her like shadows" (*Redux* 128). Leaving the bar, Harry panics when, in the "rolling balls of light before them" cast by headlights that illuminate the "white shards" of boat shapes against the "black floor" of the river, he perceives that "two brown figures are chasing them. Their shadows shorten and multiply" (137). Throughout the novel shadows chase Harry, who has become the embodiment of middle-class white, passive America—part of that all-accepting, television-watching, flag-waving silent majority. Later when Harry, having taken the black militant Skeeter and Jill into his home, "contemplates the set of shadows" sitting across from him (206), one suspects that these active and youthful character types are projections of what Harry was, and what he could yet become. Before his "shadows" arrived, Harry felt dead to the world. "I don't feel anything," he tells his mother (100). Only with the wholeness provided by the infusion of new ideas—by the shadows he takes in—does he come slowly to life again, himself re-created, his own light made stronger by the contrast. Rabbit and his shadows are tonal contrasts (yin/yang), but also moral contrasts. According to Jung, "The shadow is a moral problem that challenges the whole ego-personality. . . . To become conscious of it involves recognizing the dark aspects of the personality as present and real" (91). However, given the Jungian notion of shadows as projections, it is possible that Updike's artist-heroes may at times project their "shadows" onto objects in order to achieve formal wholeness and artistic balance, as well as ego-personality wholeness and stability.

It would be foolish to contend that racial elements are not present, since the novel is Updike's most sociologically and historically topical, but Updike is also highly fascinated by the sheer beauty of sharp contrasts. But there are certain passages that are unexplainably bizarre if content alone is considered. In the scene from *Rabbit Redux* where Rabbit watches a black man sexually exploit a white girl in his living room, for example, he sees in the dark room something so "beautiful" and fascinating in its contrast that it prompts him to turn on the light: "The black shadows of [Skeeter's] hands glide into the white blur Jill is . . . as a potter guides a lump of clay upward on the humming wheel, into a vase. She keeps rising, smoke from the vase. Her dress is being lifted over her head. 'Turn around, honey, show us your rump.' A soft slap gilds the darkness, the whiteness revolves. . . . Where her breasts should be, black spiders are fighting" (296–97). The contrast of black and white planes juxtaposed creates, for Updike and his narrative persona, a thing of beauty and artistic tension in spite of the coarse drama that gives it shape. In this instance, though such episodes will typically prompt thematic studies, it is just as likely that Updike is again treating his humans as if they were objects: formally. Form becomes content. That the scene is so conceived is upheld by Updike's otherwise curious and inappropriate use of the potter metaphor. Though his son sees the incident as a rape, Harry, sitting in his easy chair, sees nothing sexual, but rather a creative process that reminds him of his own printing occupation. Like Updike, he is fascinated by the way black ink looks upon a pure white page (*Picked-Up Pieces* 517). When Harry cannot bear to watch what he perceives as "beautiful" anymore in darkness and finally turns on the light, his initial response is shocking and unexplainable—even sadistic or misogynistic—if the potter metaphor is not seriously considered. He thinks, simply: "Nice," because "what he sees reminds him in the first flash of the printing process, an inked plate contiguous at some few points to white paper" (*Redux* 297).

In his application of Barth's Yes and No—the moral dialectic—to Updike's fiction, Hunt notes that the No exists "only by reason of the exclusion that the power of God's Yes entails, the way a shadow exists only by reason of light" (34). In this he echoes Kant, who also felt that light must precede shadow. Yet, in the Orient, "the dualism of light and darkness is summed up by the *yin-yang* symbol: each area contains the seed of its own opposite and each grows out of the other in unity and interdependence" (Piper 116). As a writer who studied art formally, Updike most certainly accepts the latter principle, realizing that shadow and light must coexist on equal planes if balance is to be achieved. In Updike's fiction, light and darkness are symbolically present in the polarities that critics have fully explored: Barth's Yes and No, Eliade's sacred and profane spaces, Kierkegaard's dialectic method, and the eros and agape forms of love. These paired opposites help create the stasis that approximates the fragile moments in a Vermeer where the ordinary becomes briefly glorious. Under a painterly reading of Updike's work, such stasis is a positive element, the result of a preference for "pictorial" fiction over the traditional narrative, and an expression of Updike's deep-seated concern for creating lasting monuments.

Because of his erratic behavior in *Rabbit, Run* and in three sequels, Harry "Rabbit" Angstrom has fairly perplexed critics. Tremendously irresponsible, he moves from job to job, leaves his wife several times, takes up with a prostitute, takes in a teenage runaway and a black militant, sleeps with his daughter-in-law, and generally behaves as if he had never grown up. But Updike would have us believe that Rabbit is also one of the few people who are fully sensitive to life. Mrs. Smith, near the first novel's end, remarks, "That's what you have, Harry: life. It's a strange gift and I don't know how we're supposed to use it but I know it's the only gift we get and it's a good one" (223).

Updike writes that "a man in love ceases to fear death" (*Assorted Prose* 286), and so while the sexual is always a predominant quest for Rabbit and other Updike heroes/antiheroes, the love of life is equally important. A man in love sees wonder in the world, and a man who *wishes* to see wonder in the world will want more than anything to be in love, to keep trying to see things with the nonjaded eyes of a young person. Ruth senses this quality in Rabbit. When Harry asks her why she likes him, she says, " 'Cause you haven't given up. In your stupid way you're still fighting" (92). While others around him have become either wearied by life or accepting of its drab reality of commonness, Harry, in *Rabbit, Run* and in three sequels, is able to see the world like someone watching a lover undress for the very first time, to see things more artistically or monumentally than they are in reality.

While numerous critics see Harry Angstrom as little more than a has-been star trying desperately to recapture lost glory, Rabbit, by virtue of his eye for light, his painterly sensibility, is infinitely more complex than the irresponsible ex-athlete who hops from bed to bed in plotlines that at times seem thin. Considered in the context of Vermeer's work, Harry's ability to appreciate the essence of life that *is* light accentuates his redemptive possibilities as well. As Oates has observed, Updike's world is "incarnational." She adds, "Updike usually affirms it in words, but the act of writing itself, the lovely spontaneous play of imagination, is salvation of a kind" (57–58). More precisely, a painterly style using color and tonal gradations to shape the fictional canvas, balancing polarities to achieve tension and stasis, and describing things with an exaggerated expressiveness—this is salvation for Updike and his characters. If, as Malraux has suggested, art is "that whereby forms are transmuted into style" (272), then Updike—especially in his attempts to render the commonplace in the scintillating style of a Vermeer—is certainly an artist of the highest order. And Rabbit? What first set him in motion is what has driven him in each of the four novels: a fascination with "*Jan Vermeer*, for salting humble bread / With Dabs of light, as well as bricks and thread" (*Midpoint* 38). Sensing darkness at the novel's end, "a dark circle in a stone façade," Rabbit sees "light, though, in the streetlights. . . . Although this block of brick three-stories is just like the one he left, something in it makes him happy; the steps and window sills seem to twitch and shift in the corner of his eye, alive" (*Run* 306). With light.

Notes

1. I have used the following editions: *Rabbit, Run* (New York: Knopf, 1960); *Rabbit Redux* (New York: Knopf, 1971); *Rabbit Is Rich* (New York: Knopf, 1981); *Rabbit at Rest* (New York: Knopf, 1990); *Assorted Prose* (New York: Knopf, 1965); *Hugging the Shore* (New York: Knopf, 1983).

2. For an account of Updike's childhood fascination with Vermeer and an early example of an interior composed in the manner of the Dutch painter, see "The Lucid Eye in Silvertown" in *Assorted Prose* (New York: Knopf, 1965), 188.

Bibliography

Published Works by John Updike

Assorted Prose. New York: Knopf, 1965.
Assorted Prose. New York: Fawcett, 1966.
Beck: A Book. New York: Knopf, 1970.
Beck Is Back. New York: Knopf, 1982.
Brazil. New York: Knopf, 1994.
Buchanan Dying. New York: Knopf, 1974.
The Carpentered Hen and Other Tame Creatures. New York: Harper & Brothers, 1958.
The Centaur. New York: Knopf, 1963.
Couples. New York: Knopf, 1968.
Emersonianism. Cleveland: Bits Press, 1984.
Hugging the Shore. New York: Knopf, 1983.
Hugging the Shore. New York: Vintage, 1983.
Marry Me. New York: Knopf, 1976.
Memories of the Ford Administration. New York: Knopf, 1992.
Midpoint and Other Poems. New York: Knopf, 1969.
A Month of Sundays. New York: Knopf, 1975.
Museums and Women. New York: Knopf, 1972.
Odd Jobs. New York: Knopf, 1991.
Picked-Up Pieces. New York: Knopf, 1975.
Pigeon Feathers and Other Stories. New York: Knopf, 1976.
The Poorhouse Fair. New York: Knopf, 1959.
Rabbit Angstrom: A Tetralogy. New York: Everyman Library, 1995.
Rabbit at Rest. New York: Knopf, 1990.
Rabbit at Rest. London: André Deutsch, 1990.
Rabbit, Run. New York: Knopf, 1960.
Rabbit, Run. 1960. New York: Modern Library, 1965.
Rabbit, Run. New York: Fawcett Crest, 1960.
Rabbit, Run. 1960. New York: Fawcett Crest, 1983.
Rabbit, Redux. New York: Knopf, 1971.
Rabbit, Redux. New York: Fawcett Crest, 1971.
Rabbit Is Rich. New York: Knopf, 1981.

Rabbit Is Rich. New York: Fawcett Crest, 1981.

Roger's Version. New York: Knopf, 1986.

S. New York: Knopf, 1988.

The Same Door. New York: Knopf, 1959.

Self-Consciousness. New York: Knopf, 1989.

Self-Consciousness: Memoirs. New York: Fawcett, 1989.

"Why Rabbit Had to Go." *New York Times Book Review* 5 Aug. 1990: 1, 24–25.

The Witches of Eastwick. New York: Knopf, 1984.

Secondary Sources

Becker, Carl L. *The Eve of the Revolution: A Chronicle of the Breach with England.* New Haven: Yale UP, 1921.

Bellah, Robert, et al. *Habits of the Heart.* 1985. New York: Harper Perennial Library, 1986.

Blake, David H., and Robert S. Walters. *The Politics of Global Economic Relations.* Englewood Cliffs: Prentice Hall, 1987.

Bradley, Bill. *Life on the Run.* New York: Quadrangle/New York Times Book Co., 1976.

Bury, Martin H. *The Automobile Dealer.* Haverford, Pa.: Philpenn Publishing, 1974.

Campbell, Jeff H. " 'Middling, Hidden, Troubled America': John Updike's Rabbit Tetralogy." *Journal of the American Studies Association of Texas* 24 (1993): 26–45.

——. *Updike's Novels: Thorns Spell a Word.* Wichita Falls: Midwestern State UP, 1987.

Carton, Barbara. "Drugs: Silent Killer of Profits." *Boston Sunday Globe* 19 Feb. 1989.

Chodorow, Nancy J. *Feminism and Psychoanalytic Theory.* New Haven: Yale UP, 1989.

Cooper, James Fenimore. *The Prairie, A Tale.* Ed. Henry Nash Smith (based on the "Author's Revised Edition"). New York: Holt, Rinehart & Winston, 1950.

Cooper, Rand Richards. "Rabbit Loses the Race." *Commonweal* 7 Oct. 1990: 315–21.

Daly, Mary. *Gyn/Ecology: The Metaethics of Radical Feminism.* Boston: Beacon, 1978.

Davis, Robert Con, and Ronald Schleifer. *Contemporary Literary Criticism: Literacy and Cultural Studies.* 2nd ed. Longman English and Humanities Series. Ed. Lee A. Jacobus. New York: Longman, 1989.

DeNeef, A. Leigh. "Of Dialogues and Historicisms." *South Atlantic Quarterly* 86.4 (1987): 497–517.

"Desperate Weakling." *Time* 7 Nov. 1960: 108.

Detweiler, Robert. *Breaking the Fall: Religious Readings of Contemporary Fiction.* San Francisco: Harper, 1989.

——. *John Updike.* Boston: Twayne, 1972.

Di Piero, W. S. "Heil Puccini!" Rev. of *Corelli's Mandolin,* by Louis de Berniéres. *New York Times Book Review* 13 Nov. 1994: 7.

Disch, Thomas. "Drop in Auto Sales Trips Up 'Megadealers'—And Their Lenders." *Wall Street Journal* 11 Dec. 1989.

——. "Rabbit's Run." *The Nation,* 3 Dec. 1990: 690–94.

Eder, Richard. "Rabbit Runs Down." *Los Angeles Times Book Review* 7 Oct. 1990: 3, 13.

Edwards, Thomas R. "Updike's Rabbit Trilogy." *The Atlantic,* Oct. 1981: 94–101.

Emerson, Ralph Waldo. *The Complete Works of Ralph Waldo Emerson.* 12 vols. Boston: Houghton, 1903.

——. "Illusions." 1860. *The Best of Ralph Waldo Emerson: Essays, Poems, Addresses.* Roslyn, NY: Walter J. Black, 1969. 269–81.

——. *Selections from Ralph Waldo Emerson.* Ed. Stephen E. Wicher. Boston: Houghton, 1960.

Falke, Wayne. "America Strikes Out: Updike's *Rabbit Redux.*" *American Examiner* 3.3 (1974): 18–21.

Falsey, Elizabeth. *The Art of Adding and the Art of Taking Away: Selections from John Updike's Manuscripts.* Cambridge: Harvard College Library, 1987.

Farney, Dennis. "Novelist Updike Sees Nation Frustrated by Its Own Dreams." *Wall Street Journal* 16 Sept. 1992: A1, A10.

Farrell, James T. *Judgment Day.* Cleveland: World Publishing Company, 1944.

——. *The Short Stories of James T. Farrell.* New York: Sun Dial Press, 1945.

——. *Young Lonigan.* Cleveland: World Publishing Company, 1943.

——. *The Young Manhood of Studs Lonigan.* Cleveland: World Publishing Company, 1944.

Flores, Ralph. *The Rhetoric of Doubtful Authority: Deconstructive Readings of Self-Questioning Narratives, St. Augustine to Faulkner.* Ithaca: Cornell UP, 1984.

Freud, Sigmund. *The Basic Writings of Sigmund Freud.* Ed. and trans. Dr. A. A. Brill. New York: Random House–Modern Library, 1938.

——. *The Complete Introductory Lectures on Psychoanalysis.* Ed. and trans. James Strachey. New York: Norton, 1966.

——. *Three Essays on the Theory of Sexuality.* Trans. and ed. James Strachey. 4th ed. New York: Basic Books, 1962.

Gado, Frank, ed. *First Person: Conversations on Writers and Writing.* Schenectady, NY: Union College Press, 1973.

Gingher, Robert S. "Has John Updike Anything to Say?" *Modern Fiction Studies* 20.1 (1974): 97–105.

Goyal, Vinod. "Beyond Contending Approaches: A New International Economic Regime." *The Hindu* 20–21 January 1995: C1.

Gray, Paul. "Perennial Promises Kept." *Time* 18 Oct. 1982: 72–81.

Greiner, Donald J. "John Updike." *American Novelists since World War II.* Ed. James R. Giles. Detroit: Gale Research Inc., 1994. 250–276.

——. *John Updike's Novels.* Athens: Ohio University Press, 1984.

Hall, Calvin S. *A Primer of Freudian Psychoanalysis.* 2nd anniversary ed. New York: Penguin-Mentor, 1979.

Higgs, Robert J., and Neil D. Isaacs, eds. *The Sporting Spirit.* New York: Harcourt Brace Jovanovich, 1977.

Hochberg, Mark S., et al. "Coronary Angioplasty versus Coronary Bypass." *Journal of Thoracic and Cardiovascular Surgery* 97 (1989): 496–503.

Holland, Joe. "Postmodern Vision of Spirituality and Society." *Spirituality and Society: Postmodern Visions.* Ed. David Ray Griffin. SUNY Series in Constructive Postmodern Thought. Albany: State U of New York P, 1988. 41–61.

Horvath, Brooke. "The Failure of Erotic Questing in John Updike's Rabbit Novels." *Denver Quarterly* 23.2 (1988): 70–89.

Hunt, George W. *John Updike and the Three Great Secret Things: Sex, Religion, and Art.* Grand Rapids, MI: Eerdmans, 1980.

Iwamoto, Iwao. "A Visit to Mr. Updike." *Conversations with John Updike.* Ed. James Plath. Jackson: UP of Mississippi, 1994. 115–23.

Jung, Carl. *The Essential Jung.* Ed. Anthony Storr. Princeton: Princeton UP, 1983.

Karl, Frederick R. *American Fictions 1940–1980: A Comprehensive History and Critical Evaluation.* New York: Harper, 1983.

Kazin, Alfred. "Easy Come, Easy Go." *New York Review of Books* 19 Nov. 1981: 3.

Kilgore, Michael. "Rabbit Tales." *The Tampa Tribune, Tampa Bay Times* 23 Nov. 1990: 20.

Koningsberger, Hans. *The World of Vermeer: 1632–1675.* New York: Time Incorporated, 1967.

Kuh, Katharine. *The Open Eye: In Pursuit of Art.* New York: Harper & Row, 1971.

Lacan, Jacques. *The Seminar of Jacques Lacan: Freud's Papers on Technique, 1953–54: Book I.* Ed. Jacques-Alain Miller. Trans. John Forrester. New York: Norton, 1988.

———. *The Seminar of Jacques Lacan: The Ego in Freud's Theory and in the Technique of Psychoanalysis, 1954–55: Book II.* Ed. Jacques-Alain Miller. Trans. Sylvana Tomaselli. Notes by John Forrester. New York: Norton, 1988.

Later, Genevieve. "The Nature of Dialogue in John Updike's *Rabbit, Run.*" Div. on Language Theory, MLA Convention. Chicago, 29 Dec. 1990.

Lawrence, D. H. *Studies in Classic American Literature.* 1922. New York: Doubleday, 1951.

Lewis, Anthony. "The Cost of Reagan." *New York Times* 7 Sept. 1989: A27.

Lewis, R. W. B. *The American Adam: Innocence, Tragedy, and Tradition in the Nineteenth Century.* 1955. Chicago: U of Chicago P, 1964.

Lowell, Robert. "Memories of West Street and Lepke." In *Life Studies and For the Union Dead.* New York: Noonday, 1969.

Lukács, Georg. *The Historical Novel.* Trans. Hannah and Stanley Mitchell. Lincoln: U of Nebraska P, 1983.

Lydon, Christopher. "Interview with John Updike." 1989. *Conversations with John Updike.* Ed. James Plath. Jackson: UP of Mississippi, 1994. 217–20.

Lyons, Eugene. "John Updike: The Beginning and the End." *Critique* 14.2 (1972): 44–58.

Mallon, Thomas. "John Updike Loves America." *Spectator* (1993), 17.

Malraux, André. *The Voices of Silence.* New York: Doubleday & Company, 1953.

Markham, James M. "Unpredictable Russians Boggle West's Brains." *New York Times* 27 Dec. 1988: A2.

Markle, Joyce B. *Fighters and Lovers: Theme in the Novels of John Updike.* New York: New York UP, 1993.

Mazurek, Raymond A. " 'Bringing the Corners Forward': Ideology and Representation in Updike's Rabbit Trilogy." *Politics and the Muse: Studies in the Politics of Recent American Literature.* Ed. Adam J. Sorkin. Bowling Green, OH: Bowling Green State U Popular P, 1989. 142–60.

Mizener, Arthur. "Behind the Dazzle Is a Knowing Eye." Rev. of *Pigeon Feathers,* by John Updike. *New York Times Book Review* 18 March 1962: 1, 29.

Mock, Michael B., et al. "Sounding Board." *New England Journal of Medicine* Apr. 4 (1988): 916–18.

Morales, Waltraud Queiser. "The War on Drugs: A New US National Security Doctrine?" *Third World Quarterly* 3 (July 1989): 167.

Mullahy, Patrick. *Oedipus Myth and Complex: A Review of Psychoanalytic Theory.* New York: Hermitage Press, 1948.

Newman, Judie. *John Updike.* London: Macmillan; New York: St. Martin's Press, 1988.

Oates, Joyce Carol. "Updike's American Comedies." 1975. *John Updike.* Ed. Harold Bloom. New York: Chelsea House Publishers, 1987. 57–68.

Ochsner, John L. "The Interaction between Percutaneous Transluminal Coronary Angioplasty and Coronary Bypass Surgery." *Surgical Rounds* Aug. 1988: 17–25.

O'Connell, Mary. *Updike and the Patriarchal Dilemma: Masculinity in the Rabbit Novels.* Carbondale: U of Southern Illinois P, 1996.

Olster, Stacey. "Rabbit Is Redundant: Updike's End of an American Epoch." *Neo-Realism in Contemporary American Fiction.* Ed. Kristiaan Versluys. Amsterdam: Rodopi; Antwerp: Restant, 1992. 111–29.

———. "Rabbit Rerun: Updike's Replay of Popular Culture in *Rabbit at Rest.*" *Modern Fiction Studies* 37.1 (1991): 45–59.

Ortega y Gasset, José. *"The Dehumanization of Art" and Other Writings on Art and Culture.* Garden City: Doubleday Anchor Books, 1956.

Piper, David, ed. *The Random House Library of Painting and Sculpture.* Vol. 1. New York: Random House, 1981.

Plath, James, ed. *Conversations with Updike.* Jackson: UP of Mississippi, 1994.

Poirier, Richard. *A World Elsewhere: The Place of Style in American Literature.* New York: Oxford UP, 1966.

Pollard, Ernest C., and Douglas C. Huston. *Physics.* New York: Oxford UP, 1969.

Pritchett, V. S. "Updike." *New Yorker* 9 Nov. 1981: 201–6.

Raban, Jonathan. "Rabbit's Last Run." *Book World—The Washington Post* 30 Sept. 1990: 15.

"Rags-to-Riches Dealer Leaves Behind Big Losses and Allegations of Fraud." *Wall Street Journal* 11 Dec. 1989.

Ristoff, Dilvo I. *Updike's America: The Presence of Contemporary American History in John Updike's Rabbit Trilogy.* New York: Lang, 1988.

Roth, Philip. *The Counterlife.* New York: Farrar, 1986.

Rule, Sheila. "New Threat Received." *New York Times* 31 Dec. 1988: A16.

Salgas, Jean-Pierre. "Hawthorne, Melville, Whitman, and the American Experience." 1986. *Conversations with John Updike.* Ed. James Plath. Jackson: UP of Mississippi, 1994. 176–80.

Samuels, Charles Thomas. "The Art of Fiction XLIII: John Updike." *Paris Review* 12 (Winter 1968): 85–117.

Schama, Simon. *Dead Certainties: (Unwarranted Speculations).* New York: Knopf, 1991.

Schopen, Bernard A. "Faith, Morality, and the Novels of John Updike." *Twentieth Century Literature* 24.4 (1978): 523–35.

Searles, George. *The Fiction of Philip Roth and John Updike.* Carbondale: U of Southern Illinois P, 1985.

Simes, Dimitri K. "If the Cold War Is Over, Then What?" *New York Times* 27 Dec. 1988: A12.

Slater, Philip. *The Pursuit of Loneliness.* 1970. Boston: Beacon Press, 1990.

Stevens, Wallace. "A Rabbit as King of the Ghosts." *The Palm at the End of the Mind.* New York: Vintage, 1972. 150–151.

Tallent, Elizabeth. *Married Men and Magic Tricks: John Updike's Erotic Heroes.* Berkeley: Creative Arts, 1982.

Tanner, Tony. *City of Words: American Fiction, 1950–70.* London: Jonathan Cape, 1970.

Tarnoff, Peter. "Bizarre Nostalgia for the Cold War." *New York Times* 19 Sept. 1989: A14.

Theroux, Paul. "A Marriage of Mixed Blessings." Rev. of *Too Far to Go,* by John Updike. *New York Times Book Review* 8 Apr. 1979: 7.

Tocqueville, Alexis de. *Democracy in America.* Trans. George Lawrence. Ed. J. P. Mayer. New York: Doubleday Anchor Books, 1969.

Twain, Mark. *The Adventures of Huckleberry Finn.* Middlesex: Penguin, 1985.

Uphaus, Suzanne Henning. *John Updike.* New York: Ungar, 1980.

Vargo, Edward P. *Rainstorms and Fire: Ritual in the Novels of John Updike.* Port Washington, NY: Kennikat Press, 1973.

Waldmeir, Joseph. "It's the Going That's Important, Not the Getting There: Rabbit's Questing Non-Quest." *Modern Fiction Studies* 20 (Spring 1974): 13–27.

Weinstein, Fred. *History and Theory after the Fall: An Essay on Interpretation.* Chicago: U of Chicago P, 1990.

White, Hayden. *The Content of the Form: Narrative Discourse and Historical Representative.* Baltimore: Johns Hopkins UP, 1987.

———. *Tropics of Discourse.* Baltimore: Johns Hopkins UP, 1978.

Wood, Ralph C. *The Comedy of Redemption: Christian Faith and Comic Vision in Four American Novelists.* South Bend: U of Notre Dame P, 1988.

Contributors

Charles Berryman is Professor of English and American Literature at the University of Southern California. His books include *Decade of Novels, Fiction of the 1970s: Form and Challenge; From Wilderness to Wasteland: The Trial of the Puritan God in the American Imagination;* and *W. B. Yeats: Design of Opposites.* He has published widely on Roth, Updike, Vonnegut, Bellow, Heller, and Doctorow.

Lawrence R. Broer is Professor of English at the University of South Florida. He earned his Ph.D. from Bowling Green State University. The author of two books, *Hemingway's Spanish Tragedy* and *Sanity Plea: Schizophrenia in the Novels of Kurt Vonnegut,* Broer has also edited four collections of critical essays on modern and contemporary fiction. In 1981 and 1984 he served as Fulbright Lecturer at the University of Paris. His numerous essays on twentieth-century literature have appeared in such journals as *Modern Fiction Studies, Studies in Short Fiction,* and the *Southern Humanities Review.*

Paula R. Buck is an Associate Professor of English at Florida Southern College. She received her B.A. from Ursinus College and an M.A.T. from Lehigh University. She recently completed her dissertation "Dorothy Parker: Playwright" and holds a Ph.D. from the University of South Florida.

Jeff H. Campbell graduated from Lamar College and Southern Methodist University and then earned his Ph.D. from Duke University. He served as Herman Brown Professor of English and Chairman of the Department of English at Southwestern University in Georgetown, Texas, before becoming Chairman of the Department of English at Midwestern State University in Wichita Falls, Texas, where he is currently Professor of English and Graduate Coordinator for the English Program. He is the author of *John Howard Griffin* and *Updike's Novels: Thorns Spell a Word,* as well as numerous essays on Updike, Bellow, Faulkner, Griffin, Dobie, and others in regional and national journals.

Donald J. Greiner earned his Ph.D. at the University of Virginia. He is presently Carolina Distinguished Professor of English as well as Associate Provost and Dean of Undergraduate Affairs at the University of South Carolina. He is executive editor of *Critique: Studies in Contemporary Fiction.* Among his many books are three on John Updike: *The Other John Updike, John Updike's Novels,* and *Adultery in the American Novel: Updike, James, and Hawthorne.* He also worries about his golf game.

Jack B. Moore is a Professor of English and American Studies, and member of the Institute on Black Life, at the University of South Florida. He received his Ph.D. from the University of North Carolina in 1963, and was Graduate Director of English, and Chair of American Studies, at the University of South Florida. His books include studies of Joe DiMaggio, W. E. B. Du Bois, Maxwell Bodenheim, and American skinheads. Among his articles on aspects of American culture are investigations of how John Updike deals with Africa in his fiction and how myths of victimization have affected American society.

Judie Newman was educated in Caithness, Scotland, and then at the Universities of Edinburgh and Cambridge. She is Professor of American and Postcolonial Literature at the University of Newcastle Upon Tyne. Her publications include *The Ballistic Bard: Postcolonial Fictions; Harriet Beecher Stowe, Dred: A Tale of the Great Dismal Swamp; Nadine Gordimer; John Updike; Saul Bellow and History;* and numerous essays on American and postcolonial novelists. She is also the Chair of the British Association for American Studies and the mother of a young son.

James Plath is an Associate Professor of English at Illinois Wesleyan University. He received his Ph.D. in American literature from the University of Wisconsin–Milwaukee, where he wrote a dissertation on "The Painterly Aspects of John Updike's Fiction." In 1994 he edited *Conversations with John Updike* for the esteemed University Press of Mississippi series, including an interview of his own that he conducted with Updike prior to the author's visit to Key West to accept the Conch Republic Prize for Literature. In his "spare time" Plath edits *Clockwatch Review,* the award-winning journal of the arts he founded in 1983, and directs the Hemingway Days Writers' Workshop and Conference in Key West each July.

Dilvo I. Ristoff is a Professor of English and American Literature and Provost of Undergraduate Studies at the Federal University of Santa Catarina, Brazil. He received his Ph.D. from the University of Southern California. For many years he was the editor of *Ilha do Desterro,* a "Journal of Language and

Anglo-American Literature." His publications include *Updike's America: The Presence of Contemporary American History in John Updike's Rabbit Trilogy*, as well as articles on Joseph Conrad, James Joyce, Ford Madox Ford, Saul Bellow, Philip Roth, John Updike, and other contemporary American writers.

Edward Vargo received his M.A. and Ph.D. in English from the University of Chicago. He is currently Dean of the Faculty of Arts at Assumption University, Bangkok, Thailand. He has also served as an Associate Professor of English and Dean of the College of Foreign Languages at Fu Jen University, Taipei, Taiwan. He is the author of one of the first full-length studies of Updike's work, *Rainstorms and Fire: Ritual in the Novels of John Updike*. More recently, he has published essays on cross-cultural readings of American literature.

Joseph J. Waldmeir is Emeritus Professor of English at Michigan State University. He is the author of *American Novels of the Second World War* and numerous essays on American fiction writers such as Henry James, Ernest Hemingway, John Steinbeck, Ken Kesey, and John Updike. He has edited *Recent American Fiction: Some Critical Views; Critical Essays on John Barth;* and, with John Waldmeir, *Critical Essays on Truman Capote*.

Matthew Wilson is presently Associate Professor of Humanities and Writing at Penn State, Harrisburg. He received his Ph.D. from Rutgers University, and has taught at Rutgers, at King Saud University, Riyadh, Saudi Arabia, and at the University of Łódź in Poland, where he was awarded a Fulbright in American Literature. In addition to several essays on composition, he has published essays on Philip Roth, John Edgar Wideman, David Bradley, and Willa Cather. He is currently working on a project to publish the manuscript novels of Charles W. Chesnutt.

Ralph C. Wood received his B.A. and M.A. degrees in English from East Texas State University and his Ph.D. in theology and literature from the University of Chicago. From 1971 to 1997 he taught at Wake Forest University, where he was the Allen Easley Professor of Religion, until his recent appointment as Distinguished Professor of Religion at Samford University in Birmingham, Alabama. His major book is *The Comedy of Redemption: Christian Faith and Comic Vision in Four American Novelists,* which concerns the writings of Flannery O'Connor, Walker Percy, John Updike, and Peter De Vries. He serves on the editorial board of the *Flannery O'Connor Bulletin,* as book review editor of *Perspectives in Religious Studies,* and as editor-at-large for the *Christian Century.*

Index

GAYLORD F